Sons of the Lion's Cub

Other Books by
Melvyn R. Werbach, M.D.

Third Line Medicine:
Modern Treatment for Persistent Symptoms

Healing Through Nutrition

Nutritional Influences on Illness (two editions)

Supplemental Chapters:
Nutritional Influences on Illness

Foundations of Nutritional Medicine

Case Studies in Natural Medicine

Nutritional Influences on Mental Illness

Botanical Influences on Illness (with Michael Murray, N.D.)
(two editions)

Textbook of Nutritional Medicine
(with Jeffrey Moss, D.D.S., C.N.S., C.C.N.)

SONS OF THE LION'S CUB

THE HORENSTEIN BROTHERS AND THEIR FORTUNE

by MELVYN R. WERBACH

III THIRD LINE PRESS
4751 Viviana Drive, Suite 201
Tarzana, CA 91356, USA

thirdlinepress@gmail.com

Sons of the Lion's Cub: The Horenstein Brothers and Their Fortune
by Melvyn R. Werbach

Published by Third Line Press, 4751 Viviana Drive, Tarzana CA 91356, USA

thirdlinepress@gmail.com

ISBN: 978-1-891710-04-9

Library of Congress Control Number: 2019933005

Publisher's Cataloging-in-Publication Data

Names: Werbach, Melvyn R., author.
Title: Sons of the lion's cub : the Horenstein brothers and their fortune / Melvyn Werbach.
Description: Tarzana, CA : Third Line Press, 2019. | Includes bibliographical references and index.
Identifiers: LCCN 2019933005 | ISBN 978-1-891710-04-9 (paperback)
Subjects: LCSH: Jews--Biography. | Jews--Ukraine--Biography. | Jewish families--Biography. | Brothers--Biography. | Wealth. | Genealogy--Charts, diagrams, etc. | BISAC: BIOGRAPHY & AUTOBIOGRAPHY / Jewish. | HISTORY / Russia & the Former Soviet Union.
Classification: LCC DS115 .W47 2019 (print) | DDC 920.0092/924--dc23.

Dedicated to my Werbach family for whom this will serve as a record of one of its early origins, and to all genealogists, intrepid researchers determined to unearth the true story of their ancestry.

גּוּר אַרְיֵה יְהוּדָה

(Gur arye Yehuda)

Judah is a lion's cub.

Genesis 49:9

TABLE OF CONTENTS

SONS OF THE LION'S CUB

INTRODUCTION:
AN EARLY ANCESTRAL LINEAGE

"You ... should know who you are and who are your ancestors, and you should instruct your children, and they to their children for all time, for the Holy One, blessed be He, only rests His presence on those of pedigree."

From the Ethical Will of Rabbi Sheftel (Shabtai) Halevi Horowitz (1590-1660)[a]

I have long known from members of my father's family that one of my 2nd great grandmothers was Tzirul Horenstein Kanfer, wife of Shmuel Kanfer of Shumsk, Ukraine (which was then part of Russia). The family lore was that she came from an extremely rich family named "Horenstein." After the passage of several decades, I was able to confirm that she was the sister of Rabbis Yakov Yosef and Naftali HaKohen Horenstein, two "billionaire" brothers who lived in the 19th century.

While unknown outside of the Jewish community, these brothers were celebrated by their fellow Jews in Ukraine because of their achievement of extraordinary financial success in a country with strong anti-Semitic sentiments, because their wealth never diluted their commitment to Hasidism,[b] and especially because of their enormous donations to charity.

New data, some of which came from the Ukrainian archives and some of which came from Horenstein descendants, have rescued the story of the Horensteins from obscurity. The two brothers provide the central focus for this book, although "Sons of the Lion's Cub" covers much more territory than the story of their lives. The book examines the Horenstein family following the brothers' deaths, analyzing the changes in the family as it coped with the disasters of the 20th century. It also goes back in time to provide a multi-generational exploration of the Horensteins' distinguished ancestral origins viewed in the context of European Jewish history.

If you have read many history books, you know that some authors view history from a distance, while others move in closer to focus on the contributions of specific people. This book does some of both, using a multi-generational family line as the connecting thread as it takes you through more than one thousand years of European Jewish history.

---

[a] Appended to *Yesh Nochlin* (1615), written by his grandfather Rabbi Abraham (son of Shabtai) Horowitz (1540-1615) and published in 1701.

[b] Hasidism: A movement of observant Jews, called *hasidim* ("pious ones" in Hebrew), founded by the *Baal Shem Tov* in Eastern Europe during the 18th century.

The results of many years of genealogical research laid the foundation of this book. The beauty of genealogy is that it makes history personal. Whether or not your ancestors are part of this particular family's story, I hope that viewing Jewish history through the eyes of a genealogist will make it more real, and thus more meaningful and memorable.

As you go through the book, you may notice something unusual in my writing style. I wondered for a long while whether I should direct this book towards an academic, scholarly audience or towards a more general audience. My decision was to do both: to seek to make the text relatively easy to follow and understand, but to include extensive footnotes and references as are found in academic texts.

Now sit back and enjoy the journey!

Melvyn Werbach

PART I

RABBI GUR-ARYE HAKOHEN HORENSTEIN & HIS TWO SONS

EVERY GUR-ARYE IS MY COUSIN
("Gur-arye" is pronounced "Gur Ahr yay.")

Have you ever felt led by some invisible force that drops evidence in front of you piece by piece until you finally are able to put those pieces together?

It was just an offhand remark, made sometime during my childhood in the 1940s. I was perhaps eight years old. We were living then in Washington Heights, at the Northern tip of Manhattan. I don't remember when my father said it, or why he said it then, but that doesn't make a difference.

"You know," he said, "you descend from a man named Gur-arye, and every Gur-arye is your cousin."

I do recall saying to myself: "What a strange first name. Why would parents want to give their son such a name?"

Yet his statement was intriguing, especially as I was born into a small family and would have liked to have had more relatives. I never knew my father's parents as his mother had died delivering his younger brother, his step-mother had been murdered by the Cossacks in Ukraine during a pogrom, and his father had died before I was born. As my mother's father died when I was six, I grew up knowing just one grandparent. Moreover, my two uncles (one on each side) were unfriendly, and I had just one first cousin on each side. (I did have a little sister, but she was too young to play with.)

I began to imagine asking every Jewish male I met named George (the usual American equivalent for Gur-arye) if his Hebrew name was Gur-arye, as then he could be my cousin. Soon I tabled the thought ... for about half a century.

Around the time of my retirement from medical practice, I finally had the time to turn my attention back to the name of Gur-arye. A Hebrew name meaning "cub of the lion," I discovered that its history is extensive, with its origin dating back to the Torah, the great book at the heart of the Jewish religion.

In the Book of Genesis (Genesis 49:9), the patriarch Jacob blesses his son Judah, referring to him as a young lion or, perhaps more accurately, as a lion's cub, with the words: *"Gur arye Yehuda."* ("[The] cub [of the] lion [is] Judah.") Simply restated, he prophesizes in these few words that Judah will grow up to be like a lion which, according to the Talmud (Hag. 13b), is the "king of the beasts."

This blessing is not only associated with Judah and his tribe, but is also closely tied to King David, a member of the Tribe of Judah, thus making the Lion of Judah one of the most common Jewish symbols.[a]

According to my father, the name Gur-arye had been passed down through many generations within the Horenstein family, a very wealthy Jewish family in Ukraine, who he knew to be our cousins. I was later to learn that we were related to them through my father's mother, Yocheved Kanfer Verbukh, as the maiden name of Yocheved's paternal grandmother was Tzirul Horenstein; thus Tzirul, my 2nd great grandmother, was my link to the Horenstein family. It was not until I did a considerable amount of research that I discovered that Tzirul's father, my 3rd great grandfather, was the first to be named Gur-arye in the Horenstein family.

Surviving Russian records state that Tzirul (Yiddish for the Hebrew name Sarah) was born in 1823,[1,2] probably in the Ukrainian town of Berestechko, part of the Volhynia gubernia. By about 1840, she had married Shmuel Kanfer, a townsman from the town of Shumsk, also in the Volhynia gubernia, and had moved there to live with him.[3] Their son Isaac (my father's grandpa) grew up to become the owner of a local tannery.

---

[a] Rashi explains that the *Gur-arye* (cub of the lion) refers to none other than King David, who in the beginning, when under the rule of King Saul, was likened to a cub, but eventually, when he was crowned, was like a lion (http://www.jewishpress.com/judaism/ask-the-rabbi/q-a-the-scepter-shall-not-depart-from-judah-part-i/2013/05/14/0/).

Isaac Kanfer, tannery owner (ca. 1840 – ca. 1924)

Judging by the standards of the times, Isaac's tannery was successful. As of 1913, it employed five workers and had an annual production of 25,000 rubles,[4] an amount that is roughly equivalent to $250,000 in 2006 US dollars. To give you a better idea of what 25,000 rubles meant, at that time the average tannery worker earned about 360 rubles a year so, to earn 25,000 rubles, it would take him almost 70 years!

According to an Israeli cousin, Isaac's family also owned forest land which produced lumber for making fine furniture, such as this cabinet that he built as a wedding gift for one of his children:

There were a couple of other reminders of our family's connection with Tzirul and the Horensteins. Ciel Arshack, my father's first cousin, was the person who introduced me to my wife. Tzirul died in 1904 and Ciel was born later that year. In accordance with Jewish naming customs, she received her name, an American-ized version of Tzirul, in honor of her late great grandmother.

Also, Ciel's sister, Edith Arshack Sonneman, once reported to me that her mother had told her that they had "wealthy and generous Radomysl Orenstein [sic] cousins." Then, in 1980, Edith had a rather strange experience. While visit-ing with her friend Sima at Sima's home, Edith's friend introduced her to her house guest, Abe Keltner, a friend of hers who lived in Canada.

Abe took a look at Edith and remarked that she looked surprisingly like a friend of his in Canada, a man by the name of George Skulsky. In fact, Abe was so struck by the resemblance that he was convinced that Edith and George were cousins. He promised that, as soon as he returned to Canada, he would inform George of their meeting, and he expected that George would want to contact her.

Sure enough, soon after Abe's return home, Edith received a letter from George with the heading "Dear Unknown Relative." In the letter, he stated:

"I am Gur-arye. My grandfather was Shamai Hornstein, who was a cousin to the Hornsteins at Radomysl, Kiev Gubernia."

They were indeed cousins!

Many years later, after both cousin Edith and my father had passed away, Edith's daughter Toby gave me a letter she had found among her mother's papers. It was a letter my father had written to Edith the same year that she had been contacted by their Canadian cousin. In the letter, he confirmed our relationship with the Horenstein family, stating that he had corresponded with a mutual 1st cousin, who knew that their Horenstein cousins were "tremendously" wealthy and lived in Radomyshl near Kiev.

His letter goes on to state that, because the Horensteins were both very rich and very religious, the Jews of the region delighted in sharing many stories about them. For example, Menachem Verbukh (my father's father) once told him the following popular anecdote:

A Hasid came to the Horensteins looking for a job.

Mr. Horenstein asked him what he can do to be helpful.

He answered that he can give him advice.

Mr. Horenstein said:

"OK. You are hired. Now advise me how I can get rid of you."

My father points out in his letter that this was, "of course," not a true story, but showed how well known the Radomyshl Horensteins were among the Jews of Ukraine.

While my family's connection with the Horensteins had aroused my curiosity, for the next half century I was too busy to pursue it. During those years, I became a physician, completed an internship in Internal Medicine, married, served during the Viet Nam War as a commissioned officer in the United States Public Health Service, completed a residency in Psychiatry, went into private practice, and had two sons. Finally, in the 1990s, I decided to close my practice in order to pursue writing as a full-time occupation.

Retirement finally gave me the time to take up genealogy as a hobby, so I began to research my family tree in earnest. I learned a great deal about family history on both my paternal and maternal sides. However, like most Ashkenazic Jews, I found that, without the aid of DNA matches, I could only go back to the 19th century, and to a limited extent to the 18th century, due mainly to the lack of earlier civil records or other early sources.

The only exception was my father's relationship to the Horensteins.

One of my early efforts to learn more about my father's family was to do computer searches for the Horenstein surname. While various sites, and especially online databases, listed Horensteins in Ukraine, my most important discovery was the personal web site of Avrom Horenstein of New York in which he had included a section devoted to his proud Horenstein family lineage.

I contacted Avrom and he agreed to mail his entire family tree to me. Soon I received a 32-foot-long paper roll that showed the descendants of his ancestor Rabbi Naftali HaKohen Horenstein (one of the two Horenstein brothers) - but my family was not included. Was I wrong? Had I found the correct Horenstein family?

For the answer, I had to go back another generation. I discovered the identity of Naftali's father from something Avrom had posted on his web site: an excerpt from a book written by Rabbi Yosef Lieberman, a Horenstein cousin.[5] According to Lieberman, Rabbi Naftali HaKohen Horenstein was the son of Rabbi Gur-arye HaKohen Horenstein.

I had found a Gur-arye! Moreover, I later learned that this Gur-arye was the first Horenstein family member to receive this name.

Everything suggested that this was indeed the correct Horenstein family. Where, however, did my 2nd great grandmother Tzirul fit into that tree?

I already knew that Yakov Yosef Horenstein was born about 1818, while Naftali, his brother, was born in 1821. Thus Tzirul, who was born in 1823, must have been their sister. While no birth document existed, the timing was perfect.

Later, I found confirmation of my theory in an 1892 record filed in the Kiev archive. It states that Gur-arye Kanfer, a permanent resident of Shumsk (where Tzirul and her husband had settled), was working for Naftali Horenstein in faraway Kiev, the city where Naftali maintained a residence. Naftali, one of the fabulously wealthy Horenstein brothers, would have been Gur-arye Kanfer's great uncle.

Tzirul Kanfer, Naftali's sister, must have stayed in touch with her brother after her marriage. Compared to the great city of Kiev, Shumsk was a small town with limited employment opportunities. It would not be surprising for the young man to have been given a job working for his wealthy great uncle.

Rabbi Lieberman's book also noted that Gur-arye Horenstein's father was Shmuel HaKohen. Now I could trace this ancestral line back six generations:

Melvyn (Menachem) Werbach (b. 1940)
son of
(1) Shmuel Verbukh (1903-1997)
son of
(2) Yocheved Kanfer Verbukh (1870-1909)
daughter of
(3) Isaac Kanfer (1840-1924)
son of
(4) Tzirul Horenstein Kanfer (1823-1904)
daughter of
(5) Rabbi Gur-arye HaKohen Horenstein (1792-1849)
son of
(6) Rabbi Shmuel HaKohen (1770-1840)

As exciting as it was to be able to connect the Horensteins with my father's family, I was blocked from proceeding further back in time by the same problem I had encountered when researching my other ancestral lines, namely the lack of earlier census records.

The Horenstein *Yichus* Claims

However, in contrast to all my other family lines, my Horenstein cousins came from a prominent rabbinical family. That was a decided advantage, as rabbis, especially those who achieved some prominence, were likely to have had their names, and even the names of their ancestors, recorded somewhere. For example, when a rabbi wrote a book, it was often customary for the publisher to promote sales of the book by providing the author's illustrious ancestry.

Also, my research on the Horenstein family found two "*yichus* claims" that various family members had made. The first is that the Horensteins descend from Rabbi Yehuda Loew ben

---

YICHUS

Yichus, a Yiddish word which refers to pedigree as modified by personal achievement. A "yichus claim" is an assertion that a person descends from a prominent and highly regarded ancestor.

Community standing within the Jewish population was an important value to Jews of this era. People's reputations were based, not only on their character and achievements, but on the character and achievements of their ancestors.

When it came time for marriage, family achievements were an important consideration in selecting a spouse, as a suitable match often meant someone who came from a family of equal importance.

Betzalel, the MaHaRaL of Prague (ca. 1525–1609), one of the most famous Euro-pean rabbis of all times.

The MaHaRaL made numerous contributions to Jewish society, both by his actions and in his writings, yet his fame today among the laity is due to a popular legend which claims that he raised a monster (the "*golem*") from the water to rescue the persecuted Jews of Prague.

The most interesting version of the Horenstein claim of descent from the Ma-HaRaL is the following piece of family folklore, transmitted via the branch of the family that emigrated in the early 20th century from Berestechko, Volhynia Gu-bernia, Ukraine to Moose Jaw, Saskatchewan, Canada:

> "*A great great grandfather, a well-known rabbi with the name of Yehuda Leib ben Betzalel, associated with the name MAHARA"L Mi Prag, wrote a book called Gur-arye.*

> "*There is a legend that one of his grandchildren was having trouble giving birth. So, he came to her in a dream and said that everything would be fine if she would name the grandchild Gur-arye.*

> "*Ever since then, the name has remained in our family.*"[6]

Was the MaHaRaL really my ancestor? To find the answer, I would need to discover the intervening generations between our lives. This task was made eas-ier by the other Horenstein *yichus* claim. This claim is that the Horensteins de-scend from Rabbi Naftali Katz (1645-1719). Like other famous European rabbis of the past, he was commonly referred to by the title of his best-known book which, in his case, was the *Smichat Chachamim*.[b,c]

It was simple to discover that the *Smichat Chachamim* descended from the MaHaRaL as the relatively few generations between them were easy to trace. Since these two prominent rabbis were the only people that the Horensteins

---

[b] Rabbi Yosef Lieberman, a great grandson of Avraham HaKohen Horenstein, wrote in *Shalshelet HaYuchasin*. Jerusalem, 5738 [1977/8], p. 39:

"*[Naftali HaKohen Horenstein was] son of the brilliant rabbi, Gur Arieh HaKohen; [who was]*

g) son of the brilliant rabbi, Shmuel HaKohen; [who was]

h) a descendant of our master, Naftali Ka"tz, author of Semikhat Chakhamim."

[c] Dov Rabinovitz, in *Sefer Mishkenot HaRo'im* (Jerusalem, 1984) states in a footnote that Shmuel HaKohen Horenstein [son of Naftali HaKohen Horenstein] was a descend-ant of the *Smichat Chachamim*.

claimed as famous ancestors, the fact that one was an ancestor of the other increased the likelihood that their claims could be substantiated.

Years went by, however, without any success in linking the Horensteins to the *Smichat Chachamin*, and I was starting to think that I would never be able to break through this "brick wall." Then, as luck would have it, I was contacted by Allan Dolgow. Allan had discovered that a small museum, located in the town of Ostroh (Ostrog in Russian) in Ukraine, had in its possession the 1795 Jewish Census for the Ostroh District. The census book was only available at the museum, but Allan, with considerable effort, had succeeded in obtaining photographs of the entire census!

This census was unusual. Only three years earlier, Russia had taken over the territory from Poland as part of the Third Partition of Poland so, when it came time for the census, the question was raised concerning whether the census should be recorded in Polish or in Russian. The new Russian government's decision was to record the data in Russian on the left side of each page, and again in Polish on the right side. Here are the two sides of a typical page:

1795 Ostroh Census – in Russian

1795 Ostroh Census – in Polish

Would the census contain the answer to the mystery of my ancestry? Rabbi Naftali Katz, supposedly my ancestor, was the *Av Beit Din* (head of the rabbinical court) in Ostroh from 1680 to 1689 and returned there in 1715. Moreover, some of his children had lived in Ostroh, suggesting that, as of 1795, he might still have descendants living there. I thought about it carefully and concluded that looking into the census would probably be a waste of time, yet I was so eager to confirm this ancestral line that I couldn't resist the desire to review it in detail.

How could I review the census in the hope of discovering the missing links? In order to do a meticulous review, the data would need to be in the form of a spreadsheet which permitted the sorting of each column of data. Translating the data from old Russian and Polish script and inputting it into a spreadsheet would be a daunting task. Although the old script was difficult to read, even for an experienced translator, the dual notations of this census provided an unusual advantage since, if words could not be deciphered in one language, the same information in the other language on the other side of the page could help to clarify the correct spelling of the data that the scribe had written down.

Allan did not have the time to take charge of the translation, so I volunteered for the project. My first task was to find a translator. Fortunately, I found Ola Heska.[d] Ola is a native of Poland who is fluent in both Russian and English. Moreover, she has had decades of experience in genealogical and archival research and translation. Working with her on the project was a pleasure.

The next step was to arrange for Ola's funding. I decided to do the project in conjunction with JewishGen,[e] a popular online site which is an affiliate of the Museum of Jewish Heritage. I thus became their Coordinator of 1795 Ostroh Census Translation Project and proceeded to raise the money to fund Ola for her efforts. She eventually translated the data and then placed it on an Excel spreadsheet so that it could be assorted by each important category. By the time she had finished, Ola had translated a total of 2,950 entries.[f]

Now I could do a detailed analysis. This was not easy, as the census was taken before the advent of surnames. Moreover, as the data was collected by the Russian authorities rather than by the Jews themselves, each resident was only identified with a single given name alongside the given name of the father. Names commonly used by Jews within the Jewish community were absent, making identification especially difficult.

---

[d] http://www.hwwd.com/genelady/index.html

[e] https://www.jewishgen.org

[f] Information on the 1795 Ostroh Census can be found at: https://www.jewishgen.org/databases/Ukraine/1795OstrogCensus.htm

For further information, and to download the entire census in Excel, go to: https://kehilalinks.jewishgen.org/Ostroh/census.asp

While the Census covered the entire Ostroh region, rabbinical families appeared to primarily reside in the original "Old Town." Within this section, houses were numbered from #1 to #236. I discovered my ancestors living there in house #106:

> Leybka Pinchasvich [Leib, son of Pinkhas], head of household, b. 1744, merchant of the 3rd guild (sells measured goods)
> Wife: Hinde Berkova [Hinde, daughter of Berko], b. 1750
> Daughter: Dynia, b. 1781
> Son: Shmuel, b. 1770; married (helps father)
> [Shumel's] Wife: Malka Mikhelyovna [Malka, daughter of Mikhel] b. 1772
> [Shmuel's] Son: Pinchas, b. 1790
> [Shmuel's] Son: Shimon, b. 1792

Let's interpret these listings. The head of the household was "Leib" who was 51 years old and the son of "Pinchas." Pinchas must have died by 1790, as that year Leib's wife gave birth to a son who, consistent with Jewish naming customs, was named Pinchas after his deceased father.

Other sources provide us with further information about this family. "Leib, son of Pinchas," the head of the household, was apparently known in the Jewish community as Rabbi Arye Judah Leib.[7] (We'll call him "Arye Leib" for convenience.) The census notes that he was a fairly prosperous merchant[g] who sold "measured goods."

Pinchas, his late father, had been known as Rabbi Pinchas of Ludmir while "Shmuel," Arye Leib's son, apparently was known as either Shmuel Asher[8] or Shmuel HaKohen; thus his full name among Jews would have been "Rabbi Shmuel Asher HaKohen."[9,h,i]

Gur-arye, my 3rd great grandfather, was an infant son of Shmuel around the time of the census. Although a later census from elsewhere stated that he was born in 1792 (three years before this Ostroh census), he is not included in the Ostroh census, a common omission for babies and very young children at the time.[j]

Another interesting finding in the 1795 Ostroh Census was that house #112 (probably located close to house #106) was the home of Rabbi Yoel Katz. A great grandson of the *Smichat Chachamim* (who the Horensteins claim as an ancestor), Yoel Katz's father was the late Rabbi Nachman Katz, who had died two decades earlier in 1774, while Yoel's paternal grandfather was Rabbi Betzalel Katz (a previous *Av Beit Din* of Ostroh), son of the *Smichat Chachamim*:[10]

---

[g] He was one of the few Ostroh residents who could afford to pay the fee to join the lowest of three Guild levels in order to gain the privileges of a Merchant of the 3rd Guild.

[h] My hypothesis concerning Gur-arye's father assumes that, although listed by the Russian authorities in the 1795 Ostroh Census merely as "Shmuel, son of Leybka Pinkhasvich" (Shmuel son of Leib, grandson of Pinchas), he was identical to the man known among Jews as Shmuel Asher, son of Leib. Moreover, I assume that he later acquired the Horenstein surname.

This issue of the identity of Gur aye's father is discussed in detail in Appendix One which starts on page 281. My conclusions:

    1. While not definitive, the evidence is strong enough to accept the hypothesis that the two men (Shmuel, son of Leib, grandson of Pinchus, and Shmuel Asher, son of Leib) are identical.

    2. The evidence for the hypothesis that Shmuel Asher HaKohen adopted the Horenstein surname to become Shmuel Horenstein is weaker, although it does appear likely.

[i] The Horensteins were Kohanim, i.e. members of the priestly caste believed to descend from Moses' brother Aaron. "HaKohen" was an appellation used by the family to indicate a male family member whose intense and ongoing Jewish studies had earned him the title, although no family member is known to have functioned as a pulpit rabbi.

[j] According to the years of birth listed on the relevant censuses, Gur-arye was one of three brothers born to his parents in the year 1792. The brothers, then, were either triplets (very unlikely) or the listed years of birth were not precise (quite likely).

Rabbi Naftali Katz, the *Smichat Chachamim*
↓
Rabbi Betzalel Katz
↓
Rabbi Nachman Katz
↓
Rabbi Yoel Katz

Nachman Katz and Arye Leib were cousins, since both descended from the *Smichat Chachamim*. They were also related through marriage. Arye Leib's first marriage was to a daughter of Nachman Katz, making Nachman his father-in-law.

Following his son Simcha's birth, Arye's wife probably died from complications of childbirth (then a common occurance); thus "Hinde Berkova" (Hinde, daughter of Berko), listed as his wife in the 1795 Ostroh Census, was his second wife.[k]

Now, which family did Hinde come from? As the census fails to identify her family, I have had to make an educated guess based on various lines of evidence. I concluded that she was most likely Hinde Yekels, daughter of Rabbi Dov Ber ("Berko") Yekels, who, like Arye Leib, was a member of the Ostroh *chevra kadisha*.[11] (If you wish to review that evidence, see Appendix One which starts on page 281.)

I then traced Hinde's ancestry and made yet another interesting discovery. Like Arye Leib's lineage, her lineage traces back to – the *Smichat Chachamim*!

Now I had discovered not only one ancestral line, but two lines that descended from the *Smichat Chachamim*. Moreover, from now on my research would proceed faster, as I had broken through the "brick wall" and entered into a major rabbinical lineage.

Compared to my effort to reach this point, it was relatively easy to discover how my 5th great grandparents each descended from the *Smichat Chachamim*:

---

[k] We know this because the *Pinkas* (minutes) of the Ostroh *chevra kadisha* for a particular sunday in the Hebrew year of 5529 (1768-1769) state:

> ``Behold, on this day none other than the rabbi, master and teacher, Nachman, son of the genius, rabbinical court chief, our teacher, Mr. Betzalel K''atz, came before us wanting to bring his beloved young grandson, Mr. Simcha ... the son of his son-in-law, the rabbi, Mr. Arye Judah Leib ... to serve in the chevra kadisha."

This wording contrasts with that of a similar note later in the same *Pinkas* which states that Arye Judah Leib presented his son Shmuel. Rabbi Katz – not identified as Shmuel's grandfather – was just present to sign the document (Accounts Book of the Ostroh *Chevra Kadisha*, p. 84 - quoted by Menachem Mendel Biber in *Markezet LeGedolei Ostraha* [1907], Entry 149).

5th great grandfather:

Arye Judah Leib (1744-aft. 1806), son of Pinchas (abt. 1730-1786), son of Saul Fishel (abt. 1710-aft. 1765), son of Jacob Fishel Kloizner (abt. 1690-1730), son of the wife of Efraim Fishel (abt. 1675-abt. 1715), daughter of Shprintze Katz (abt. 1670-?), daughter of **Natfali Hirsh Katz** (1645-1719).

5th great grandmother:

Hinde Yekels (1750-?), daughter of Perl Katz Yekels, daughter of Betzalel Katz (abt. 1680-1717), son of **Natfali Hirsh Katz** (1645-1719).

The family line from the *Smichat Chachamin* to the MaHaRaL is well-established:

Natfali Hirsh II Katz (the *Smichat Chachamim*) (1645-1719), son of Yitzchok II Katz (1608-1670), son of Naftali Hirsh Katz (abt. 1580-1648), son of Vögele Loew (abt. 1560-1629), daughter of **Yehuda Loew, the MaHaRaL of Prague** (abt. 1525-1609).

I had finally validated the Horenstein *yichus* claims!

Now that I had confirmed my descent from an important rabbinical line, I became so intrigued that I wanted to continue my research into the Horenstein family and their ancestry. There were two directions in which I could do further research:

1. I could investigate the lives of Gur-arye's two sons (my "extremely wealthy" Horenstein cousins) and their progeny. These sons were legendary among the Jews of Ukraine at that time, but as little about them had ever been published, they had been forgotten in the history books.
2. I could research the earlier ancestry of my 3rd great grandfather, Gur-arye HaKohen.

I found myself equally drawn to discovering both stories, so I decided to take on both projects, and both – as you will learn - turned out to be fascinating. Researching Gur-arye's wealthy sons led me to understand why the Jews of Ukraine loved to tell tales about their extraordinary lives. After setting the stage, we will review the story of their lives – and more – in the rest of Part One.

Researching Gur-arye's ancestors led me back many centuries to discover a rich history of important contributors to Jewish life and wisdom. This history forms the basis of Part Two.

What makes this book different from most history books is that we will be viewing Jewish history through a genealogical perspective as we identify some of the exceptional members of a European Jewish ancestral line and place them within their historical framework.

We will start our historical journey by examining Jewish life in Poland in the 18th century, setting the stage for the birth of the first Gur-arye, father of the rich Horenstein brothers, towards the end of the century.

JEWISH LIFE IN 18ᵀᴴ CENTURY POLAND

A s of the 18th century, the ethnic identity of the population of the Polish-Lithuanian Commonwealth was widely mixed, with ethnic Poles constituting only about half of the population. In addition to Lithuanians, Ukrainians, and Belarusians, as well as Tatars and Romany, the inhabitants of many cities and towns included Germans, Italians, Scots, Armenians, and Greeks.[12]

There was no sense at the time of belonging to the Polish nation. Identity instead was characterized by a multiplicity of loyalties. People felt patriotic in regard to their local area, but not in regard to Poland.[13]

Habit of a Polish Jew in 1768.
Juif Polanais.

In 1765, 750,000 Jews were living in Poland, constituting 5.35 percent of the population. The extent of their impact on Polish society, however, was much greater than this figure suggests. Jews resided mainly in urban areas where only 20 percent of the country's population lived.[14] In fact, about half of the urban population was Jewish.

As a substantial majority of Jews lived in communities of 500 or more people, they were a considerable – and quite visible - portion of the population of the larger towns and cities.[15] This explains why, in the travel literature of the period, the most recurrent observation about Jews in Poland-Lithuania was their large numbers.[16]

As the 18th century progressed, the role of

Jews in the economy became increasingly significant. This was partly because of their growing numbers and partly because they were prominent in commerce, making major contributions to the economy. Jews were mainly responsible for transforming the use of grain (rye) from primarily an export commodity to its utilization locally for producing alcoholic beverages. Finally, as the efficiency of serf labor declined, Jews, as lessees of estate monopolies, saw to it that these estates remained productive.[17]

Jewish Autonomy

Growth in the Jewish population was paralleled by increasing Jewish autonomy that, in some ways, approached self-government. Their varied institutional structures were the most elaborate and widely-branched in European Jewish history.[18] They included artisan guilds, voluntary societies, communal governments, regional assemblies – and a national parliament named the Council of Four Lands.[19]

Polish Jews had enjoyed some measure of self-rule since the second half of the 13th century. After the middle of the 15th century, the Polish kings encouraged their Jews to organize into compact groups, primarily to expedite the collection of taxes. Regional councils developed and, by 1580, the Jews of Greater Poland, Little Poland, Ruthenia (East Galicia and Podolia) and Volhynia had organized the Council of Four Lands. While regional councils continued to be active, the Council of Four Lands was to serve as the central body of Jewish authority in Poland for two centuries. (Initially Lithuania was also a part of the council but, starting in 1623, it had its own central organization.)[20]

Membership on the council totaled around 20 to 25 elders, most of whom were delegates from regional councils as well as the larger communities.[21] Meetings were held twice a year, usually at the spring fair in Lublin and the summer fair at Yaroslav. At first, rabbis only participated in deliberations. Later, however, there were separate rabbinic and lay boards. These eventually merged, with rabbis taking over some of the lay leaders' roles.[22]

Pages from the Minutes of the Council of Four Lands

The Council had a wide range of responsibilities. It represented Polish Jewry in both the king's court and the Polish parliament, collected state taxes, regulated religious observances, organized courts, and even sat as a court of last appeal.[23]

By the 18th century, a kind of Polish-Jewish aristocracy had developed which consisted of a relatively small number of families known for their *yichus*, many of which bore one of the prominent ancestral surnames. It was members of these select families who dominated the rabbinate, the societies, and the governmental organizations.

The Polish Magnates

Polish Magnate Costumes (1697-1795)

The magnates were a group of immensely wealthy Polish aristocrats who controlled vast landholdings, including numerous private towns. During the 16th to 18th centuries, their relative power increased at the expense of both the Crown and the gentry.[24] As political power decentralized, Jews gradually shifted the focus of their political alliances from the crown to the magnates, especially since, by the 18th century, one-half to two-thirds of Polish Jews lived in cities, towns, and villages that were owned by magnates.[25]

The Polish nobility partnered extensively with Jewish merchants who built and ran mills and distilleries, transported wheat to the Baltic Ports and shipped it to the West. Their profits were then invested in wine, cloth, dyes and luxury goods which they sold to the nobility. Jews also became the intermediaries between the magnates and the peasants who lived on their vast landholdings.

Decline of the Polish-Lithuanian Commonwealth

Polish *Sejm* during the reign of August II the Strong (1709-1733)

The general *Sejm* was the parliament of the Kingdom of Poland. In the mid-17th century, it enacted a procedure, known as the *liberum* veto, which required unanimous consent in order to pass all measures.[26] Many historians believe that it was a major cause of the deterioration of the Commonwealth's political system, as foreign powers began to bribe *Sejm* members in order to affect the parliament's decisions to their advantage.[27]

Thus, by the mid-18th century, the Commonwealth was in a state of disorder and, due to the influence of foreign powers, no longer completely sovereign.

Dissolution of the Commonwealth

Allegory of the First Partition of Poland, 1772 *(crop)*

(Catherine II of Russia is on the left, while Joseph II of Austria and Frederick the Great of Prussia are on the right.)

Starting 1772, Russia began to acquire territory from the disintegrating Poland. There were roughly 900,000 Jews in Poland at the time, roughly one-eighth of the population.[28] Russia had found it difficult to tolerate a few thousand Jews; now it was to gain hundreds of thousands of them.[29] In the First Partition, Russia took White Russia, while Austria took Galicia, and Prussia took Pomerania and part of Posen.

The Second Partition took place in 1793, this time between Russia and Prussia. Russia annexed Volhynia gubernia, along with part of Kiev, Podolia gubernia, and the region of Minsk, while Prussia acquired the remainder of Great Poland, with Dantzic and Thorn. It was this second vast swatch of territory that contained hundreds of thousands of Jews.[30]

In the Third, and final, Partition (1795), Russia received the provinces of Vilna and Grodno, a territory which had been the backbone of Polish Jewry. Prussia absorbed the remainder of Great Poland as well as the region of Bialystok, while Austria added the provinces of Kraków and Lublin.[31]

The Jews quickly discovered that the attitude of the Russian government to its Jewish population was far different from that of Poland. Suddenly they became inhabitants of an empire in which Jews, despite their important economic contributions, were clearly unwelcome. Laws were enacted to see that the new Jewish residents did not disperse any further towards the East of the Russian Empire, thereby creating the Jewish Pale of Settlement. Moreover, the taxes of Jewish members of the mercantile class in the cities were doubled. If they did not wish to continue to pay the high taxes, they were invited to leave the Russian Empire, but only after paying the double tax for three years.[32]

Dissolution of the Council of Four Lands

The 18th century was largely a period of stagnation for the Jewish councils, with a sharp decline in their number of meetings and amount of legislation. Meetings of the Council of Four Lands were preoccupied with endless discussions or procedural matters, and complaints were raised of corruption including the misappropriation of funds. The Council took on ever-increasing amounts of debt to non-Jewish bodies, while faced with a government which was hostile to their collection of funds for the use of the Jewish community, arguing that all income from Jews should go to the state.[33]

Thus, as the Polish economy declined, the Council of Four Lands fell heavily into debt and declined with it. In 1764, the Polish parliament abolished both the Council of Four Lands and the Lithuanian (Jewish) Council with the hope that direct taxation would increase the income from its Jewish citizens.[34] During the last third of the 18th century, regional representatives met in councils sporadically before they too disappeared.[35]

Jewish Communal Institutions in the 18th Century

The *Kahal*: Local Jewish Self-Government

For the Jewish communities of the region, the 18th century was marked by profound changes in governance by the large institutions which had traditionally exerted a major influence on their lives. They had lived in Poland; now they would be living in Russia. They had been under the supervision of the Council of Four

Lands; now that council was gone. Their local *kahal* was now the only governing body devoted to the Jewish community that continued to function.

The term *kahal* ("assembly"; "community") refers to the organization which served as the institutional leadership of individual European Jewish communities. The start of the institution dates back to before the Crusades when it began to shoulder the collective responsibility of the Jewish community to the government in regard to taxes.[36]

Its leaders, whose numbers were usually proportionate to the size of the local Jewish population, consisted of some of the most prosperous and prominent community members, in the belief that such members could best make decisions on behalf of every resident. *Kahals* were formally recognized by both the state and by the owners of private towns. Both groups also recognized their courts, which decided cases on the basis of *Halakhah* (Jewish law).[37]

The *kahal's* responsibilities included all the functions of a municipal administration and more. It collected local and national taxes as well as funds to pay for its activities. Until their demise, tax monies had also gone to the regional councils and the Council of Four Lands. In addition, some of the *kahal's* income was used for "gifts" to churchmen and government officials for protective purposes.[38]

Its judiciary system included both lay and rabbinical courts. A board of education supervised schooling from the elementary to advanced levels. Matters related to housing, health and welfare, utilities and safety, public morality, commerce, and defense were also within its purview.[39]

In addition to the *kahal* officers, there was a broader council from which committees of supervisors were chosen. For the larger towns these included a variety of overseers: synagogue overseers, overseers of funds for the land of Israel, overseers of funds for the redemption of captives, overseers of charity collection, overseers of education, overseers of the *hekdesh* (funds for the poor and the sick) and overseers for visiting the sick (*bikur holim*), as well as tax assessors and account keepers.[40] There also were a number of salaried officials, including the *sofer* (scribe) who was responsible for keeping the records, as well as judges, preachers, cantors, and the town's rabbi.[a,41]

Sometimes a *shtadlan* (a specially qualified official lobbyist) was employed whose responsibilities included interceding with government officials or the town owner on behalf of the community as well as accompanying and assisting residents who appeared in Christian courts. In the 18th century, Jewish communities tended to rely on a *shtadlan* appointed by the regional councils or, until it was dissolved, the Council of Four Lands.[42]

Kahals functioned fairly smoothly until the Cossack uprisings in the mid-17th century, after which the ability of Jewish communities to fund them was greatly

---

[a] The selection of the rabbi, who was generally appointed for a 3-year term, had to be approved by the town's owner or provincial governor. Such approval required the applicant to make a substantial payment.

reduced, forcing them to seek loans from the abbots,[b] the only capitalists at that time. Increasing debts led to bitter struggles between the *kahal* elders and the Jewish masses throughout the 18th century, at least partly due to the greed of their administrations.[43]

This dire situation led to the Constitution of 1764 which prescribed a census of the entire Jewish population in Poland and Lithuania so that poll taxes[c] could be paid by individuals directly into the government treasury. Subsequently the relationship of the *kahals* with the government continued to evolve until the government abolished most of them in 1844.[44]

The *Chevra Kadisha*

The primary task of the members of each town's *chevra kadisha* was to prepare bodies for burial according to Jewish law and to protect them from desecration until burial. It also organized funerals, maintained the cemetery and participated in other charitable causes.

Like membership in the *kahal*, membership in the *chevra kadisha* was considered to be a great honor. Initiation was offered to the children of the richest and most prominent families, sometimes in return for a sizable donation. Often children were enrolled at the time of birth, although membership was limited to males over the age of 13.

Once inducted into the society, young members would first begin to learn the art of preparing the dead for burial by watching others. Then, when they were older, they would be allowed to wash bodies, dig graves, and instruct families in the proper rules for mourning. Males prepared the bodies of men, while female members of the burial society (or of a parallel society for women) prepared the bodies of women.

The manner of burial reflected the social status of the deceased. That power was frequently used by burial societies to require payment of a considerable sum of money to arrange the most elaborate burials, a practice which sometimes led to harsh criticism. When it was in existence, the Council of Four Lands had tried to intervene by stipulating the maximum sums that could be paid for burial.[45]

Hasidism: A New Religious Movement

While the *kahal* and the *chevra kadisha* continued longstanding traditions within the Jewish community, a revolutionary religious movement started about 1736 when a different type of Jewish leader emerged from a small shtetl in backward Podolia gubernia in the Ukraine.

---

[b] Abbot: The man in charge of an abbey of monks.
[c] Poll tax: A tax levied on every adult, without reference to income or financial resources.

Israel ben Eliezer, an orphan and man-of-the-people, was not a scion of a famous rabbinical line. So far as we know, he never preached in a synagogue. With little formal learning, we have no evidence that he ever wrote down his thoughts, although his homilies (sermons) were put down in writing by disciples.[46]

Called the *Ba'al Shem Tov*[d,e] ("Master of the Good Name") or the *Besht* (an acronym based on the initials of his name), he travelled around the country preaching, writing amulets, curing illnesses, purging evil spirits and, most of all, inspiring his fellow Jews. As his reputation increased, he moved to Miedzybóz (about 74 miles from the town in which Gur-arye HaKohen, father of the Horenstein brothers, would later be born). There he began to hold court. People began to travel long distances just to see him.

He revived the ancient concept of the *tzadik* – a religious leader who was a superior human being because of his special capacity to adhere to God. He also invented a new theory of prayer which he saw as a supernatural act which breaks down the barriers of existence and reaches into the world of the divine.[47]

Baal Schem Tow ישראל בעל־שם־טוב

To do so, he said, you do not read, but look at the prayer and concentrate on the letters until their shapes dissolve. Their divine attributes become visible as you annihilate your personality and become nothing. While your mouth continues to speak the words of the prayer, divine energy supplies your thoughts.[48]

There is no evidence that the *Besht* himself developed a large following. In fact, the very concept of starting a religious movement would have been foreign to his worldview,[49] yet his mystical interpretation of prayer led to a different form of worship as his small circle of followers gradually spread his teachings. Instead of praying in traditional synagogues, they went to *shtiblekh* (prayer

---

[d] *Ba'al Shem* or *Ba'al Shem Tov*: A man who knew the secret names of God and could manipulate them to serve his desires.

[e] The first recorded *Ba'al Shem* was Rabbi Eliyahu *Ba'al Shem* of Chelm (1516-1583), the Horenstein brothers' 11th great grandfather. (The original version of the *golem* legend credits its creation, not to the *MaHaRaL* of Prague, but to Rabbi Eliyahu.)

houses), where followers, usually poor, assembled in rustic clothes and broad fur hats. Some would drink or smoke. They prayed at the top of their voices while joyfully swaying and clapping hands.[50]

While this behavior was difficult enough for traditional Jews to accept, even more outrageous to them was the principle, declared by the *Besht*, that man is saved by faith, not by religious knowledge. This contradiction with the fundamental dogma of rabbinic Judaism – namely that a man's worth as a Jew was measured by the extent of his knowledge of Talmud – was intolerable to many. Traditional rabbis thus saw these new "*tzadiks*" as dangerous rivals who gained the confidence of the masses by feeding on superstition.[51]

Yet the new form of Judaism proved highly appealing, especially for the lower classes for whom Talmudic rabbis often spoke over their heads, making their lengthy religious services boring. They therefore flocked to the miracle-working *tzadiks* who offered them something better: a joyous religious experience along with practical advice and their blessing.[52]

It would be a mistake, however, to view the appeal of the *tzadiks* as limited to the lowly, since their new supplicants represented Jews from the entire socioeconomic range. In fact, some members of the Polish Jewish bourgeoisie warmly received the Polish *tzadiks* and were happy to finance, promote and protect them.[53] Their donations facilitated the rapid expansion of the Hasidic movement despite apparently more sophisticated rivals.[54] The *Besht*, after his arrival in Miedzybóz, was quite comfortable being embraced by the local elite and resided in a *kahal*-owned home tax-free. When a local conflict arose, he was careful to remain neutral.[55]

According to one author:

> "All the merriment, religious ecstasy, comforting advice, inspiring sermons, and putative miracles ultimately rested upon a sturdy foundation of patronage."[56]

While adherents to the movement gained the title of *Hasidim* (pious Jews), they were quite different than the "old-style" *Hasidim*, especially in their rejection of asceticism. The *Besht* and his followers did not believe that physicality threatened the spirit, or that it could be demonic, as everything could be elevated to the spiritual plane. Thus, many of these new *Hasidim*, as well as their *tzadiks*, did not hesitate to display wealth, and sometimes even flaunted it.[57]

They saw no conflict between business and sanctity. For example, according to the Seer of Lublin:

> "When a merchant travels on business, he should say to himself: 'I am traveling for business so that I will have money to serve God by paying for my son's tuition, so that my sons will be Talmudic scholars ... and so that I can marry my daughters to Talmudic scholars, and sanctify the Sabbath, and give charity....'"[58]

These novel practices quickly spread over Poland and into Lithuania. Despite the attempts of the traditionalists to suppress it, the movement quickly spread west into Germany and then worldwide.[59] As you shall soon learn, the beliefs and practices of this *Ba'al Shem Tov* were to profoundly influence the lives of the fledgling Horenstein dynasty.

Rabbi Israel ben Shabbetai Hopsztajn, Magid of Kozienice (1736-1814)
and his followers. (Woodcut created ca. 1800.)

Part I: Chapter Three

RECONSTRUCTING THE LIFE OF RABBI GUR-ARYE HAKOHEN HOREN-STEIN

Born Ostroh?, Ca. 1792; died Aleksandriya (Rovno Uyezd), 1849

For several generations, Gur-arye's family had lived in the province of Volhynia in the Ukraine. They were wealthier than most residents, yet of moderate means. Usually the men supported their families primarily through business enterprises; yet they were also rabbis and often served as *Av Beit Din*, either in their own community or, when they were more widely known, in larger Jewish communities within the region.

In Gur-arye's time, there were four principal communities in Volhynia: Ostroh, Ludmir, Kremenets and Lutsk. His ancestors were deeply involved with the first two of them, namely Ludmir and Ostroh, so we will examine these communities in some detail before we review Berestechko and Aleksandriya, the other two towns in which he resided.

❧ Ludmir (Volodymyr- Volynskyi) ☙

Great Synagogue of Ludmir

Ludmir, the town's Yiddish name, is known outside of the Jewish world as Volodymyr-Volynskyi. It had been an important regional center of Volhynia since the 10th century.[60]

The Horensteins' ancestral connection to the town goes back to the *Av Beit Din* Rabbi Isaac Betzalash (ca. 1535- ca. 1575) who served there in the mid-16th century around the time that the King of Poland, Sigismond August, gave Jews the right to choose their own rabbis. A prominent rabbi and scholar, he founded a large yeshiva.[61]

The son of Rabbi Isaac's daughter Chana was Rabbi David Halevi Segal (the TaZ) (ca. 1586-1667). He became the Chief Rabbi of the large city of L'vov and one of the greatest authorities of Jewish law of his time. From 1634 to 1643, Rabbi Yom Tov Lipman Heller, a famous Talmudist and a Horenstein ancestor from a different lineage, served as community rabbi. It was not long after his tenure that the town fell victim to a Cossack onslaught.

The Khmelnytsky Uprising (1648-1657)

Bohdan Khmelnytsky

Engraving by Willem Hondius

The Uprising was a Cossack[f] rebellion in the Polish-Lithuanian Commonwealth with disastrous consequences for the Jewish communities within its boundaries. The rebels created a Cossack Hetmanate[g] in Ukrainian lands under the command of Hetman Bohdan Khmelnytsky. Allied with the Crimean Tatars and local peasantry, they fought against the armies and paramilitary forces of the Commonwealth. Mass atrocities were committed by the Cossacks against the civilian population, especially against the Jews and the Roman Catholic clergy.[62] Jews were slaughtered because, as agents and managers for the Polish nobles, they were seen as their immediate oppressors.[63]

---

[f] Cossacks: Christian horsemen who lived on the steppes of Ukraine and were hired by the Czar as soldiers whenever there was a war or military campaign that necessitated ruthless warriors.

[g] Hetmanate: A Ukrainian Cossack state ruled by a hetman.

Ludmir, like other Volhynian Jewish communities, was victimized by the Uprising, during which many Jews were either captured or murdered. Of the 159 Jewish homes before the uprising, only 39 remained yet, only four years later, community leaders began to participate in the Jewish regional council once again.[64]

It was not long afterwards that the philanthropist Rabbi Efraim Fishel Kloizner (ca. 1650-1721), a Horenstein ancestor, became the community leader of Ludmir for the Council of Four Lands as well as the head of the regional council for Volhynia. In 1705 he was chosen to be *parnas*[h] of the Council of Four Lands.[65,66] Known as Rabbi Efraim the Lobbyist, he was "one of the primary speakers among contemporary Polish Jewry."[67]

To honor his outstanding service to the community, two Polish-Lithuanian kings awarded him the status of Royal Servant. This honor granted him permission to live anyplace throughout the kingdom, to construct beer breweries and liquor distilleries on his lands in Ludmir, and to be judged in the king's court.[68]

Rabbi Jacob Fishel Kloizner (ca. 1690 – ca. 1730), his 3rd son, instead of following his father's focus on social activism, became *Av Beit Din* of Ludmir in 1713 – although he did participate that year in a meeting of the Council of Four lands. He also served as head of the Ludmir Yeshiva.[69,70]

Rabbi Jacob Kloizner's 1st son, Rabbi Saul Fishel (ca. 1705 – after 1765), followed in his father's footsteps. In 1720, while his father was still *Av Beit Din* of Ludmir, he accepted an appointment as *Av Beit Din* for the smaller town of Berestechko. Following the death of his father, he replaced him as *Av Beit Din* of Ludmir. The Horenstein connection with the TaZ and his ancestry was established with Saul's marriage to the daughter of Rabbi Israel Charif Heilprin, the TaZ's 2nd great grandson.

Due to Saul's participation in meetings of the Council of Four Lands, he was selected to serve as a trustee for the entire province of Volhynia.[71] One of his responsibilities as a trustee was financial matters, and a record has survived detailing one of his interventions in this capacity:

In 1758, Rabbi Saul of Ludmir, together with Arye Leib, the rabbi of Kremenets, acting in their capacity as trustees for the province of Volhynia, made a formal protest against the Jewish community of Ostroh. The rabbis claimed that the province's trustees faithfully took care of the Ostroh community's business. However, despite promising to pay their expenses, the Ostroh community had now refused to do so. The rabbis noted that a district council had certified this debt, and the Ostroh community had acknowledged it, but the Ostroh community still had failed to pay what it owed.[72,73]

About 1764, Rabbi Saul became ill. Despite the tension there had been between them, the Ostroh *chevra kadisha*, in a show of respect, sent him a bottle of cherry liquor.[74] He died not long afterwards.

---

[h] *Parnas:* The president/trustee of the congregation.

Rabbi Saul's son was Rabbi Pinchas of Ludmir (ca. 1725-1786), Gur-arye's paternal great grandfather. It appears that Rabbi Pinchas never became *Av Beit Din*, although he did achieve the distinction of being considered "among the most honored residents" of Ludmir.[75]

Both of his sons did become *Av Beit Din*. Gur-arye's paternal grandfather, Rabbi Arye Leib (1744 – after 1806) served as Ludmir's *Av Beit Din*,[76] while his brother, Rabbi Yisaachar Ber, became *Av Beit Din* of Tul'chyn, located in the adjoining province of Podolia.[77,78]

Rabbi Arye Leib was Gur-arye's last ancestor to be born in Ludmir as he eventually decided to leave the town of his birth and move to the town of Ostroh where he was to spend the remainder of his life.

᧤ Ostroh ᧤

Ostroh has a long and distinguished history. Founded in 893, the town was originally surrounded with a fortress ("*ostroh*" in Russian) for its defense. It became the seat of the powerful Ostrohski princely family in the 14th century who developed it into a center of commerce and learning. In the second half of the century, Ostroh was annexed by the Grand Duchy of Lithuania along with the rest of the Volhynia region. In 1569, while still remaining a private town owned by hereditary princes, it became part of the Kingdom of Poland.

Jews lived in the area at least since the 15th century, as demonstrated by two tombstones from 1445 and documents dating to 1447. There were 1,000 Jews in the area by 1565 when Ostroh had become a leading center for Jewish learning and scholarship. In 1603, the princes divided the town into two sections, causing the formation of two Jewish communities, each of which was administered by four elders. By 1765, these sections registered 213 and 202 Jewish dwellings, with 934 and 843 Jews living in them, respectively. An additional 652 Jews lived in neighboring villages.[79]

The Ostroh Jewish community was one of the original four leading Volhynian communities represented on the Council of Four Lands.[80] Throughout the life of the Council, the town remained an active participant.[81]

The Ostroh yeshiva, founded before the start of the 16th century, was one of the most important centers of Jewish learning in Poland, and some of the country's most eminent rabbinical scholars served as its principals. Gur-arye's ancestors were major contributors to the yeshiva's development and reputation, starting with Rabbi Kalonymus Kalman Haberkasten (ca. 1490 – ca. 1550), Ostroh's first known rabbi and principal of the yeshiva. Other ancestors who achieved the honor of being appointed principal of the Ostroh yeshiva include Rabbi Solomon Luria (ca. 1510–1573), Rabbi (ca. 1535–1631), and Rabbi David HaLevi Segal (ca. 1586-1631). (We will discuss the three of them later in the book.)

When Bohdan Khmelnytsky's Cossacks arrived in Ostroh, they were as merciless as they were in Ludmir. The Jewish community was viciously attacked and Jewish life in the town was utterly destroyed. Even worse, a year and a half later the killers returned to attack and ransack the town for a second time.

Everyone who failed to escape was massacred. Men, women, and children were slain on the streets and squares. Their homes, which were made of wood, were destroyed down to the foundations so that the Cossacks, along with local Christians, could better search for the treasures they believed the residents had hidden.[82] They even denigrated the town's Great Maharsha Synagogue by turning it into a stable.[83] Jewish Ostroh was so totally destroyed that, even 11 years later, only five Jewish families were living in the town's two sections.[84]

Recovery from Catastrophe

Jewish Ostroh soon began to arise again due to the efforts of Rabbi Samuel Shmelke Zak, Gur-arye's 4th great grandfather, who became the ailing town's rabbi and yeshiva principal. A wealthy man, he loaned a large sum of money to the Council of Four Lands to re-establish the yeshiva and maintain the students.[85] He also underwrote the cost of restoring the Great Maharsha Synagogue to its former glory.[86]

When Rabbi Zak died in 1680, he was succeeded by Gur-arye's illustrious 3rd great grandfather, Rabbi Naftali Hirsh Katz, known as the *Smichat Chachamim* (who we will eventually discuss in detail). At one point, Rabbi Katz left Ostroh for

Posen, and then went on to Frankfurt and Prague, but he returned to Ostroh in 1715.

Rabbi Katz was followed by Rabbi Joel Heilprin, another of Gur-arye's 3rd great grandfathers, who was *Av Beit Din*, not only of Ostroh, but also of L'vov. He was succeeded by Naftali Katz's son, Rabbi Betzalel Katz, who died in 1717.

In 1737, Rabbi David Heilprin, son of Rabbi Israel Charif Heilprin (yet another of Gur-arye's 3rd great grandfathers), became Ostroh's rabbi.[87]

Jewish Ostroh in the 18th Century

When the hereditary Polish princes divided Jewish Ostroh into two parts, the *kahal* was also divided into two *kahals*, with each under its own rabbi. It did not take long for internal dissensions between the *kahals* to arise. These weakened their ability to function both within Ostroh as well as between Ostroh and other Jewish communities within Volhynia.[88]

There is no known record of Gur-arye's family belonging to either of the Ostroh *kahals*. In addition to the friction between the two *kahals*, accumulated debts had caused the *kahals* to become embroiled in some controversy, so they may not have wished to become involved.

Also, despite their distinguished ancestry, Gur-arye's family lacked a prestigious family name. As men with these names dominated local and regional *kahals* (as well as supra-communal bodies like the Council of Four Lands),[89] their *yichus* may not have been considered adequate to warrant invitations to join, despite their descent from many of these same families.[i]

Besides the local *kahal*, there were a number of benevolent societies and foundations in Ostroh, the most important and prestigious of which was the *chevra kadisha* (burial society). This was the community institution with which Gur-arye's family was traditionally involved.

After his move to Ostroh, Rabbi Arye Leib earned a decent livelihood as a merchant selling "measured cloth goods." Like his ancestors, he became active in the *chevra kadisha where* he was elected to be its treasurer.[90]

His father, Rabbi Pinchas, moved from Ludmir to Ostroh late in life to live with his son who had made the move earlier.[91] There Rabbi Pinchas displayed the same social activism as his immediate ancestors. He joined his son in the *chevra*

---

[i] Their ancestral lines include members of the following families: Averbuch, Babad, de Falaise, de L'Esoile, de Lunel, de Vitry, Drucker, Eberle, Heilprin, Heller, Heshel, Horowitz, Isserles, Jaffe, Kalonymos, Katz, Katzenellenbogen, Klauber, Kloizner (the Horensteins' direct paternal line), Landau, Lipshitz, Loew, Luria, Margoliot, Meisels, Mintz, Munk, Rapaport, Rokach, Segal, Shachna, Shmelke, Shor, Shrentzel, Sirkes, Sofer, Spira (Shapira), Stern, Tauber, Taussig, Teomim, Trèves, Tzarfati, Wallerstein, Yalish, and Zak.

kadisha where he was elected *gabbai*.[j] By 1780, despite having lived most of his life in Ludmir, he had become one of the Ostroh *chevra kadisha's* chief executives.[92] Rabbi Pinchas died there on July 7, 1786.[93]

Gur-arye's father, Rabbi Shmuel Asher HaKohen (1770-1840), was Rabbi Arye Leib's first son[94] At the time of the 1795 Ostroh census, he was making his living by assisting his father in his business. Although we don't know the specifics of his subsequent career, he was to become an important member of the Jewish community as, more than half a century after his death in 1840, Rabbi Menachem Mendel Biber wrote:

> *"Rabbi Shmuel Asher left his mark on our city [Ostroh] till this day [1907], and his descendants are well known and are honorable people in our city."*[95]

Ostroh at the Time of Gur-arye's Birth

The 18th century was a difficult economic time for Polish Jewry, and the Jews of Ostroh were no exception. Although the town's Jewish population between 1765 and 1787 was relatively stable, the number of Jewish homes within the town decreased from 415 to 282 in the same time period, suggesting that declining incomes had forced more families to share their homes with other families.

Crowded living arrangements were not unusual, even for the families who were comparatively well off financially. Like its effect on housing, the town's economic decline had detrimental effects on the Jewish community's cherished institutions, especially those related to Jewish education and other community services.

Beside the serious economic stress, there was major political unrest. Volhynia had been an administrative division of the Polish Crown since the Union of Lublin in 1569. Polish control ended, however, in 1793, when the region was annexed by the Russian Empire as part of the Second Partition of Poland. While the Russian forces advanced, the retreating Polish army destroyed the bridges over the Horyn River to slow their progress. Polish residents ran away as the Polish army retreated, leaving only the Jews who hid in the Great Maharsha Synagogue.[96,97]

---

[j] *Gabbai:* Sexton; the person who organizes the running of a Jewish religious service and determines who will receive honors during the portion of the service when the Torah is brought out of the ark.

Great Maharsha Synagogue of Ostroh

The Russians, unaware of the departure of the Polish army, started to shell the town. Thinking that the imposing synagogue was a fortress, they focused their guns on it, shelling it heavily.

The situation appeared desperate when an elderly Jewish man took the risk of leaving the building to walk over to the Russian camp in order to speak to the general in charge of the operation.

A helpless elderly Jew approaching the camp could well have been killed by the soldiers, but the commander ordered his forces not to shoot him. He approached the commander, explained that the Polish army had evacuated Ostroh along with the Polish residents, and assured him that his forces could enter the town without encountering any resistance. Fortunately, the commander believed him and ordered all shelling to be stopped. With the crisis averted, the Russians occupied the town without incident.[98]

The Birth of Gur-arye

Malka bat Mikhel, the wife of Rabbi Shmuel Asher HaKohen, gave birth to Gur-arye ben Shmuel HaKohen around 1792.[k]

Ashkenazic Jewish naming customs call for children to be named after a deceased ancestor, with the first son usually being named after a paternal grandfather or great grandfather – yet "Gur-arye" (the lion's cub) was not an ancestral name. Moreover, according to the 1906 edition of the Jewish Encyclopedia,

> *"The form "Gur-arye" is quite rare, and is to be found only among the Italian Jews."*[99]

Why, then, would the family name the baby Gur-arye? The most likely explanation is that he was named after his paternal grandfather, Rabbi Arye Judah Leib, who served as treasurer of the Ostroh Chevra Kadisha. I suggest this because the next two Horenstein family members who were named Gur-arye were not named after the first Gur-arye; they were great grandchildren of Arye Judah Leib through other family lines.

As explained in Chapter One, there is a family legend that the MaHaRaL himself – through a dream – had communicated to his descendants that he wished the name Gur-arye to be passed down in the family. As Gur-arye ben Shmuel HaKohen was the first Gur-arye in the family, the legend probably originated some time after his birth.

Since the birth of Gur-arye ben Shmuel, his rare Hebrew given name has been fairly common among his descendants. (Its English equivalent is usually "George.") While not exclusive to the Horensteins, rarely will you find "Gur-arye" used by others, except when it is used as a surname (as in "Jacob Gurarye").

In Chapter One, I discussed my discovery of Gur-arye's family in the 1795 Jewish Census for the Ostroh District, part of the "All-Russia Census" conducted only two years after the Russian annexation of Ostroh. A careful review of the relevant entry helps one to understand the living conditions of Gur-arye's family around the time of his birth.

I had noted that Arye Leib (Gur-arye's grandfather) and his family lived in house #106 in Old Town; what I didn't mention is that they shared the house with a second family. The two families were of roughly equal means, as both Heads of Household were Merchants of the 3rd Guild, a designation which granted certain mercantile rights to the title holder in return for a considerable

---

[k] Based on the 1851 *Revizskaya Skazka* (census) for Aleksandriya, Rovno uyezd, Volhynia gubernia, which states that he was 42 at the time of the previous (1834) census. His year of birth is probably inaccurate, as he also had two brothers whose years of birth on other censuses were also 1792 – yet there is no reason to suspect they were triplets, or that any two of them were twins.

fee. As few Ostroh merchants could afford to buy these rights, the two families were better off financially than most of their neighbors.

Moreover, both Heads of Household were sellers of "measured cloth goods." They were merchants, not peddlers, so they must have sold their merchandise out of a store. Unlikely to be competitors, they were probably business partners who decided to extend their joint tenancy to their living facilities, a move that meant that they were unable to afford "single family housing." Most likely, the front section of their shared home was designed to be their store, a common arrangement.[i]

If we add up the number of listed individuals living together in house #106, there were 6 in Arye Leib's family and 13 in the other family. Thus, a total of 19 people, ranging in age between 3 and 85 years old, lived in the house – although it is likely that unlisted babies (including Gur-arye and his brother Avel) also lived there. Living space was probably very cramped, with a single kitchen serving the needs of both families.

Ostroh is transferred to Russia

Gur-arye's birth came at a historic time of transition for Ostroh. The province of Volhynia had been part of Poland since 1569, so Ostroh residents watched with dismay as Poland, starting in 1772, was progressively swallowed up by the major powers of the region. Their time for the change in nationality came in 1793 when Russia annexed Volhynia. Suddenly, their world was turned upside-down. Knight Tadeusz Czacki, son of Felix, had been the hereditary Polish owner of their part of the town. Russia quickly confiscated the area from him "due," according to the introduction to the Census book, "to the rebellion that emerged in Poland."

A new national government meant major administrative changes. New local government functionaries, loyal to the Czar of Russia, had to be installed. All national laws and regulations had to be changed to those of the new government. Polish had been the official language in their area; now Russian became the official language. As Yiddish was the native tongue of the Jews, Polish or Ukrainian had been their second language. Now it also became an asset to learn to read and speak Russian.

The Rise of Hasidism

As the popularity of the Hasidism of the *Ba'al Shem Tov* spread during the 18th century, Ostroh soon became a center for the young movement,[100] bolstered by the vacuum in Jewish life created by "poverty, ignorance and a sense of helplessness."[101] Indeed, during the last two decades of the century, Hasidism gained numerous adherents throughout Volhynia.[102]

---

[i] My grandfather's store and home in Felshtin, another town in western Ukraine, had a similar design.

One of the first Hasidic communities in Ostroh was founded mid-century by Yehuda Leib (died 1765), a disciple of the *Ba'al Shem Tov*, and his son Yakov Yosef (known as Rav Yevi). Rabbi Meir Margoliot of Brody, a personal friend of the *Besht*, was appointed Rabbi in 1777. He was succeeded by two students of Dov Ber of Mezeritch, an important propagator of Hasidism.

Gur-arye's family had close ties with the Hasidic rebbes. I already mentioned that, in the mid-18th century, Rabbi David Heilprin, Gur-arye's 3rd great grand-father, was Ostroh's rabbi. A prosperous member of an illustrious family, he was an ardent supporter of the young Hasidic movement, bequeathing substantial sums of money to many of the associates of the *Ba'al Shem Tov*, the movement's founder.[103]

Since his time, Gur-arye's family continued to interact with Hasidic rebbes in Ostroh. For example:

1. Among members of the *chevra kadisha*, Rabbi Arye Leib Heilprin, an early adherent to Hasidism, was a leader when Rabbi Pinchas, Gur-arye's paternal grandfather, became the society's *gabbai*.

2. Rabbi Pinchas' uncle by marriage was Rav Yevi (Yakov Yosef ben Yehuda Leib), the disciple of the Magid of Medzirech who established the dynasty of Ostroh *tzadiks*.

From the little we know, it does not appear that Gur-arye's immediate ancestors became *Hasidim*. Even the single description we have of him as a married adult suggests that he did not embrace the Hasidic movement until some time after his marriage, long after he had left Ostroh:

> *"Gur-arye was considered 'well-to-do' and was well respected in his local community. He was devoted to Torah study. Khaya, his wife, ran the household 'extensively and properly'. In short, the life they led was typical of that of a pious, patriarchal Jewish household of that period."*[104]

This is does not seem to be the portrait of a *Hasid*. If he were one, his Hasidic dress and lifestyle would be so obvious that we would expect the writer to mention it. Also, he states that Gur-arye was "devoted to Torah study." Hasidism emphasizes enthusiastic worship over Torah study,[105] unlike the rabbinic tradition of Gur-arye's ancestors where the study of Torah is an end in itself, and prayer, while important, is only secondary.[106]

∽ Berestechko ∾

BERESTECZKO. Rysował B. Podbielski. (Opis w następnym N-rze).

Located at the upper reaches of the Styr River, halfway between Ostroh and Ludmir, Berestechko is the third Volhynian town to which the Horenstein ancestors were closely tied. Only 12 of the town's 1,000 Jews had survived the Khmelnytsky Uprising in 1648-1649 but, like other Jewish communities, the Berestechko community had gradually regrown and re-established itself.

This was the town where Rabbi Saul Fishel, Gur-arye's 2nd great grandfather, as well as Rabbi Fishel's son, Rabbi Efraim Fishel, had served as *Av Beit Din* in the mid-18th century. Both were to move on later to assume the same position in a larger town (Ludmir for Rabbi Saul; Dubno for Rabbi Efraim Fishel).

Towards the close of the 18th century, Berestechko suffered from a serious pestilence, but quickly recovered following the Third Partition of Poland as it became a transit point for Austrian-Russian trade.[107] This started the town on a growth spurt with a rapid rise in the Jewish population.[108] By the middle of the 19th century, there were four synagogues in town, two of which were Hasidic.[109]

Berestechko census records prior to 1850 have been lost, but we know from the 1816 Aleksandriya Census that Gur-arye's brother Avel moved *from* Berestechko in 1814 when he was roughly 22 years old.[m] So Avel had lived in Berestechko earlier, in all likelihood with his parents as well as with young Gur-arye and his other siblings. The family probably moved there following the death of Arye Leib. Shmuel (his son) may have been attracted by its booming economy. Perhaps cousins whose families had lived there since the time of their Fishel ancestors had invited him and his family to live there.

Aleksandriya

Aleksandriya was a private village in the Rovno district within the province of Volhynia, The Horyn River flows through it before it reaches Ostroh which lies roughly 29 miles to the southeast. Located just nine miles north of the city of Rovno (Rivne), the village was named after the Polish nobleman Aleksander Ostrohski since, like Ostroh, it was owned at the time by the Ostrohski family.

Like other Volhynian towns, the Jewish community was largely destroyed during the Khmelnytsky Uprising in the mid-17th century. It had reconstituted by 1700 when it came under the leadership of Ostroh, its mother community.[110] Thus Ostroh and Aleksandriya had longstanding ties between them.

In the mid-18th century, after it had passed through three other noble families, Aleksandriya was transferred to the authority of the princes of the Lubomirski dynasty[111] who, at the start of the 19th century, founded both a paper mill and a cloth factory in the town, thus expanding the employment opportunities for its residents.[112]

The expanding economy, along with the Lubomirskis' liberal policies towards Jewish residents, made Aleksandriya an attractive location for Jews seeking job opportunities. In 1756, while the city of Rovno had over 1000 Jewish residents, only about 300 Jews lived in all of the 47 villages that were part of the Rovno district. By 1847, Aleksandriya itself had grown to have a total of 278 residents, the majority of whom were Jewish.[113]

The local census record states that, in 1814, Gur-arye's brother Avel, now about 22 years old, moved with his immediate family into his brother-in-law's house in Aleksandriya.[114] Gur-arye and his immediate family followed them sometime during the next two decades as, by the next census in 1834, they were living in Aleksandriya where they were listed as "town dwellers." [115] Gur-arye was to remain there for the rest of his life, while his parents and other siblings remained in Berestechko where his father died in 1840.[116]

---

[m] In addition, the 1816 Ostroh census fails to include Shmuel Asher and his family, indicating that they were no longer living in Ostroh.

The Marriage of Gur-arye and Khaya

Around the same time as the 1816 Aleksandriya Census, Gur-arye, now about 24 years old, married Khaya. The couple was to have at least four children: The first (Yakov Yosef) was born about 1818, then Naftali was born in 1821, Sarah ("Tzirul") was born 1823, and finally Feiga Bluma was born about 1825.

Both Yakov Yosef and Naftali, the Horenstein brothers, were to become extremely successful entrepreneurs. Before we discuss each of them in detail, this is what we know about Gur-arye's two daughters:

Sarah (Tzirul) Horenstein (1823-1904)

Born in 1823,[117] Tzirul (my 2nd great grandmother) married Shmuel Kanfer of Shumsk, another town within the province of Volhynia.[118] While we have no early records, by 1850, when she was about 27 years old, the couple was living in Shumsk[119] where Shmuel probably ran a small tannery. There is nothing to suggest that he was Hasidic, or even that he came from a rabbinical family.

We know from surviving documents that Tzirul must have maintained contract with her younger brother Naftali after her marriage. From at least 1892 to 1893, Tzirul's young grandson, Gur-arye Kanfer (undoubtedly named after Gur-Arye Horenstein, the first family Gur-arye), worked for his granduncle Naftali as a shop assistant in Kiev.[120] Also, as of 1913, her son Chaim owned one of the five tanneries in Radomysl together with his son and a 3rd party.[121]

Radomysl, while close to Kiev, was a rather distant location from Shumsk, so why would Kanfer family members wish to establish a tannery so far away? Moreover, another tannery was owned by one of Naftali's sons (named Gur-arye after his late grandfather), so why would he want competition, even from a cousin?

The decision to open a tannery in Radomysl must have been based on the Kanfer's familial tie to the Horensteins. Since we can assume that they were not in competition, Gur-arye Horenstein must have collaborated with the Kanfers so that each tannery produced different products. They may even have had a joint marketing arrangement.

Tziporah (Feiga Bluma) Horenstein (born about 1825)

Feiga Bluma, the other known daughter, was ""*a tall, austere and respectable-looking woman who wore glasses.*"[122] In contrast to her older sister, she married a local man with the surname of Kremenstein and thus remained in Aleksandriya when her brothers moved away. When her husband died young, she assumed control of his business, a factory for cremating tar, and subsequently ran it herself. She also owned shops for rent, and some plots of land for her sons.[123]

A prosperous, independent businesswoman, she owned a large house in the center of Aleksandriya which she ran "like a prominent person" with her own horses, a wagon and a driver.[124]

Later she married a man with the Rapaport surname, but he died shortly after the marriage, making her a widow for the second time. Following his demise, she donated a plot of land for constructing a new synagogue with the stipulation that it would be registered under the Rapaport name.[125]

Since the days of Prince Stanisław Lubomirski (1704-1793), the Jews had enjoyed a good relationship with the Lubomirski nobles who owned most of the lands in the entire Rovno area, including the forest in which Feiga Bluma's factory was located. To honor this Polish noble family, she named the new structure the Lubomirski Synagogue.[126]

While we don't know the year that she built the synagogue, Feiga Bluma could have named it after this Polish noble family in order to specifically honor Zenaida Hołyńska Lubomirska, the wife of Duke Kazimierz Lubomirski, the Lubomirski prince who owned the lands. (We will discuss him soon.) Zenaida had become so close to the Jewish residents that, when she died in 1892, they gave her an impressive funeral and even mourned her in their synagogues as a "righteous gentile."[127]

Appellations and the Horenstein Surname

For many centuries, Jewish traditional family names (often called "appellations") were adopted by sons who were proud to publicly display their kinship with prestigious ancestors. Examples are the Katz, Loew, Luria, Rapaport, Horowitz, and Katzenellenbogen families.

Appellations were entirely voluntary. Few rules governed their usage. Sometimes, when the mother's family was more prestigious than the father's, sons would choose the appellation of their mother's father, thus inadvertently creating a problem for future genealogists attempting to decipher a family line.

These appellations had a variety of origins. Some, for example, referred to the town where the family's patriarch lived. Examples are Horowitz (from Hořovice, Bohemia), and Katzenellenbogen (from Katzenellenbogen, Germany).

The Horenstein surname, by contrast, had a much later origin. Hereditary surnames such as "Horenstein" were first mandated in 1804 by Czar Alexander I. The adoption of these surnames was imposed in order to better identify and track Jews for the dual purposes of tax collection and military service. While Jewish families were eager to use the appellations of prominent ancestors to show off their *yichus*, their attitude towards these mandated surnames, imposed by a Czarist government to facilitate tax collection and military conscription, was quite the opposite. Although they were usually permitted to choose their own surname, Jews initially minimized their usage, reserving them for official government records.

Prior to the Czar's imposition of hereditary surnames, Horenstein rabbis commonly used the "HaKohen" appellation, a reference to the family tradition that they were patrilineal descendants of Aaron, the first Jewish priest and brother of Moses. Even after surnames became mandatory, rabbinical Horensteins continued to place the HaKohen appellation before their Horenstein surname for another century and a half.[n]

Surviving records indicate that the Horenstein surname was first recorded the 1816 Aleksandriya census by Avel, Gur-arye's brother. The next countrywide Russian Census was in 1834, and by then all the family members identified themselves as Horensteins.

We don't know who selected the surname, although the very earliest it could have been selected would have been in 1804 when Jewish surnames were first mandated. Since Arye Leib, Gur-arye's grandfather, was alive until 1806 or even later, he may have made the selection, especially as both of his known sons, Shmuel Asher and Duvid, were recorded in later censuses as Horensteins.[128]

While we can only guess why "Horenstein" was chosen, the Memi De-Shalit Database of Jewish Family Names[o] notes that:

"Horenstein may be derived from the name of Aaron, Moses' elder brother, the first high priest of the Jews and the ancestor of the Kohanim."

If the first syllable of the surname was chosen for this reason, its meaning would duplicate that of the family's "HaKohen" appellation.

An alternative possibility is that the first syllable of the surname could refer to the Horyn River. Berestechko is not on the Horyn, but the Horyn flows south from Aleksandriya to Ostroh, the town in which the family's ancestors had lived for centuries. Thus, the local river provides a natural connection between the two towns, making it a masterful choice for the new surname.

"Stein" at the end of the surname is the German word for "rock" or "stone." It was common for Jews in Russia to use German words in their surnames, and "stein" was a frequent choice for the ending syllable. Not only is "stone" a symbol of strength, but stone was used to build both the house of David (2 Samuel 5.11) and the house of God (1 Kings 5.31-32). The English translation of "Horenstein" could thus be "rock of Aaron."[p]

---

[n] The last HaKohen Horenstein was Shlomo HaKohen Horenstein, who died in 1965.

[o] From *Beth Hatefutsoth* (The Nahum Goldmann Museum of the Jewish Diaspora), Tel Aviv.

[p] Several unrelated families in the Ukraine, some of whom were not Kohans, also chose the Horenstein surname.

Becoming a Ruzhiner Hasid

Dov Ber of Mezeritch

By the 1760s, the *Hasidim* had become influential throughout Volhynia. Dov Ber, the famous Magid of Mezeritch, in contrast to the isolation of the *Ba'al Shem Tov* from communal activities, was so involved with the Jewish communities that he had become a decisive authority in Volhynian public affairs. As the influence of the *Hasidim* grew, the administration of the Jewish communities came under their control, and all appointments required the consent of the *tzadiks*.[129]

Both of Gur-arye's famous sons were raised as Ruzhiners, so it is likely that the charisma and brilliance of Rabbi Yisrael Friedman of Ruzhin (who was about the same age as Gur-arye) convinced him to join the burgeoning movement. A direct descendant of Rabbi Dov Ber of Mezeritch (the most important disciple of the Ba'al Shem Tov), Rabbi Israel began to attract masses of followers as soon as he succeeded his late brother as the *Rebbe* of Prohobisht, and then Skvyra.[130] He quickly proved to be a charismatic leader, known for his aristocratic demeanor.

As increasing numbers of followers flocked to the *rebbe's* small town, his home became too small to receive all the visitors, so he moved to the larger town of Ruzhin. There he attracted thousands, soon making the Ruzhiner dynasty the largest and most influential Hasidic community in the southwestern region of the Jewish Pale of Settlement.[q,131]

His presentation differed markedly from that of most Hasidic *rebbes*. While they would wear white clothes, he wore fashionable woolen clothes sewn with buttons. He traveled in a silver-handled carriage drawn by four white horses,

---

q Pale of Settlement: The area of the western part of the Russian Empire in which Russian Jews were allowed to live from 1835-1917.

wearing a golden *yarmulke*[r] and stylish clothing with solid-gold buttons, accompanied by an entourage of attendants. Even his children dressed like nobility and were attended by servants in livery.[s,132]

As a *tzadik*, it was said that he comported himself this way only to elevate God's glory, while he personally took no pleasure from it. Despite living in a palatial home with splendid furnishings, he would constantly humble himself before God by voluntarily submitting his body to fasts and painful afflictions.[133]

Gur-arye must have had a difficult internal struggle, and we do not know if his family put pressure on him to remain "with the flock." Becoming a Ruzhiner would greatly change, not only on his life, but also the lives of his wife and children. No longer would the family be associated with a traditional synagogue; now they would pray and study with other Ruzhiners, and his sons would be raised as, and would be dressed as, Ruzhiners. Outside of business and communal activities, they would mainly associate with those who, like them, professed allegiance to the rabbinic dynasty of Rabbi Israel of Ruzhin.[134]

Death of Gur-arye

Gur-arye ben Shmuel HaKohen Horenstein died in Aleksandriya in 1849, only eight years following the death of his father. Living with him at the end of his life were his wife Khaya, his younger son Naftali, now 29 years old, and Naftali's wife and children.

Yakov Yosef, now 31 years old, had moved to Ludvipol. Tzirul, Gur-arye's older daughter, was probably married by then and living in Shumsk.[135] Feiga Bluma, his younger daughter, was also probably married, living with her husband in Aleksandriya.

Gur-arye and his Life: An Analysis

Other than a single reference to him in an article about his wealthy sons, we are missing a description which breathes warmth into the dry facts of the life of Gur-arye ben Shmuel HaKohen. He had famous ancestors and famous children, but the lack of information on him beyond government documents suggests that he never achieved, or perhaps never sought, recognition in the Jewish world.

From the little we know, he appears to have been a quiet, inwardly-looking man who was devoted primarily to his family and to religious study and

---

[r] *Yarmulke:* Skullcap; a small brimless cap worn by Jews, especially during religious services.

[s] David Assaf, in The Regal Way: The Life and Times of Rabbi Israel of Ruzhin (2002), notes that, while nobody disputes that Rabbi Israel owned a lot of property and lived in a magnificent palace, many authors have vastly exaggerated depictions of his wealth, his palace, and his carriage.

observance. As a businessman, we don't know what he did for a living, but he seems to have been successful enough to have been an adequate provider.

In earlier generations, his ancestors, almost all rabbis, were often *Av Beit Din*, Talmudic scholars and community leaders. We often know little about the source of their financial support, but many had substantial financial assets which mitigated the need for the community to provide them with an adequate income. We do know that Gur-arye's grandfather, Arye Leib, was a rabbi and a leader of the Ostroh *chevra kadisha* but, after moving to Ostroh, earned his income as a 3rd Guild Merchant.[t]

Shmuel HaKohen, Arye Judah's son, followed in his father's footsteps, functioning primarily as a merchant, and Gur-arye did the same. While these men were rabbis and remained devoutly religious, business interests had an equal footing with religious practice and communal responsibilities. This important shift in emphasis within the family was not limited to a couple of generations, but was to continue with Gur-arye's progeny.

We can also learn something about Gur-arye by examining the personalities of his two sons, as we know much more about them than we do about him. While their personalities were different, they were both devout *Hasidim* who were widely known for their generosity to the community and especially to the poor. This generosity was a quality that their father had likely modeled for them during their youth.

He was the first Gur-arye in the family, but certainly not the last. What seems to shine through the few facts we have is that this "lion's cub" was respected both within and outside of his family. Otherwise his given name would not be bestowed on Horenstein progeny even today, in the hope that the many family Gur-aryes which have followed him would grow up to exhibit the fine qualities of his character.

---

[t] Rights to conduct trade were dependent upon a merchant's guild. Catherine II, in 1775, set 500 rubles of declared capital as the requirement for joining the 3rd guild, 1,000 rubles for the 2nd guild, and 10,000 rubles for the 1st guild, with the fee for joining a guild set at one percent of declared capital. Only the most successful merchants could afford to join even the lowest guild [https://novossiltzeff.com/other-information/the-russian-guilds/]

RABBI YAKOV YOSEF HAKOHEN HORENSTEIN OF KORETS

Born Aleksandriya, 1818-1819; died Korets, 1876

Yakov Yosef was Gur-arye's oldest son. Scholarly like his father, he immersed himself in Torah study in his early years. He married Margulia, his first wife, around 1832. Between 1833 and 1847, the couple had five children.[136] We know from *Shalshelet HaYuchasin* (ca. 1977), a book written by Rabbi Yosef Lieberman, Yakov Yosef's 2nd great grand nephew, that he supported the family with the modest wages he received by working as a clerk for the owner of the local forest.[137] He would have had little money left over after expenses to put into savings.

From Forest Clerk to Wealthy Businessman

This young Ruzhiner *Hasid*, sole support for a wife and several children, a mere clerk for a rich forest owner, was to soon become one of the wealthiest Jews in the Ukraine. Fellow Jews throughout the region were intensely curious as to how a Jew – and especially a *Hasid* – became so wealthy, and so fast?

Usually mysteries like this go unsolved, but we are fortunate in this case to have a folk tale, also included in Lieberman's *Shalshelet HaYuchasin*, which claims to explain the mystery:

> *"One day, Yakov Yosef traveled to see the holy Rabbi of Ruzhin. During his meeting, he handed the rebbe a 'kvitel'.[a] In the note, among other things, he asked the rebbe to bless him with wealth and stated that, with this wealth, he would be able to serve God generously.*

> *"The holy man blessed him with all of his petitions - except for his request for wealth.*

---

[a] *Kvitel:* Yiddish for "little note," a *kvitel* refers to a note with a petitionary prayer that is given to a Hasidic *rebbe* in order to receive the latter's blessing. It may be a general request for health, livelihood or success, or a specific request such as recovery from illness, the ability to bear children, a wedding match, etc., and is usually given together with a sum of money which is used by the *rebbe* for the upkeep of his court or for distribution to charity (Wikipedia.org).

"Yakov Yosef returned to visit the rebbe several more times, each time making the same request, until finally Rabbi Friedman said to him,

> 'If I bless you with wealth, I am afraid of what that wealth would do to you and your children'.

"Yakov Yosef replied:

> 'I hereby promise the master that the wealth shall not bring harm to me or my children'.[b]

"When the holy man heard his words, he blessed him with wealth.

"After he returned home from the rebbe's house, he happened to sit beside a Russian nobleman and began to converse with him. The nobleman liked Yakov Yosef and asked him what he did for a living. When he heard that he earned his livelihood from the forestry business, he told him that he had a large forest which he would be willing to sell to him for an inexpensive price.

"Yakov Yosef replied:

> 'I don't own anything, so how can I buy a large forest'?

> 'No matter', answered the nobleman.

> 'Take it now, and at the end of one year, after having made your profit from it, you will give me its price'.

"Yakov Yosef left his job and arranged to cut timber in the nobleman's forest. As the nobleman had predicted, when he sold the wood the first year, he was easily able to pay the price for the forest."[138]

This is a typical Hasidic folk tale, designed to show the insightfulness and power of a famous *tzadik* when a *Hasid* applies to him for assistance. It has two parts. The first part is proposed to explain the second part, namely Yakov Yosef's chance meeting with the Russian nobleman, as the result of his promise to the *rebbe* to "serve God generously with his wealth" and to not let the wealth "bring harm" to him or his children.

Even if we assume that the discussion between Yakov Yosef and the Ruzhiner *rebbe* over wealth was fanciful, the second part of the tale, namely the chance

---

[b] "To bring harm" probably means to succumb to the baser temptations of wealth, such as laziness, narcissism and devaluation of the poor.

meeting with a generous nobleman, may have a kernel of truth. Discovering the historical reality requires some investigation as we aren't told the identity of the nobleman, the year of their meeting, or even the location of the nobleman's forest.

Who was this mysterious nobleman who practically gave Yakov Yosef a piece of his extensive forest landholdings in the area, and started him on the path to a fortune? Since the noble Polish Lubomirski family owned these lands, he must have been a member of this family. In the previous chapter, we discussed how, after his brother Avel moved to Aleksandriya, Gur-arye (Yakov Yosef's father), followed him there. This small private town outside of the city of Rovno, both of which were part of the immense holdings of the Lubomirski nobles, was where Yakov Yosef grew up.

Lubomirski family tradition was one of service to the Polish nation. Family members held the most important offices in the state, such as *starosts*[c] and governors. Four representatives of the family held the office of Grand Marshal of the Crown. They performed important political functions, such as chairing the *Sejm*, forming a private army, and repeatedly representing the king at all the courts of Europe. Many times they had a decisive influence on the choice of monarchs. They were defenders of the nobility, who often entrusted them with their vote at the *Sejm* and in the election of kings.[139]

The Rovno branch of the large noble Lubomirski family resided in their local castle, which had been rebuilt for them by Jan de Witte in rococo style:[140]

---

[c] *Starost:* A Polish nobleman who possessed a *starosty* (castle and domain conferred for life).

Lubomirski Palace, Rovno

The Rovno Lubomirskis, known for their good relations with the Jews, wanted to attract more Jews to the area to help develop the city,[141] which was to become the center of their financial empire in Volhynia.[142] They did so in at least two ways:

- At the beginning of the 18th century, they granted Jews living in their towns the same land ownership rights as Christians, as well as communal and juridical autonomy.[143,144]
- On July 13, 1749, Prince Stanisław Lubomirski granted a charter to the Jewish residents of the Rovno area, establishing a full-fledged Jewish community with all its own institutions.[145]

These efforts to appeal to Jews were quite successful leading, over the next century, to a dramatic increase in the Jewish population.[146]

In the late 1700s, the owner of the vast Lubormirski properties in the Rovno area was Prince Fryderyk Wilhelm Lubomirski. Born in 1779, he was only a teenager when he was listed as a general in the Polish army until its defeat by the Russians in 1793.[147]

Fryderyk married Franciszka Załuska about 1808.[148] Kazimierz, their only child, was born in Chernivtsi, in the province of Podolia, in 1813.[149]

Fryderyk's focus was on developing the Rovno section of his holdings. He was known as a philanthropist and amateur builder, and he and Franciszka initially maintained an active social life, with their palace serving as the center for Rovno's high society.

His life took an unexpected turn, however, when, not long after Kazimierz's birth, his marriage fell apart. Fryderyk remained in Volhynia where he brought up little Kazimierz, while Franciszka stayed mainly in Warsaw. In 1816, she began an affair with Antoni Malczewski, a well-known poet, and went with him for a famous romantic tour of Europe during which he became the first Pole to climb Mont Blanc.[150]

That same year, Fryderyk was appointed Vice-Governor of the province of Volhynia. His father died in Rovno the following year, so he assumed the entire responsibility of administering the family's vast real estate holdings in addition to his official duties as Vice-Governor. He also served as Chamberlain of the Russian Emperor (manager of his household), although his position was probably purely honorary.[151]

Meanwhile, young Kazimierz grew up in the Lubomirski palace where he took music lessons from the bandmaster of the palace's own orchestra. That experience set the stage for a highly unusual career for a Lubomirski noble. Following his high school graduation in Klevan (not far from Rovno), he moved to Europe around 1830 to study music more seriously in Dresden, Germany with the intention of composing parlor music.

Prince Kazimierz soon established himself as a composer, and his young adult life was spent traveling around Europe as well as organizing weekly concerts in his salon in Warsaw.[152] In 1852, he was elected deputy president of the Society for the Support of Impoverished Musical Artists.

He composed many pieces for voice and piano, as well as small instrumental pieces, over his career. Although he is largely forgotten today, he achieved considerable reknown at the time.

Kazimierz married Zenaida Hołyńska, the "righteous gentile" I mentioned earlier. The couple had two children but did not return to live in Rovno until after

1860 when Kazimierz had become partially paralyzed and no longer able to fully engage in music composition and performances. By then his father had been dead for 12 years.[153]

Following Kazimierz's move to Europe in 1830, his father had been left in the palace without any family. Fryderyk continued to carry out his many responsibilities, but lost interest in participating in the glamorous lifestyle of the nobility. For some years, he continued to live alone in the palace, escaping in the summers to the family's manor house in Aleksandriya, the same town in which Yakov Yosef and his family lived.[154] (We have no way of knowing whether the fact that they were neighbors during the summers led to a deepening of Fryderyk's relationship to Yakov Yosef.)

In 1840, after living alone in the palace for two decades, he built an unimposing, one-story structure on a little hill behind Rovno and surrounded it with a garden, while he let his grand palace deteriorate.[155] His new residence, which looked like a country house, seemed so modest that people in his social class thought it was unsuitable for a member of a family with such an important surname and plenty of money. Fryderyk didn't care what others thought, as this was the way he wanted to live.[156]

Was Prince Fryderyk Lubomirski the "wealthy Russian nobleman?"

We noted earlier that Rabbi Yosef Lieberman, a Horenstein cousin, reported that the young Yakov Yosef was employed by "a local forest owner" as a clerk, information that was probably passed down from generation to generation through family sources. He apparently was unaware that, in the area where Yakov Yosef lived, the local forests were owned by the Lubomirskis.

Thus, when Lieberman reported the folk tale ("it is said that") concerning how Yakov Yosef became immensely wealthy, he failed to realize that the "local forest owner" was probably none other than the "Russian nobleman" of the Hasidic folk tale!

Let us examine this hypothesis in some detail. Usually the Polish nobility kept to themselves, but we already know that Fryderyk was not a typical noble. Also, for the Rovno Lubomirskis, Yakov Yosef's Judaism, even his Hasidic dress, would not have been an obstacle to forming a personal relationship.

At the time that Yakov Yosef was apparently employed by Fryderyk, the Polish prince was living alone in the palace except for his servants. Deserted by his family, he could have substituted an active social life, including palace festivities, to make up for his lack of family, but we already know that the glamour of palace social life failed to appeal to him.

If Yakov Yosef were indeed Fryderyk's clerk, he may have been the only person with whom he spent considerable time; therefore, Fryderyk may have gotten to know him quite well. Not only would he have appraised his dedication to his work and the quality of his service, but Yakov Yosef may have revealed to him his keen desire to become wealthy – a goal that, realistically, a simple clerk could never achieve in Czarist Russia without outside financial assistance.

While we have no facts concerning Fryderyk's relationship with Kazimierz, we can speculate that Fryderyk may well have been displeased that his only son, then about 28 years old, was "fliting" around Europe, likely living primarily on family funds, rather than assisting him in managing the vast Lubomirski properties. Just five years older than Kazimierz, Yakov Yosef could well have been embraced by Fryderyk, either consciously or unconsciously, as a substitute for his absent son.

As their relationship matured, Count Lubomirski may have been inspired to do something remarkable for his ambitious young clerk, something that could indeed start him on the road to fulfilling his dream.

He could, of course, simply have given him a piece of his vast forests. Although such a generous gift would have had considerable value just as real estate, for its full value to be realized, its owner would need to take the responsibility of hiring a crew to fell the mature trees. Then he would have had to negotiate the sale of the raw timber to local timber merchants, or perhaps make arrangements to transport the timber from the forest to lumber mills which would then transform it into boards and other commercial products.

Thus, if Yakov Yosef were truly determined to start a personal fortune, he would have had to be willing to expend considerable time and effort to maximize the forest's economic potential. The folk tale suggests that Fryderyk found the perfect way to test his determination: Rather than simply turning the ownership of a local forest over to Yakov Yosef, he offered him ownership of the forest for a price well below its market value.

He knew that Yakov Yosef could not possibly afford to buy the forest, even at such a low price, but the other part of his offer would make that possible, if Yakov Yosef were up to the task: He would grant Yakov Yosef the right to harvest the trees for one year without any charge. During that year, he could sell the timber however he wished. Fryderyk set the price low enough so that Yosef Yosef could then afford to purchase the forest – but only if he handled this opportunity well.

This was a spectacular, once-in-a-lifetime opportunity for a young man with little money and a wife and young children to support - so Yakov Yosef accepted the offer, moved with his family to a poor little town just below that area of forest, and began on his road to riches.

Of course, most of this is pure supposition, but it is the best we can do without further factual data, such as a document which legalized the property transfer from Prince Lubomirski to Yakov Yosef.

The available historical record is consistent with this speculation. As you may recall, the 1834 Aleksandriya census listed Gur-arye and his family, including Yakov Yosef, as ordinary "Town Dwellers."[157] Fryderyk moved out of the palace to take up residence in his new home in 1840, around the same time as Yakov Yosef moved away from the rest of his family with his wife Margulia and his children to settle in the little town of Ludvipol, about 29 miles away.[158] (Perhaps the two moves were somehow related to one another.)

⇜ Ludvipol (Sosnove) ⇝

Built in the 13th century and long settled by Jews, Ludvipol was one of the smallest communities in Volhynia province, with only 286 residents as of 1847.[159] The town was so small that locals would say that

> *"when a carriage or a wagon entered [Ludvipol], the head of the horse would be at one end of the town while the back wheel would be at the other end."*[160]

The town was located by the Sluch River, a tributary of the Horyn. Most importantly, above it there were thick pine forests,[161] owned by the Rovno Lubomirskis.

Ludvipol's inhabitants were generally poor. Even by 1910, six decades after Yakov Yosef moved to the town, only a small portion of the townspeople were making enough money to live comfortably, so we can expect that they were not faring any better when Yakov Yosef arrived in 1841. With a source of lumber in the forest just above them, the town's lumber merchants were the exception, as they made a good living.[162]

Craftsmen constituted the bulk of the population. Due to "oppression and lack of rights," they were unable to find adequate work to support their families, resulting in considerable poverty. Even the shopkeepers were suffering due to lack of capital.[163]

Why would this young clerk with a decent job, responsible for a wife and young children, want to move to Ludvipol? It would seem to make no sense as it would be foolish for him to seek employment there as a clerk; yet it was during the relatively few years during which he resided in this poor little town that Yakov Yosef amassed a small fortune in the lumber industry. Despite the factual distortions that occur both in a folk tale and in family lore after being handed down from person to person over a period of 130 years, there seems to be no other possible explanation for the sudden, steep rise in Yakov Yosef's financial assets.

Magulia died in 1847, probably due to complications of childbirth.[164] By the following year, about 8 years after his arrival in Ludvipol, he had paid a tax of 200 rubles (at least half of a year's income for the typical Russian worker) which granted him the special rights and privileges of a Ludvipol Merchant of the 3rd Guild. He also had applied for an international passport.[165]

That was only the beginning. The folk tale states that, "in the course of time," he re-sold a small portion of his forest for a large sum at a substantial profit.

Within a few years after that sale, he had paid the Czarist government at least 2,300 rubles, 12 times as much money as he had paid to become a 3rd Guild Merchant, to become a Ludvipol Merchant of the 2nd Guild.[166] This granted him many more rights, in fact most of the rights of a Merchant of the 1st Guild.[167]

While still living in Ludvipol, he married Sura Raitsia and had two more children. The first, a daughter born about 1854, was named Margulia, undoubtedly after her father's late wife.[168] Duvid Shulim, their second child, was born about 1856, also in Ludvipol.[169]

∾ Zaborol ∾

While Yakov Yosef had already achieved considerable financial success, his fortune continued to rapidly increase over the next several years until it was well beyond the reach of all but the richest Jews in the entire Ukraine. Around 1858,[170] he left Ludvipol to move to a lavish estate in the private village of Zaborol, another village owned by Polish magnates, located nine miles north of the city of Rovno. Not only was his estate luxurious, but, according to a witness, it was like a "miniature Jewish kingdom," with many servants, a house of prayer and even its own *mikva* (ritual bath).[171]

The estate's main building was massive. One visitor recounted how, while walking through the building, she found herself in a room full of mirrors. As she had never seen so many mirrors, she became frightened. She then began to wander around, trying to find a way out of the building, winding her way through a labyrinth of many rooms. With great difficulty, she eventually succeeding in leaving.[172]

How was it possible for a young clerk, a Ruzhiner *Hasid* of modest means, to become so wealthy within two decades while residing in a small, poverty-stricken town? It would be difficult to find an alternative explanation to that provided by the folk tale.

Now that he was a wealthy man, Yakov Yosef's lifestyle changed dramatically. According to Rabbi Yosef Lieberman:

"After he became wealthy, Yakov Yosef used to sit in the beit midrash (Jewish house of study) busy with Torah, prayer and Kabbalah.[d] He dressed in silken clothes and white socks every day of the week. He was openhanded to everyone.

"When he traveled in his covered wagon, he used to stand in the city's Jewish street and distribute golden dinars without limit to the masses. When he said the Shacharit (morning) prayers, at the point of

'And You are governor of all',

he put his hand into his pocket, took out one of the golden dinars and two silver dinars, approached the poor and let them take whatever they wanted."[173]

Noa Ironi, writing in the Aleksandriya yiskor book (*Pinkas HaKehilah Alexandrija/Sefer Iskor*), provides a similar picture:

"The (H)orenstein family members would appear in the town riding a chariot with three graceful horses. All the city would gather around.

'The gvirim (very wealthy people) are coming'!

"The rumor would quickly spread among the town's beggars and they would encircle them like flies. The guests then would generously give alms and everyone was happy."[174]

While we do not have a complete record of his holdings, Zaborol was an administrative center for the extensive Zaborol-Horodyshche forests.[175] We know that Yakov Yosef bought the village of Horodyshche from Horodyski himself,[176] most likely to produce lumber from the surrounding forest land. That purchase probably prompted his move to the village.

Around this time in his life, Yakov Yosef began to diversify his holdings well beyond forest lands. He became one of the first Jewish beet sugar manufacturers, establishing the Zhytyn sugar refinery just south of his Zaborol estate.[177,178] Also, on the northeast side of the village of Mizoch, 25 miles south of Aleksandriya and just south of Rovno, he became owner of the Karwice sugar refinery, probably in partnership with his brother Naftali (as ownership later passed to Naftali's son

---

[d] *Kabbalah:* The ancient Jewish tradition of mystical interpretation of the Bible.

Avrum). This enterprise initiated the industrial development of the village.[179] He even developed a farm for cattle which were fed the beetroot remains from the refinery.[180]

Sugar beet mill, France - ca. 1843

Yakov Yosef also became the owner of distilleries, such as the Sroten-Goworen Distillery.[181] In addition to his own investments, he would partner with his younger brother Naftali to invest in still other business enterprises.

Throughout his life, despite his many businesses and burgeoning fortune, Yakov Yosef remained a devoted *Hasid*. Like his father, he was a *Ruzhiner*, a follower of Rabbi Yisrael Friedman of Ruzhin. After the *rebbe's* death in Sadigura in 1850, Yakov Yosef became a follower of the *rebbe's* sons: first Sholom Yosef Friedman, who died after just one year, and then Avraham Yakov Friedman, the first Sadigura *rebbe*.[182]

Several times a year, Yakov Yosef would travel to visit his *rebbe*, Rabbi Avraham Yakov Friedman, in Sadigura, riding in a coach drawn by four horses at the cost of several thousand rubles – a fortune for most people in a society where the average worker earned about 360 rubles a year. Along the way he would pick up other *Hasidim* who wished to make the pilgrimage.

Rabbi Avraham Yakov Friedman

An ardent supporter and close companion of Rabbi Avraham Yakov, he so generously provided for the needs of the *rebbe* and his court that his reputation spread throughout all of Jewish Ukraine.[183]

Once, according to another folk tale, Yakov Yosef was in Sadigura for the holiday of *Shavuot*.[e] At the time, he was engaged in a lumber contract for the Czar. There had been a severe drought so, since the lumber was to travel by boat, he had not been able to deliver any lumber to fulfill the contract.

He was very worried that he could be arrested and jailed for the rest of his life and thus fail to provide funds for the sustenance of his family.

---

[e] *Shavuot*: A major Jewish festival held late May or early June, 50 days after the second day of Passover. Originally a harvest festival, it now also commemorates God's giving of the Torah to the Jews.

uss aus der Bukowina   Palais des Wunderrabbi in Sadagora

Home of the Sadigura Rebbe

According to the tale, the eve of the first day of *Shavuot*, in the dimness of the early morning, the Master returned home from the *mikveh*.[f] He was alone in his large parlor when Yakov Yosef entered. With tears in his eyes, he explained to the *rebbe* how his life was hanging in the balance.

The *rebbe* replied,

"Look, although the eyes of a living being cannot see at a great distance, I see a cloud through the window which looks like the palm of a human being. Undoubtedly rain has fallen there."

Hearing this, Yakov Yosef calmed down and cheered up. He then returned to his inn in a happy mood.

On the day following the two days of the holiday, a telegram arrived at the inn informing him that there had indeed been a large rainfall in the area where the

---

[f] *Mikveh:* Bath used for ritual immersion.

lumber was located. Moreover, it turned out that a close friend[g] had received a confidential letter on that first day of Shavuot which also stated that a large amount of rain had just fallen in that area.[184]

While folk tales usually go unconfirmed by other sources, in this case the author of the tale reported that a remarkably similar story had been told to him personally by none other than Naftali Horenstein, Yakov Yosef's younger brother:

> *"There was not enough water for the barge from Prussia, and (Yakov Yosef) went to the Master, Avir (Rabbi Avraham) Yakov," ... to pour his heart out to seek some sympathy against his misfortune.*

> *"And, on the day of Lag Ba'Omer[h] (between late April and late May), great amounts of snow fell there until the lumber could be transported on the water.*[185]

---

[g] Fishel of Myhkolaiv (later of Proskurov)

[h] *Lag B'Omer*, a minor Jewish holiday, occurs in late April to early May, on the 33rd day of the Omer, the 49-day period between Passover and Shavuot, and is a break from the semi-mourning during that interval.

❧ Korets ❧

Around the early 1860s, Yakov Yosef moved his family once again, this time 17 miles south of Ludvipol to the town of Korets, located by the Kortchek River which wraps around the town.[186] His brother Naftali and his own family joined them there.[187]

During the 19th century, the population of Korets increased to 4,000 people, with Jews accounting for 70 to 80% of the population. By late in the century, the town's population had jumped to 12,000, 80% of whom were Jewish.[188]

He was to remain there the rest of his life and to exert an important influence on its growth and economy. Soon he became known as "Yakov Yosef of Korets."

His worth at this time was estimated to have increased to several million rubles.[i,189]

Yakov Yosef probably selected Korets for his residence as it was the primary location of the wood industry.[190] He bought or leased local forests and built a lumber mill to process and sell the lumber made from his trees.[191] He also opened two banks.[192] Soon he became a major employer for the town's Jewish population.[193] According to Dov Bernstein, writing in the Korets yisgor book:[194]

> *"The phenomenon of a great master, such as, R' Yakov-Yossi Horenstein, the owner of large estates, dense forests, and large economic enterprises - was 'out of the ordinary'."*

He quickly became, not only one of the town's biggest employers, but also one of the its biggest benefactors. In 1866, after Czar Alexander II survived an attack by his enemies, Yakov Yosef donated money to build a new Jewish hospital, named the Alexandrovski Hospital in the Czar's honor.[195] Among his other donations were funds to build a *beit midrash*[196] a *Talmud Torah,*[j] and a town library.[197]

His business enterprises also extended well beyond Korets. In 1870, he signed a 30-year contract for logging rights on the 8100-acre estate of Count Aleksandr Vladislavovich Branitskiy at Migalki village in Radomysl Uyezd (near his brother Naftali's estate). Five years later he passed the contract on to the Zussman family which, in turn, passed it on to Naftali in 1879.[198]

By 1870, Yakov Yosef had paid the required tax to become a Kiev Merchant of the 1st Guild.[199] While retail trade was limited to Kiev (his town of registration) and then to three shops, he now had the right to carry on every kind of wholesale trade, to own ships, to possess warehouses, to manufacture everything except hard liquor (and to possess landed property with serfs for this purpose), to engage in banking, to have insurance offices, to undertake all government contracts, and to enter into contracts of any amount.

In addition, he was freed from corporal punishment, exempt from military service and the capitation tax, admitted at court and permitted to wear a sword and to "drive around the town in a closed carriage with two horses."[200] As long as his payments for these privileges were continued, he and his immediate family were no longer restricted to living within the Jewish Pale of Settlement, but were permitted to live anywhere in Russia.[201]

Since Korets was still his primary residence, he could have chosen to become a Korets Merchant of the 1st Guild. His decision to make Kiev the location of his 1st Guild designation indicates that he was spending considerable time doing

---

[i] The printing of the number of rubles listed in the original article is blurry, but it was either three or eight million rubles.

[j] *Talmud Torah:* School for teaching the fundamentals of Judaism.

business in Kiev, probably including projects with Naftali, his younger brother, who was also staying in Kiev on occasion.

This designation placed him in the top rank of Russian businessmen, but it was dwarfed by the Czar's decision, which had also been made by 1870, to grant his petition to become an Honored Citizen *(pochetnyi grazhdanin)*, the highest designation of *any* citizen of the Russian Empire.[202] The title, established in 1832 by Emperor Nicholas I, was bestowed on the upper echelon of merchants and industrialists as well as non-government officials who had higher education and legitimate children of personal (as distinguished from hereditary) nobles. Honored Citizens had additional rights and privileges beyond those given to Merchants of the 1st Guild, such as the right to participate in urban self-government.[203]

Like his previous estate in Zaborol, Yakov Yosef's home in Korets resembled a palace, complete with servants and attendants, horses, carriages, stables and cellars. It was said to overflow with all sorts of luxuries. Open to everyone passing through town, it was always swarming with people. Its atmosphere was "a blending of the Jewish way of life and wealth, full of joy, singing and commotion."[204]

Yakov Yosef always gave generously to the poor, although his method of making these donations was often rather unusual. He did not actively supervise the spending of the funds he donated to charities, nor did he pre-determine a fixed amount of money to give to the needy. Instead, he would simply hand out money whenever he saw the need. Often, he would send out his servants to find poor people deserving of a donation, and then to bring them to him so that he could personally present them with the money.[205]

There are a number of tales about the unusual manner in which he made his charitable contributions:

- One year Yakov Yosef found that his fields were producing little in the way of crops, which told him that there was a significant drought. Certain that, the following spring, prices would rise causing the poorer Jews to starve, he purchased a large amount of produce in the autumn to store in his warehouse. Then, when autumn came and the prices rose as he predicted, he ordered his warehouse manager to distribute the stored produce to the poor.

- There was a time, on the eve of Passover, that his porter came to him and, with tears in his eyes, requested that he give him 10 rubles (about 2 week's wages) because his wife had died and he did not have enough money to pay for the burial. Yakov Yosef immediately gave him a check for the money. The porter then left and quickly disappeared from the estate.

  As he was quite surprised at his disappearance, Yakov Yosef went to investigate the matter and discovered that the porter's wife was alive and well. He searched out the porter and, when he found him, the man confessed to his lie.

  Yakov Yosef replied:

"You're such a fool. For 10 rubles, was it worth your while to 'kill' your wife and to 'orphan' your children? If you had spoken to me about your financial plight plainly and forthrightly, would I have refused you?"

And, with that, Yakov Yosef gave him another check for 10 rubles and sent him back to his courtyard.

- Once an emissary visited him to collect financial support for the *Yeshiva* (Jewish school for advanced education). They arrived at a compromise between the amount that the emissary requested and the amount Yakov Yosef wished to donate, and the emissary was about to leave.

  Suddenly, the postman came in and brought a telegram. After reading the telegram, Yakov Yosef called the emissary back and asked him for a receipt for a sum much greater than what he had received. When he saw the surprise the emissary's face, Yakov Yosef explained that:

  "They informed me in the telegram that several of my barges sank in the water, and the damage is great. Now, do you understand? To Satan I've 'donated' such a huge sum, shouldn't I do the same for the Yeshiva? Therefore, I have decided to increase the amount of my contribution."

- While on a business trip, Yakov Yosef stopped over in a small town to spend the Sabbath during one of the four times of the year when there are special Torah portion readings. As it was his custom to receive the *Maftir aliyah*[k] for these special Sabbaths, he visited the *beit midrash* early in the morning and told the *gabbai* to call him up for *Maftir*.

  The *gabbai* replied,

  "The town's rich man has already bought the rights to all the Maftirs for the entire year."

  Yakov Yosef said,

  "I will pay handsomely."

  "How much?" asked the *gabbai*.

  "A lot." answered Yakov Yosef.

---

[k] *Maftir aliyah:* The honor of being the last person called upon to read from the Torah.

They met with the rich man to discuss the issue. In the end, he agreed to make a concession for this *Maftir* so that Yakov Yosef could do the last reading from the Torah.

So, at the appropriate point in the service, Yakov Yosef was called up. When the *gabbai* came to the phrase

"For his promise to donate ....,"

Yakov Yosef interjected,

"the amount that this town's rich man is worth!"

The congregation was stunned into silence.

After the Sabbath's end, representatives of the congregation met with the town's rabbi, the rich man and Yakov Yosef. The rich man reported that his worth amounted to 1,800 rubles. Yakov Yosef promptly paid the full amount in cash.[206]

The Death of Yakov Yosef

In March of 1876, death came to Yakov Yosef while he was still at the height of his career.[207,208] Rabbi Nechemiah Hershenhorn, Rabbi of Korets and its surrounding region, wrote a eulogy which was published in the local newspaper:

"Rabbi Yakov Yosef ... was a great man.... For his entire life his hand was open to aid the distressed without making distinctions in religion and faith....

"And, he never said, "Enough!"[209]

Zalmen Kobylański, a Korets resident, wrote:

"This was a man of lofty status who offered his life as a total sacrifice on the altar of Torah and wisdom ... and whose home was open wide to any person in poverty or ailing in spirit. He was the leader of the respected merchants who were known throughout the land for praise and reputation....

"The poor of our city will wail because Yakov, their father, has died.... All residents of the city, the learned, the enlightened and Hasidim rose up in unity to eulogize Yakov and to cry over him and to accompany him to his everlasting resting place.... He spoke pleasantly with each person, and on his face one could discern an expression of truthfulness."[210]

The editors of *Halvri*, the newspaper in which the above obituary was published, added the following:

"We request that [you, the readers] inform us about his last will and testament because he has for certain left much for charity."[211]

Following their father's demise, Yakov Yosef's children moved to Kiev and other large cities, while his palatial home near Korets became vacant and slowly deteriorated.

Five years later, on June 17, 1881, a great fire broke out in Korets, killing 20 residents and destroying hundreds of homes and shops. All of the synagogues, Hasidic *shtiblekh[I]* and *batei midrash* were destroyed.[212]

Although Yakov Yosef had died five years earlier, Herzel Frankel, writing in the Korets yisgor book, states that, following the fire, Yakov Yosef funded a magnificent synagogue for which he "commissioned famous artists from Odessa, and they built the synagogue for beauty and glory." It was located prominently on a hill by the bank of the Kortchik River and "gave the impression that the safety of the entire (Jewish) community lay in its hands."[213,214] This synagogue became known as "Reb Yakov-Yosi's Shul."[215]

As the Korets yisgor book was published in 1959, 78 years after the Korets fire, it is understandable why Frankel could have mistakenly assumed that Yakov Yosef paid for the construction of the synagogue that bore his name. An article published in *HaMelitz* in 1883, only two years after the fire, provides a more likely scenario:

"At the time of the awful fire that occurred in our town in the [Hebrew calendar] year 5641..., the notables of our town made known that the House of HaShem is a necessary thing in order to bring together the hearts of the people of the town who are distant. And, they consulted each other and decided that it is incumbent on the entire community to cover the costs of building a synagogue from donations."[216]

This building was to be *"of stone, tall and magnificent ... such as never before seen in our town."[217]* Among the contributors to the new building were Yakov Yosef's three sons as well as the wife (probably the widow) of his fourth son.[218]

While the unfinished synagogue had not been named at the time the article was written, the Korets yisgor book article suggests that, following its completion, it became known as "Reb Yakov-Yosi's Shul" to honor him for his numerous contributions to the city.

Yakov Yosef's Descendants

Yakov Yosef was survived by three sons, Leibush, David and Moshe. All were extremely pampered growing up. After their father's demise, all three left Korets

---

[I] *Shtiblekh:* Small places used for Jewish communal prayer.

for Kiev and other large cities where they were said to "revel in the caprices of the wealthy." While they were reveling, the Horenstein Korets estate was neglected and slowly deteriorated, and the family businesses that they had inherited went progressively downhill.[219]

For example, at a time when only the ruling class would travel by train in First Class, Leibush, his eldest son, regularly traveled that way. Moreover, it was said that Leibush would stay in Kiev at the Hotel Evropeyskiy, the most elaborate hotel in the city, where he would take baths in pure *Eau de Cologne*.[220]

Despite their extravagances, Yakov Yosef's sons would travel to visit Rabbi Avraham Yakov of Sadigura. According to a folk tale, the *rebbe* once said to Leibush:

"I feel pity, Leibush, on account of your father's labors. Promise me that you will behave properly, and then I will give you my word that you will earn a good livelihood for your entire life."

Leibush replied:

"Rebbe, I cannot promise you. It is difficult for me to break away from my habits!"[221]

You will recall the earlier folktale that, when Yakov Yosef was but a poor clerk, Rabbi Avraham Yakov Friedman of Ruzhin was reluctant to "bless him with wealth" because of his concern about the effect on the children:

'If I bless you with wealth, I am afraid of what that wealth would do to you and your children'.

"Yakov Yosef replied:

'I hereby promise the master that the wealth shall not bring harm to me or my children'.

Typical of folktales, despite Yakov Yosef's promise, his wealth did indeed bring harm to his sons – by weakening their character, causing them to succumb to the baser temptations of wealth.

The fate of Yakov Yosef's three sons has been lost to history. One of his daughters (either Mirium or Sheindla) is said to have married Rabbi Pinchas (Rabinowitz) from Sokolovka.[m] The rabbi's father, also a rabbi, was murdered in 1919

---

[m] While there are 14 towns with this name in Ukraine, this is probably the Sokolovka which is 19 miles north of Uman.

in a pogrom in Uman.[222,223,224] The couple's subsequent fate is unknown.

Meanwhile, another Horenstein dynasty, that of Yakov Yosef's brother Naftali, was developing in Radomysl. The Radomysl Horensteins were to be even more celebrated among the Jews of Ukraine than Yakov Yosef. This was because Naftali's sons, who were raised quite differently, were to further extend and enhance their family's wealth and reputation.

Part I: Chapter Five

RABBI NAFTALI HAKOHEN HORENSTEIN
OF RADOMYSL

Born 1820-1823; died 1899

"Whoever may come to write the history of Jewish Ukraine - and will want to high-light a wealthy Jewish bourgeois family that, in the 19th and early 20th centuries, helped the economic development of the previously backward and later highly-developed Ukraine - will have to concern themselves with the Radomysler Horenstein family."

Nakhman Mayzel (1887-1966), Yiddish scholar and literary critic (*Morgn Frayhayt*, 1943)

A few years younger than Yakov Yosef, the story of Naftali HaKohen Horenstein is remarkably similar to that of his older brother. Both built great fortunes - sometimes by working as partners - and each lived in elaborate estates located in small villages just outside of cities. Moreover, both had the same intense commitment to the Ruzhiner Hasidic movement and both were equally well known for their generous gifts to charities.

Born in Berestechko sometime between 1820 and 1823, Naftali's family had moved to Aleksandriya by 1834. As a young adult, he became an important force in Rabbi Yisrael of Ruzhin's growing Hasidic movement, and his activities in this movement was one of the reasons for Naftali's fame among the Jews of the region.

We do not have a physical description of Yakov Yosef, but we have three physical descriptions of Naftali. We thus know that he dressed in the traditional long caftan of Hasidic Jews and that he was tall and powerfully built, with broad bones, large, thick hands, and a red beard with curly side locks.[225,226,227]

In 1838, Rabbi Yisrael Friedman of Ruzhin was accused of complicity in the death of two Jews who had been accused of being informers. Although he was never formally charged and no trial was held, Russian authorities imprisoned him for two years, probably because Czar Nicholas I had been told by his agents that the *rebbe* was trying to establish his own kingdom and was fomenting opposition to the government.

On his release he moved to Kishinev, then to Iasi and other places before finally settling in 1842 in Sadigura in the Austrian Bukovina. With their *rebbe* living so far away, young Reb Naftali of Aleksandriya became the leader of the orphaned Ruzhiner *Hasidim* in Ukraine.[228]

Naftali would travel as far as necessary in order to visit with his *rebbe*. According to a folk tale, one trip that Naftali made to Sadigura to visit *Rebbe* Yisrael was particularly notable:[n]

> "It was Sukkot[o] at the home of the famous Reb Yisrael (Friedman) Ruzhiner. The rebbe was sitting in a lovely sukkah,[p] in which were strung out candles and lamps, and which was decorated with drapery and carpeting. Surrounding him were 'refined' Jews, the ones with respectable ancestry and wealth, and Naftali Horenstein was among them.
>
> "Suddenly, a drape caught on fire from above. The sukkah ignited, and the walls were engulfed in flames.
>
> "There was tumult and an outcry. Everyone became unhinged. But Naftali, tall and robust, jumped up onto a bench and immediately put out the fire with his hands, severely burning his hands and fingers.
>
> "Afterwards, he went into the rebbe's house to see him. When he entered, Moshe David, the rebbe's court gabbai, showed him Naftali's hands. The rebbe took his hands and stroked them, saying:
>
> "Naftali, travel home, and for this, God will send good fortune into your hands!"
>
> "And the rebbe's blessing, the Hasidim say, came true. Things began to go very well for Naftali; he became very wealthy and whatever he undertook was met with good fortune, as the rebbe had foretold. And the Ruzhiner Hasidim therefore felt as though they shared in Naftali's fortunes because it was their rebbe who had pronounced the blessing."[229]

How did Naftali acquire his fortune? We know that Yakov Yosef transitioned from clerk to wealthy entrepreneur within relatively few years. In order to reduce the ever-increasing responsibility of managing his rapidly growing financial empire, Yakov Yosef must have enlisted Naftali's assistance. Working with his wealthy older brother probably started him on his own path to riches.[230]

In 1858, Yakov Yosef was able to afford to be an Aleksandriya Merchant of the 2nd Guild, while younger brother Naftali was an Aleksandriya Merchant of the 3rd Guild, a less privileged designation, but still an indicator of his increasing wealth.[231]

---

[n] This visit must have been before 1850, the year of the *rebbe's* demise.

[o] *Sukkot:* Booths or huts. A weeklong Jewish harvest festival which commemorates God's protection of the children of Israel when they left Egypt.

[p] *Sukkah:* A temporary hut constructed for use duing Sukkot.

With so much in common, the relationship between the brothers during childhood and adolescence was probably fairly good. It began to deteriorate, however, after they became business partners, both due to differences in personality and behavioral traits and to the stresses they were experiencing as joint owners of growing businesses.

In terms of their psyches, Naftali appears to have been the stronger and healthier of the two. Yakov Yosef had a bigger ego, most likely due to underlying insecurities. Compared to Yakov Yosef's regal style of living, Naftali was more humble and earthy.[232,233]

Naftali had a fiery, hot-blooded temperament. We do not know if Yakov Yosef was equally prone to anger, but either way we would expect that anger would have erupted between the brothers when one refused to agree with the other's proposals.[234]

Over time, disagreements between the brothers mounted, probably concerning how to conduct business operations. As logging contracts and the number of factories which they operated in partnership increased, and as their business operations became more complicated, these differences put increasing stress on their relationship and gradually impeded their ability to agree on business decisions.

Disagreements between the two brothers began to cause serious problems in their relationship, making it increasingly difficult for them to spend time together.[235] As their relationship deteriorated, their arguments increased.[236]

According to a folk tale, the matter came to the attention of their *rebbe*, who at this time was Rabbi Avraham Yakov Friedman[q] The Horenstein brothers were visiting the *rebbe* on a Jewish day of celebration around the mid to late 1850s. Yakov Yosef placed 49 bottles of fine wine on the *rebbe's* table to represent the 49 Sefirot[r] of the Omer.[s] The *rebbe* looked over the wine bottles and said,

"The midot-sefirot are not completely established within you."[t,237]

---

[q] Rabbi Avraham Yakov became the Sadigura *rebbe* in 1851 after the deaths of his father, Rabbi Yisrael, and of his brother, Rabbi Sholom Yosef.

[r] Kabbalistic theosophy views the *sefirot*, literally "emanations," as the building blocks of creation; the primary values of the world.

[s] Counting of the Omer: Observant Jews verbally count each of 49 days starting the second day of Passover. They believe that this was commanded in the Torah in order to prepare for the giving of the Torah by God on Shavuot.

[t] The *midot-sefirot*, emotions of the *sefirot*, refers to the six elements of a person's emotional make-up: Kindness (the quality of giving and revealing to others), Might (the quality of withholding and concealing from others), Beauty (merging the first two qualities to bring about the quality of mercy), Conquest (the quality of overcoming all obstacles), Majesty (the quality of grandeur and splendor), and Foundation (the desire and ability to influence others).

There happens to be another version of this story. While the occasion for the meeting was probably the same, in this version, instead of a statement about the *midot-sefirot*, the *rebbe* simply diagnosed Yakov Yosef as

"a man with a problematic personality"

thereby indicating - just as in the first version - that he held Yakov Yosef to be the brother responsible for their difficulty.[238]

This second version goes on to state that, after the holiday, the *rebbe* traveled to the countryside to "breathe in some fresh air," and Yakov Yosef followed him. The *rebbe* then told him that Naftali had visited him earlier with complaints that,

"when he was helping you in the lumber business and the two of you disagreed, you did not properly deal with him [i.e. you insisted on having your own way].

"If you decide to reconcile with him, then you should be a partner with your brother in this forest, you both shall be successful, and people shall refer to you as 'the rich Horenstein family'."[239]

This version of the story thus claims that, when Yakov Yosef and Naftali were worked together in the lumber business, Yakov Yosef maintained sole owner-ship. Thus, when the brothers disagreed, Yakov Yosef always had the final say, to Naftali's displeasure. The *rebbe*'s prediction was that they would both be suc-cessful if, from now on, they were equal partners in their joint ventures.

It is striking that, in both versions of the story, the *rebbe* believed that Yakov Yosef, because of his own psychological problems, was responsible for the diffi-culties in their relationship.

Yakov Yosef did begin to partner with Naftali, but this failed to resolve their differences. Naftali then decided he could no longer live in the same town as Ya-kov Yosef. He therefore left Korets to relocate in a small village in the Radomysl area.[240]

❧ Radomysl ❧

Радомысль.   Видъ съ Тетерева на городъ.

View of Radomysl from the Teterev River. Early 20th century

Radomysl is within the Kiev province, only 57 miles by modern roads from the great city of Kiev and roughly 122 miles from Korets. It is on the west bank of Teterev River, a tributary of the Dnieper River which empties into the Black Sea. It had long been primarily a Jewish town.[u]

---

[u] In the year 1797 a total of 1,424 people (80% of the total population) were Jewish. In 1847 the population had increased to 2,734 and it further increased to 7,502 (67%) in 1897 [http://www.wikiwand.com/en/Radomyshl].

Map of Radomysl 1848

Naftali probably chose Radomysl because it was a largely Jewish town located close to Kiev, an important city in which to conduct his growing business. Jews had long been prohibited from residing in the city. However, following the ascension of Czar Alexander II to the throne in 1855, the traditional anti-Semitism of the Czarist government was fading, so it appeared that a Kiev residence would soon be a possibility. Indeed, four years after the start of the reign of the new Czar, Jewish 1st Guild merchants were granted permission to reside there.

This was around the time that Naftali arrived in Radomysl. With his lower rank,[v] permanent residence in Kiev was still illegal, although he could commute between his new home and Kiev in order to conduct business.

---

[v] As of 1858, he was listed as an Aleksandriya Merchant of the 3rd Guild, the lowest rank of the three Guilds.

The Reform of 1861 gave Jews the right to buy land, and Naftali became the first Radomysl Jew to become a landowner.[241] His initial land purchase was a small one: he acquired one dessatina (1.09 hectares = 2.7 acres) of field land in Mykgorod.[242,243,w] The small size of this purchase, as well as his designation as a 3rd Guild merchant, suggest that he was a man of moderate means at the time.

In 1851, a tannery had been started in the Radomysl suburb of Rudnya.[244,245] Naftali purchased the tannery after his arrival and, over time, made it into the largest tannery in the area.[246] By the time of his death in 1899, the tannery, with an employee staff of 40, was producing 12,500 items, for an annual revenue of 164,500 rubles.[247]

Vegetable leather tannery – 19th century

The law issued July 10, 1864 forbade Jews from buying real property, but this did not stop Naftali from his plans to log some of the region's vast forestland. He thus began to negotiate long-term logging contracts.

The first lease we know of he negotiated around the mid-1860s with a man named Potemkin who had recently bought estate land to farm in the area of Priborsk on the coast of the Teterev River. Naftali completed the contract to cut down the estate's vast forests over the next several years; then he sold it about

---

w Also known as Mychesk, it is separated from Radomysl by the Myka River.

1877 to a new owner.[248] This forest was so large that, according to his children and grandchildren, he could have cut trees for decades without exhausting it.

Despite Naftali's separation from Yakov Yosef, the two brothers continued to form business partnerships. For example, in 1869, Naftali and Yakov Yosef signed a 36-year lease with Count Khodkevich covering the use of 8100 acres of forest land in the Vahovskaya Dacha within the Kiev gubernia, much of which they logged until sometime after 1891.[249,x]

In 1871, Naftali signed a 36-year contract with Lieutenant Vladimir Morozov for his Lubovichskoye estate in Lubovichi which consisted of 5549 acres. This contract included, not only the right to log the forest, but usage of the arable lands, pastures and other lands, as well as usage of the buildings and the winery.[250] His other investments in Lubovichi (as listed in 1887) consisted of a tar works and a distillery.[251]

By 1876, Naftali could afford to pay the large fee to become a Radomysl Merchant of the 1st Guild with all its attendant privileges.[252] In 1879, he acquired from the Zussman family the remainder of a 30-year logging rights contract on the 8100-acre estate of Count Aleksandr Vladislavovich Branitskiy in the Radomysl area.[y,z]

Naftali thus became one of the largest Jewish timber merchants in Ukraine, with holdings covering as much as 54,000 acres of woods, land, fields and rivers.[253] While his logging contracts did not give him land ownership as Jews were prohibited from owning such lands, he still ran into difficuly when, in 1891, the

---

[x] In 1891, the General Governor informed the Kiev Governor that he had received information that Naftali and Yakov Yosef (who had died 15 years earlier) were abusing their lease of Count Khodevich's Dacha by:

> "totally deforesting the … entire territory, not even sparing young trees. In addition, they are using the areas free of trees for pastures and building houses and, against the law of May 2, 1882, have accommodated there as well as in neighboring villages numerous co-religionists who are making it difficult for the local farmers to access their fields and pastures, openly selling vodka and oppressing the hired workers, using various excuses to not pay them the salaries that were agreed upon (Kiev state oblast archive, fond 2, opys 207, sprava #208, 1891)."

The Manager of the State Property to the General Governor investigated and found no basis for the allegations. However, since the Horenstein brothers could theoretically still "abuse" the land during the remaining years of the contract, they were given 6 months to prepare "a simplified plan for the usage of the lands during the remaining period of the above contract for the approval of the Committee (Kiev state oblast archive, fond 2, opys 207, sprava #208, 1891)."

[y] Yakov Yosef had originally acquired the contract in 1870; then, five years later, he had passed the contract on to the Zussmans.

[z] at Migalki village.

Governor General of Kiev, Podolia and Volhynia decided to cancel his logging contract with Count Branitskiy on the grounds that it illegally gave him ownership rights to the land.

Naftali appealed to the Kiev Governor's office, noting that the contract was not for the purchase of real property, but for the purchase of moveable property (logs), as it was limited to the right to fell trees for removal from the Count's estate. The decision of the Kiev Governor is not known, but his argument does appear to be persuasive.

Naftali also purchased or built distilleries.[254] One of his distilleries (valued at 10,000 rubles[b]) was in Lubovichi,[255] most likely at the Lubovichkoye estate where he was leasing both the forest land and the facilities. It was operating by 1877.[256]

Later on, he purchased or built paper factories which probably made use of the lumber produced from his logging contracts. He also purchased or built beet sugar refineries.[257]

His most unusual pursuit was between 1874 and 1878 when he became the "box-tax lease holder"[aa] for the Jewish community of Radomysl. Funds were collected by him from the Jewish residents and then deposited with the Radomysl City Council.[258]

By 1880, his Kiev business dealings had increased so much that he had established a Kiev residence and had paid the fee to become a Kiev Merchant of the 1st Guild.[259,bb]

He was listed the following year as leasing a sugar beet refinery in the village of Luka, Tarashcha uyezd.[260] His largest sugar beet refinery, however, was the Yanushpol' (Ivanopil') beet-sugar works in Volhynia Gubernia.[261,262,263] This factory, by the early 20th century, had a yearly income of 3 million rubles[264,265,266] and was one of the largest sugar factories in the entire gubernia.[267]

[aa] Box Tax: A special tax that was only levied on Jews. It consisted of a "general tax" which was levied on every animal which was slaughtered kosher, and on every pound of meat sold as kosher, as well as a "subsidiary tax" which consisted of a certain percentage on the rents of houses, shops and warehouses, a certain percentage on the profits of factories, breweries, industrial establishments and other trade enterprises, a certain percentage on the capital bequeathed by Jews, and a tax on apparel specially worn by Jews such as the skull cap (Appendix: an abridged summary of laws, special and restrictive, relating to the Jews in Russia, brought down to the year 1890, in The Russo-Jewish Committee of London, The Persecution of the Jews in Russia. Philadelphia, Jewish Publication Society of America, 1891).

[bb] The location was 28 Malo-Vladimirskaya Street.

Also, by 1887, Naftali had acquired a sizable tree resins[cc] factory.[dd] Like his paper factories, this factory must have used some of the lumber he owned as the result of his lumber contracts.[268] He probably shipped the lumber to the factory via barges on the Teterev River.

Naftali's Family

Naftali married three times and raised a large Hasidic family. Like him, his sons – as well as his grandsons - were tall, broad-shouldered and red-haired[269] with thick red beards. They also shared with their father his fiery temperament.[270,271] Due to their extensive knowledge of Torah, their religious devotion, and as a sign of respect, members of the Hasidic community addressed them as rabbis.

Starting with the 1st half of the 19th century, the local Teterev River was filled with lumber rafts all the way from Radomsyl to just north of Kiev where the Teterev empties into the larger Dnieper River.[272] Naftali and his sons made good use of this mode of transportation. They would cut down trees in their large forests and send them floating on lumber rafts which went to Yekaterinoslav,[ee] Pinsk, Danzig, and Memel. In the earlier years, he required his sons to ride on the rafts to ensure that these expensive barges arrived at their destinations.[273]

[cc] Tree resins, especially from coniferous trees, are important chemicals in the production of varnishes, adhesives and food glazing agents.
[dd] Located in the hamlet of Yahnovka on the coast of the Teterev River above Kuhari.
[ee] Now called Dnipropetrovsk.

Timber Rafts on the Volga by Frederic DeHaenen, ca. 1913

All six of Naftali's sons worked with him on his various enterprises, with different sons taking on different responsibilities:

Shmuel, his 1st son, became a Kiev banker.

Zalman, his 2nd son, became the official owner of a massive beet sugar refinery when only 22 years old.

Avraham, his 3rd son and the family "aristocrat," represented the family's interests in Kiev.

Berko, his 4th son, became the family's "ambassador" to Germany, traveling there to negotiate sales with the German merchants.

Yoel (Evel), his 5th son, and Gur-arye, his 6th son, stayed in the "lowlands," taking the family's lumber rafts down the Dnieper River to Cherkasy, Kremenchuk, and Yekaterinoslav where they would unload the lumber[274]

Naftali also had three daughters: Bina (b. 1851-52) and Khaya Ester (b. 1855-63) by Breine, his first wife, and later Chana (b. after 1875) by Miriam Shipra, his second wife.

For years, the Horenstein businesses prospered. Naftali and his sons bought and sold sugar factories, paper factories, distilleries, forests, and more.[275] The sons would return home to Radomysl before the start of the Sabbath. Each would then submit his report on their business activities: One had bought a sugar factory, one a large forest, and the third had bought a manufacturing factory.[276]

The Zavod Estate

Natali built a large enough estate to accommodate all of his growing family along with servants and guests. Its location, which was within the Radomysl district, is referred to in Jewish sources as "Zavod." Most likely, the estate was in the village of Piskivka ("Peskovskiv Zavod"), northeast of the city but still within the Radomysl district.[277,278] (Using modern roads, Piskivka is roughly 28 miles from the city of Radomysl and, like Radomysl, roughly 56 miles from Kiev.)

The Horenstein "court"[ff] in Zavod included his six sons and three daughters, his sons-in-law, daughters-in-law, and grandchildren, as well as teachers, wet-nurses, attendants and servants. In addition, there were carriages, horses and stables, wine cellars, and their own *beit midrash*.[3] Guests, who included friends, rabbis and emissaries, were always present.[279]

The court was marked by frequent celebrations: circumcisions, bar-mitzvahs, engagements, and weddings. Weddings, which were almost constant, were celebrated in large wedding tents. It was said that Naftali would get irritated by all the *mazal-tovs* (congratulations) he received every day: a *mazal tov* for a new grandchild, a *mazal tov* for a son-in-law's new daughter, etc. After he received each *mazel tov*, he would say angrily, "Again, again!"[280]

For every celebration, Sadigurer and Boyaner *Hasidim* would come from the surrounding regions. *Farbrengens*[gg] in the court were said to have lasted weeks on end, with prayers held in the *kloyz* (study house). Everywhere there was joy as well as dancing in the style of the Boyaner *Hasidim*.[281]

When a family wedding was held at the estate, things were especially lively. Preparations continued all around the year which included bringing in tailors to "rejuvenate" the entire family with cloths and satins. (Even the young people wore satin clothing on the Sabbath and holy days as well as for celebrations.) The brides and their mothers made trips to Kiev, Warsaw, or even to Vienna, to visit the wealthy fashion pavilions in order to choose wedding gowns in the latest styles.[282]

[ff] In the Hasidic world, "court" refers to a Hasidic sect; it is used here as life at Naftali's estate in some ways resembled such a court.

[gg] *Farbrengen:* A gathering of *Hasidim* and their *rebbe* at a table consisting of refreshments while the *rebbe* inspires them with moral lessons.

Guests came from all over - close and distant relatives, *Hasidim*, and even *Mitnagdim* (Jewish opponents of Hasidism). There were cantors, other singers and klezmer bands from far and wide, including the famous "Podtzahor" from Berdichev with his large band.[283]

Dance of the Jester [at a Hasidic Wedding] (1902)

Famous table-waiters came from Kiev and Warsaw. Hungarian wines were poured generously from large Bessarabian casks. The poor and needy were not forgotten as they received both meals and gifts. Life did not return to normal for weeks as visiting *Hasidim* lingered at the estate long after the ceremonies had ended.[284,285]

Several times a year, Jewish festivals were celebrated at the estate in the Hasidic manner with much singing and dancing. Almost the entire population of Radomysl - including the largely Jewish work force of the local Horenstein sugar factory - participated, in addition to visitors from elsewhere.[286] Often the Jewish Horenstein employees celebrated their own Hasidic festivals.

These festive celebrations became so well known by Jews throughout the Ukraine that a Yiddish folk song was composed which became quite popular:

"At Horenstein's in Zavod, where they dance the Korochod."[287]

Even when there was not a special event, there were usually house guests. Naftali supported Jewish religious scholars and hosted them at the estate so that they could pursue their studies.[288] Other house guests included Naftali's rabbinic grandsons, as well as cantors - and even traveling alms collectors.[289]

A center for the Hasidic movement in the Ukraine,[290] the Horenstein estate in Zavod had its own little synagogue in the courtyard. Enough men attended so that services were held, not only on the Jewish Sabbath, but also on weekdays. Sometimes a service was even repeated when there was not enough room for all who wanted to attend.[291]

Music was an important part of the Horenstein lifestyle. Often excellent singers, the Horenstein men loved to perform as cantors in the synagogues they supported.[292]

The Kiev Residence

Naftali continued to make frequent trips to Kiev to conduct some of his business. Now that he could legally reside there, he wanted to lease a suitable residence for him and his large family. It appears that he initially rented apartments at 28 Malo-Vladimirskaya Street where he is recorded living as of 1881.[hh,293] A few years later, he and his wife, along with those of their children who desired a Kiev address, as well as these children's families, moved into a magnificent mansion at 12 Bibikovsky Boulevard.[ii,jj]

Originally constructed in 1830, the mansion was expanded to its present size in 1875 when the property was bought by Nikola Artemiyovych Tereshchenko, founder of one of the largest joint-stock sugar companies in the south-west region of Russia and considered to be one of the 100 most famous Ukrainians. When the expansion was completed, Tereshchenko and his family had moved from Moscow to Kiev to settle into the mansion.[294]

[hh] Since renamed Olesya Gonchara Street.

[ii] Since renamed Shevchenko Boulevard.

[jj] The building is now the State Museum of the Ukrainian poet, Taras Shevchenko.

Nikola Artemiyovych Tereshchenko

Exterior, Tereshchenko Mansion; early 20th century

Lobby, Tereshchenko Mansion; early 20th century

Horenstein family stories leave no doubt that 12 Bibikovsky Street was the location of their Kiev residence.[295] Records showing when the Horensteins moved into the building, or where they lived within it, have not survived but, as of 1884, the mansion itself consisted of one residence with 39 rooms, and a two-story wing which had a carriage shed on the ground floor and a 14-room residence above.[296] We can assume that the Tereshchenko family lived in the 39-room residence, while Naftali and his family lived in the 14-room wing above the carriage garages.

There are no known photos of the Horenstein residence, but several rooms of the luxurious Tereshchenko residence were photographed in the early 20th century.

Boudoir, Tereshchenko residence, 12 Bibikovsky St.; early 20th century

Radomysler Horenstein *Yichus*

Despite its interest in appealing to the masses, Hasidism retained the importance of *yichus* from the start. In assessing a rabbi's *yichus*, Hasidic Jews particularly valued his ability to inspire through worship, preaching and teaching, and were less concerned about his Torah learning. Family status, including the fame of his ancestors, was important, but it had to be accompanied by the proper humility and worthy deeds.[297]

Unless they were community leaders, most of the first generation of *Hasidim* following the *Ba'al Shem Tov* were scions of the most illustrious Jewish families in eastern Europe. The *Besht* and Dov Ber of Mezeritch did have humble backgrounds, but they secured higher social credit through their marriage strategies.[298]

The Horensteins were probably only aware of two famous ancestors: the *Smichat Chachamim* (Rabbi Naftali Katz) and, a few generations further back, the MaHaRaL of Prague (Judah Leib ben Betzalel Loew). With these two distinguished Jews as ancestors, they could claim considerable *yichus* despite lacking a centuries-old appellation from a widely-known rabbinical family.

Generally, marriages of Naftali's children and grandchildren were designed to enhance the family's *yichus*, either by marrying into other wealthy Jewish families or by marrying descendants of famous Hasidic rabbis. Because of the latter, some of Naftali's descendants can be traced backwards to the *Ba'al Shem Tov* (1698-1760) as well as to a number of first and second generation Hasidic *rebbes* who followed him.

Conversely, Hasidic rebbes delighted in having their children marry into the Horenstein family, as the family derived its *yichus* from both its distinguished ancestors and its great wealth.[299] This tradition apparently started with Naftali's daughter Bina (b. 1851) who married Moshe Averbuch, the *Ba'al Shem Tov's* 4th great grandson.[kk]

Rachel Horenstein Landau (born 1882), Naftali's granddaughter, proudly wrote out a list of some of these Hasidic ancestral lines, titled "Fathers of the Family: Righteous Ones."[ll] On the list she names more than ten Hasidic rabbis who lived in the second half of the 18th century and whose descendants married Naftali's descendants. These rabbis include, for example, Yakov Yosef of Polonnoye, a leading disciple of the *Ba'al Shem Tov* (1698-1760) and the first theoretician and literary propagandist of Hasidism.

[kk] *Yisrael ben Eliezer (the Ba'al Shem Tov)* →*Adel* → *R' Baruch of Mezhibozh* → *daughter of R' Baruch* → *Yisrael Averbuch of Mezhibozh* →*Avraham Dov Averbuch of Tul'chyn* → *Moshe Averbuch*

[ll] See Appendix Two which starts on page 286.

Three Horenstein descent lines can be traced back to the famous Rabbi Levi Yitzchok of Berdichev,[mm] while two of Naftali's granddaughters[nn] married two sons of Rabbi Yitzchok Friedman, Admur of Sadigura and the main propagator of Rumanian Hasidism - who was himself a grandson of Rabbi Yisrael Friedman, founder of the Ruzhiner Hasidic Dynasty.

Some family members married members of the Schneerson Lubavitch dynasty, including Naftali's grandson, Moshe HaKohen Horenstein, who married Chaya Muscha Schneerson, sister of Rabbi Sholom Dov Ber, the 5th Lubavicher *rebbe*, in 1892. Their son, Menachem Mendel HaKohen Horenstein, then married Sheindel Schneerson, daughter of the 6th Lubavitcher *rebbe* (Yosef Yitzchok Schneerson) and sister-in-law to the 7th (Menachem Mendel Schneerson), while Naftali's great granddaughter married a grandson of Rabbi Menachem Mendel Schneerson.

Menachem Mendel HaKohen
Horenstein &
Sheindel Schneerson Horenstein

[mm] One of these is that of Miriam Shipra, Naftali's 2nd wife.
  Levi Yitzchok of Berdichev → *Meyer* → *Esther Rachel* → *Gitele* → *Miriam Shipra*
The other two lines descend via Israel, Levi Itzak's other son:
  Levi Yitzchok of Berdichev → *Israel* → *Belle Derbarmdiger* → *Yosef Derbarmdiger* → *Belle Derbarmdiger* → *Perla Czernobilsky* → *Rachel & Pinchas Trachtenberg*
(Rachel married Avraham Yosef HaKohen Hornstein, while Pinchas married Fanya Horenstein.)
[nn] Berta, daughter of Shmuel, and Perl, daughter of Zalman

This custom of marrying to enhance *yichus* had benefits for both the groom's and bride's families as the enhanced prestige and wealth of their children facilitated their advancement within the Jewish world, no matter what endeavors they wished to pursue.

The Late 19th Century

By late in the century, Naftali and his family, now widely known as the Radomysler Horensteins, had become one of the most famous Jewish families in the Ukraine.[300] With their family life still centered in Radomysl, they were quite different from the other wealthy Jewish families – such as the Brodskys, Zeytsevs, Halperins, Libermans, Saxes and Gepners – who lived in Kiev full-time where they transacted their business and enjoyed an opulent urban lifestyle.[301] According to one writer, while these other rich families made generous charitable donations to both Jewish and non-Jewish causes, "their Jewishness was otherwise subsumed by their efforts to outdo each other in displaying their wealth and living a life of luxury."[302]

As devout *Hasidim*, the Jewishness of the Radomysl Horensteins was never subordinate to their business enterprises or lifestyles. Consistent with Hasidic values, Naftali's wealth was obvious, yet he lived a fairly modest lifestyle for a man of his means, earning more money than he spent.[303]

Tiferet Yisrael synagogue, Jerusalem

Like his older brother, he became widely known for his deeds of charity and generosity – such as donating large sums of money to help to build the *Tiferet Yisrael* synagogue in the Old City of Jerusalem for the *Hasidim* from Sadigura and its environs,[304] a project which underwent construction between 1870 and 1872.

This synagogue served as the center for the Hasidic community of Jerusalem until its destruction by the Jordanians in 1948. Its gutted remains stood on *Tiferet Yisrael* Street for many years as a memorial, although in 2012, the Jerusalem municipality announced its approval for plans to rebuild the synagogue, and the cornerstone was laid in 2014.

Also very much like his brother, Naftali would sometimes throw money out to anyone on the street who happened to be standing near his "golden" carriage as it passed through Kiev. A specific instance, according to a Horenstein family member, took place around 1880 when a granddaughter, who was born very prematurely, survived her first few months of life. To celebrate, he took her with him on a carriage ride to celebrate her good health and, as his carriage moved through the area, showered the people lining the street with money.[oo]

The Horensteins and the Ruzhiner Hasidic Court

Devout Ruzhiner *Hasidim*, the Horensteins were followers of Rabbi Yisrael Friedman until his demise in 1850. They then followed the *rebbe*'s sons: Sholom Yosef Friedman who died after just one year, and then Avraham Yakov Friedman, the first Sadigura *rebbe*, until his demise in 1883.

Upon their father's death, both Yitzchok Friedman, Avraham Yakov's eldest son, and Yisrael Friedman, Avrahm Yakov's younger brother, became the Ruzhiner *rebbes* of Sadigura. Soon, however, the Hasidic community decided that it was too confusing to have both *rebbes* hold court in the same town so, in 1887, the *rebbes* cast lots to determine which one would remain. The results determined that Reb Yisrael Friedman would continue to hold court in Sadigura and become the second Sadigura *rebbe*, while Reb Yitzchok Friedman would move to Boyan to become the first Boyaner *rebbe*.

Rabbi Yitzchok Friedman of Boyan

[oo] The granddaughter was Wilhelmina ("Mina") Horenstein Kronstein, who was to live for a century. Her parents were Abraham and Breindel Teomim Horenstein. The incident was related by Mina to Beatrice Dhillon, her granddaughter.

When Naftali learned of the *rebbes'* separation, he decided to make a pilgrimage with his sons and sons-in-law to both towns, and thereby to evaluate the two *rebbes* in order to determine which one the family would choose to follow.

To the Radomysler Horensteins, the purpose of their trip was momentous, so they first made extensive "preparations for spiritual elevation through the execution of thought and of deed."[305] When they believed that were ready, they traveled first to Sadigura to become more familiar with *Rebbe* Yisrael and his teachings. Once they felt satisfied, they continued on to Boyan to see *Rebbe* Yitzchok, known as the *Pachad Yitzchok*. They found themselves awed by his wisdom. Thus, as a family, they decided to submit themselves to the *Pachad Yitzchok* and become Boyaner *Hasidim*.[306]

A Story from the Boyaner Court

The Boyaner court has reported the following story concerning Naftali's relationship with the *Pachad Yitzchok* at a later point in their relationship:

Naftali had once presented the *Rebbe* Yitzchok with a *kvitel* (petitionary prayer) and requested that the *rebbe* inset it into his *siddur* (prayer book) so that he would always be reminded to grant a blessing and good wishes for Naftali's welfare.

Sometime later, the *rebbe's* attendant related that the *siddur* from which the *rebbe* prayed also contained the *Hagaddah* (the text recited at the first two nights of Passover at the *seder* dinner), and he noticed that Naftali's *kvitel* was inserted at the place where *"Pour Out Thy Wrath upon those who do not know you ...."* appears in the *Hagaddah*.[pp]

In September of 1894, after the end of the Sabbath before *Rosh HaShannah* (Jewish New Year), Naftali had gone out for *Silichot*[qq] when a fire broke out in his estate, and his entire house burned down along with his possessions. Among these was the *tallit* (Jewish prayer shawl) of the *Pachad Yitzchok* which Naftali had purchased so that his body would be enwrapped with it after 120 years (the number of years that Moses was believed to have lived). Only a small piece of the silver ornamentation on the collar survived the flames.

Naftali was greatly sorrowed by the fire, particularly over his loss of the *tallit* of the "old *Rebbe*" from Sadigura. Because of this, Naftali's family members sent a *kvitel* to Rabbi Yitzchok in which they described their father's great sorrow over the burning of the Old Rebbe's *tallit*, and requested that the *rebbe* do something to "strengthen his broken heart."

On the eve of Sukkot of the year 5655 (October 1894), the *rebbe* sent Naftali a letter written in his own hand:

[pp] *Hagaddah:* The text recited on the first two nights of the Jewish holiday of Passover.

[qq] *Silichot:* The Jewish penitential poems and prayers recited in the period before the High Holidays.

"... I was informed of the fire which HaShem[rr] has brought down upon his home, including upon the prized possession that my dear friend owned, and which caused damage and emotional distress. However, 'Just as one says a blessing over the good, one must also say a blessing over the bad'.

"And, so, I hereby (turn) to him that he not allow his heart to fall.... On the contrary, he ought to give praise and thanks to **HaShem ... who has poured out his wrath** [bold type added] upon wood and stone, and that he should have faith in G-d and that this should be in order to sweeten the judgments and be a special sign towards a long and good life.

"And, I hereby give him a blessing that HaShem ... should lengthen his days and years and remove all adversaries from him. And, seeing as this thing occurred on the eve of Rosh HaShanah – 'A year and its curses has ended; a year shall begin with its blessings'.

"Like the person who requests goodness from Him, his friend, who makes his request for his wellbeing and for good things for him and for a long life and for many years, and who grants goodness to him and to all of the nation of Israel,

"Yitzhak, son of our teacher and master, Rabbi Avraham Ya'akov ...."

When the *rebbe*'s assistant saw the letter's contents, he trembled when he read *"HaShem has poured out his wrath"* as he remembered that he had seen Naftali's *kvitel* inserted into the *siddur* of the *Pachad Yitzhak* at the location of "Pour out thy wrath" in the *Haggadah* - and he even recorded this fact in the margins of the letter.[307]

[rr] *HaShem:* Literally, the name - referring to the name of God.

Home of the Boyaner Rebbe, ca. 1930s

Naftali's Last Years

Later in life, according to one writer, there was a change in Naftali's personality: he became mercenary and strict. While he maintained a fatherly, family-like relationship with his employees, he could also act like a lord and order them around. They also received low wages compared to their duties. When asked, Naftali would justify these small salaries by saying:

"With small salaries, the thievery is small; with big salaries the thievery will be big!"[308]

Death came to Naftali in Radomysl at the very end of the 19th century on November 28, 1899. By that time, it was estimated that he was worth as much as 10 million rubles.[309]

Yoel Natan Meizlish-Hammerman, Naftali's son-in-law, published the following obituary:

"The death of this excellent man, who, from his contributions, laid the founda-tion stone for every charitable institution founded in this city, is a great loss for this city. His home was open wide to every man in distress and difficulty who turned to him for help, large or small.

"And, especially he used to help and support his relatives and family members: those who fell upon the wayside, those who joined his commercial houses to earn a respectable living, and those to whom he gave enough money to enable them to earn a living for themselves."[310]

THE 20ᵀᴴ CENTURY: NAFTALI'S PROGENY

The Radomysler Horensteins after Naftali

In dramatic contrast to Yakov Yosef's sons, Naftali's sons, who had been raised quite differently, continued their father's life's work after his demise just as he had taught them. In fact, they continued both their father's businesses and his charitable giving in a manner so similar to Naftali's style that, for those who did not know these six men personally, their individual identities seemed irrelevant. Ukrainian Jews thus began to speak of "Horenstein" when referring to any of his six sons, a tradition that long continued.

For example, after my father's death, my cousin Toby Sonneman gave me a letter that he had written to her late mother in 1980:

"Our uncle Yakov [Kanfer] went to them [the Horensteins] during 1914 asking for a job in one of their factories so that he wouldn't have to go into the army. Somehow he wasn't successful. He then quoted them a well-known saying:

'If your brother or relative does not want to help, but says let someone else help, then God will never forgive him.'

The specific identity of which of Naftali's six sons Yakov approached about the job was not worth mentioning. After all, they were "the Horensteins."[a]

---

[a] Another example is in a book by Liudmyla Gladysh titled Keys to the Town of Radomyshl (2007, Zytomyr, Polissya) *(in Ukrainian)*. "The greatest landlords in the town were ... Grinzevich ... and manufacturer Horenstein who was considered to be a millionaire in Radomysl." (At least two of Naftali's sons, both wealthy manufacturers, were living in Radomysl at the time.)

Latkes for Hanukah

Three years after Naftali's death, the great Yiddish writer Sholem Aleichem, who resided in Kiev, was a family guest for the annual *Hanukah* festival held at the family's Radomysl estate in Zavod. At the end of the visit, he thanked the family for its hospitality and, in particular, for the latkes.

"I shall tell the whole world about them and write a eulogy as soon as I get back.

"Don't worry," he added, *"all names and places will be changed. You won't be embarrassed, I promise."*[311]

One year later, he published a fictional short story entitled "Latkes for Hanukah." Since the story was based on the author's actual visit, here is a summary which also removes its fictional elements so that you can have a glimpse of what it was like to celebrate a joyous occasion at the Horenstein estate:

The narrative opens on the eve of *Hanukah* with the sexton inviting the town's citizens to the family's manor house for the annual celebration following the kindling of the first *Hanukah* light, a ritual familiar to followers of the Boyaner *rebbe*. When the holiday arrives, hundreds of people are served, helped by all the resident teachers and laborers employed by the family and assisted by a large temporary staff.

"And there, high above the crowd at separate tables for men and women, sat the [Horenstein] Family. The brothers with their sons and daughters, and their in-laws, all well-dressed and groomed in their Hasidic outfits with small silk skull caps and polished shoes. The women beautifully attired in silk and velvet brandishing expensive jewelry with pearls and sparkling diamonds....

116

"Then the singing started. They were all the specially composed tunes for that particular Hasidic order and no other Jew was permitted to take part unless he could prove to be a Hasid and follower of the rabbi of Boyan....

"[Then] they were pushed onto the dance floor whether they liked it or not, joined hands with their hosts, circling the tables in a kind of Hora dance, clapping their hands, stamping their feet, some of them performing acrobatic gyrations much to the amusement of the [Horensteins]. When they were tired of singing and dancing they went back to their vodka, shouting l'chaim [to life] to their hosts and wishing them 'good luck'. They even chatted with them amicably, exchanging pleasantries - even slapping each other on the shoulder.

"This holiday mood made the people forget their troubles and woes and abandon themselves to the illusion that all was well. But it was getting late and time to go home.

'Good night, a Happy Hanukah to you all and your families, be well and prosper and, God willing, may you come next year again to enjoy our hospitality.'

"They pushed to the front where the [Horensteins] were sitting and accepted their good wishes, formally responding with 'the same to you'."[312]

THE SIX SONS OF NAFTALI

Following Naftali's demise, Gur-arye, his youngest son, took over the administration of the Radomysl estate in Zavod, and four of his other sons established an in-town office to manage the family businesses.[313] They also established a special office just for the distribution of charity. Its yearly turnover amounted to 200,000 rubles. Shmuel, the first-born son, served as the administrator.[314]

While the sons had been partners in the various Radomysler Horenstein enterprises, after Naftali's death they began to separate their lives, although sometimes they would own a business in joint partnership. An example is a list of "Accountable Enterprises" in the 1909 Tax Records of the Radomysl Area which includes the Board of Directors of one of the Horenstein factories. The executive director was Yakov Yosef of Korets, even though he had died in 1876, 33 years earlier. He supposedly received the largest annual salary (6000 rubles). The other directors descended exclusively from Naftali: Shmuel, Yoel (Evel) and his own son Yosef Yitzchok (Ossia), and Gur-arye.[b,315]

---

[b] This is consistent with my impression that Yakov Yosef's sons were uninvolved with their late father's business interests, although, as his heirs, their late father's annual salary may have been going to them.

Some of Naftali's sons remained in Radomysl, while others established homes in several smaller cities in the region where the family owned factories, plants, banks, and other large businesses. Each built his own home "according to his fashion."[316] While their houses were not the equal of their father's Radomysl estate in Zavod, they were still expansive, large homes where *Hasids* and aristocrats, prayer *minyans* (quorums) and modern pianos coexisted.[317]

The children and grandchildren who remained in Radomysl followed a religious lifestyle but, when they ventured into the outer world, the men changed from their long coats into shorter ones and "fixed up" their beards. However, rarely did a member of those generations become clean-shaven, and all of them preserved their Hasidic appearance and traditions.[318]

SON #1: Rabbi Shmuel HaKohen Horenstein

Born Aleksandriya, 1840-1841; died Radomysl, 1919

Shmuel, Naftali's first son, was born when Naftali and Breine were still living in Aleksandriya and about the same time as Yakov Yosef and his family left Aleksandria to log the Lubomirski forest above Ludvipol. He spent his childhood there, moving with the family to Radomysl when he was about 18 years old. The most religious son, he was considered to be a Torah scholar. Everyone viewed him as "pure and honest."[319]

He married a woman from Lublin. They were together for 30 years and had no children.[320] He then married a woman who, according to one source, was the daughter of Rabbi Yisrael Friedman (1853-1906), the 2nd *Rebbe* of Sadigura,[321] while another source says that she was the granddaughter of Rabbi Akiva Eiger.[322] They had four children, one of whom married Rabbi Shlomo Chaim Friedman, the Sadigura *rebbe*.[323]

Shmuel had left Radomysl well before his father's demise to become a banker in Kiev.[324] In 1895, he was also listed in Kiev as a grocer, apparently in partnership with his brother Avraham.[325]

Outside of Kiev, Shmuel had other business interests. He owned at least three saw mills, two of which[c,326] he co-owned with his brothers Berko, Yoel (Evel), and Gur-arye. He also owned a third saw mill[d,327] and a lumber store.[e,328]

Shmuel conducted himself like a rabbi. On the Sabbath, he wore a velvet *Kasket* (skullcap) together with a long, black garment. Even in Kiev, during the time of the "contracts," when all of Ukraine's gentry and peasant-landowners used to convene, Shmuel would walk around Kretschatik Street in his Hasidic

---

[c] One was in the village of "Otsytel" (perhaps "Ostila" in Yiddish); the other was in the village of Varkovichi which is between Rovno and Dubno.

[d] Located in the village of Poedinka, Zhitomir Uyezd.

[e] Located in Lelchitsy, Minsk Gubernia.

attire with a wide, red handkerchief around his neck.[329]

On the Sabbath, he and his wife would host many guests, providing only the best - and generously. The tale is told that, on one Friday night, when they were serving fine fish, Yosel, his only son, wanted to add something to it, either *chrayn* (horseradish), or lemon. Shmuel said to him,

> *"Feh! To shabbas fish, one adds condiments? Is pure shabbas fish too shabby for you?"*[330]

Yosel, a Boyaner like his father, had a personal relationship with Rabbi Yitzchok Friedman of Boyan. Anecdotes concerning his contact with the *rebbe* have been published.[331] One of his daughters married the son of the Sadigura *rebbe*, a marriage which caused quite a stir since, at the time, a virtual war was prevailing between Boyaner and Sadigura *Hasidim*.[332]

Shmuel eventually returned to Radomysl to live where he remained the rest of his life.[333] His last years were marked by losses in every direction. In 1918, although he was now elderly, Shmuel was thrown out of his house by the Bolsheviks. Afterwards he had to live in a neighbor's kitchen. While his wife had escaped earlier to Vienna, she died that same year when she was run over by an automobile.[334]

The Declaration of the Radomysl District Revolutionary Committee of July 31, 1919 mentions his son Yosel's cloth factory as one of the first enterprises in the Radomysl area to be nationalized.[335] That same year Shmuel died, in the throes of the Ukrainian Revolution and the Jewish massacres.[336] Yosel and his wife Rebecca, a daughter of Shmuel's brother Evel, were later murdered during the Holocaust in Babi Yar.[337]

SON #2: Rabbi Zalman Shaul HaKohen Horenstein

Born Aleksandriya, 1842-1843; died Warsaw, 1930

Zalman, the second oldest son, was a Torah scholar like his older brother. By around 1863, when he was only 22 years old,[338] he was first listed as the owner of the massive Yanushpol' beet sugar works in Volhynia.[339] The large refinery, located next to the town (now named Ivanopil'), was a major employer of the town's Jewish residents, most of whom were *Hasidim*. As of 1897, the town's Jewish population was 1,251 out of a total of 5,085 (25%), and the Horenstein factory was one of the two Jewish-owned sugar refineries.

Zalman and his family resided next to the refinery, and members of both his own family and his wife's family were employed there.[340] A devout *Hasid*, Zalman became famous in the area because of his many charitable acts. Friendly and easy-going, he was worldly, modern, and fairly intellectual.[341]

Aharon Liebersohn, writing in *Yalqut Vohlyn* (1945), described him as follows:

"This was a kind-hearted Jew, a Torah scholar, G-d fearing and a doer of good deeds, who became famous as a benefactor and as one who acts with loving-kindness, and whose name brought forth blessings."[342]

He was respected by the Duchess Lubomirska of Kiev gubernia, and the local nobility, with whom the Horensteins engaged in business, trusted him.[343]

Estherel, Zalman's wife, was a descendant of Yakov Yosef of Polonnoye, the *"Toldot"* (author of *Toldot Yakov Yosef*), as well as a grandchild of the Ostroher *rebbe* (probably Elyakim Getz).[344] Through their childrens' marriages, Zalman and Estherel became connected to great Rabbinic lineages (the Bohushers, the Landaus, and the Blochs).[345]

A saintly woman, through her goodness she became well-respected throughout the entire region. Their home was a kind of hostel, open to the needy and to the sick, for whom Estherel was like a real mother.

There were maid-servants for the houseful of guests, which used to come to them in the home to "recover," and Estherel had both male and female relatives around her to provide their support. Each of these guests was respectfully catered to with various foods and milk, like in a fine hotel; often Estherel herself would do the serving. One time, when a maid-servant left milk out for the family members and a guest drank it up, the maid-servant got angry. Estherel chastised her, saying "the guest gets priority."[346]

When anyone wanted to borrow money, she would silently pawn her jewelry so, before a Jewish holiday or a celebration, Zalman would have to buy the jewelry back. She also used to provide dowries from the bank for orphaned young women and poor brides. In addition, the couple distributed thousands of rubles to charity every year.[347]

During the First World War, Zalman thought of selling the factory and immigrating to the Land of Israel. Neither Estherel nor the relatives who worked for him liked the plan, so Estherel asked one of the chief clerks to use his influence to convince her husband to postpone it. The clerk's efforts were successful, so Zalman kept the factory and he and his family remained in town.[348] That turned out to be an unfortunate decision.

As of 1919, Zalman still owned the sugar refinery,[349] while Naftali's grandson Israel Yakov (son of Gur-arye) served as a member of its governing body in Kiev.[350,351,352] There were several pogroms in Yanushpol' that year. Soldiers of the Ukrainian People's Republic, operating under the authority of Simon Petlyura, killed 30 Jews in one; in another, Red Army cavalrymen went on a spree of robbery, beatings and rape.[353] The refinery was confiscated by the Ukrainian government to be used for "defensive purposes," and two million poods[f] of coal

---

[f] A *pood* was a Russian weight measure equaling 36.11 pounds in use until 1924.

as well as one-half million poods of sugar were confiscated, while he and his family were thrown out of their home.[354]

Zalman and his sons were permitted to register as "workers for the Fatherland," and were thus freed from going to the front, but Zalman was stripped of his wealth and forbidden to involve himself in public works.[355] His wife Estherel died that same year.

In 1920, their son Yosef David was captured by the Bolsheviks during their retreat from Kiev; his fate was never discovered. The following year, Zalman, now penniless, died in Berdichev.[356,357]

Rabbi Moshe HaKohen Horenstein

One of Zalman's sons, Moshe HaKohen Horenstein (born in 1869) owned a lumber mill in Yelna, Smolensk gubernia, near their estate.[358] He also owned and operated a beet sugar refinery. Chaya Mushka, Moshe's wife, was the daughter of Rebbe Shmuel Schneerson of Lubavitch and sister of the 5th Lubavicher *rebbe*, Rabbi Sholom Dov Ber.

Moshe HaKohen Horenstein

Chaya Muscha Schneerson Horenstein

Moshe is the subject of a Hasidic folk tale:

"After Rabbi Moshe Horenstein married the sister of Rabbi Sholom Dov Ber of Lubavitch (in 1892), he noticed that his new brother-in-law would not use sugar on Passover. Rabbi Moshe failed to understand why: he himself owned and operated a sugar refinery and knew that no leavened substances are involved in the sugar-making process.

"Rabbi Moshe resolved to provide the Rebbe with sugar for Passover so, despite his confidence that his sugar was 100 percent kosher for Passover, he took extraordinary precautions, purchasing new equipment and taking personal charge of the production every step of the way.

"On the day before Passover, he brought the sugar to the Rebbe. He then proceeded to describe the entire sugar-distillation process, pointing out that there are absolutely no grounds for concern, especially as he, Reb Moshe, had personally overseen the making of these sugar cubes.

"As Rabbi Moshe spoke, he noticed the grave look on the Rebbe's face. The more he elaborated, the more serious the Rebbe's expression grew. When Rabbi Moshe

finished, the Rebbe took a sugar cube and broke it in two. Out fell a grain of wheat...[359]

Tragically, Moshe's lumber mill, which was uninsured, was destroyed in a fire, but that was not the end of the matter. In November of 1901, a nobleman whose lumber was lost in the fire sued him, alleging that he burnt down his own factory in order to damage the nobleman's merchandise. Moshe was arrested and imprisoned without bail while awaiting trial.

A few days after Moshe's arrest, Rabbi Sholom Dov Ber left Lubavitch to travel to Moscow. There he hired a prestigious lawyer to provide Moshe's defense. Eventually, the lawyer succeeded in obtaining his release from jail.[360,361]

Moshe and his family later moved to Warsaw and still later settled in Otwock (Poland) where he became administrator of a Jewish orphanage, supported by the American-Jewish Joint Distribution Committee.[362] He died in Warsaw on June 23, 1930.

SON #3: **Rabbi Avraham HaKohen Horenstein ("Avrum")**

Born Aleksandriya, 1844-1846; died Vienna, 1919

The family "aristocrat," Avrum Horenstein, like all of Naftali's children, was good-looking.[363] He has been described as "half-Enlightened and half-Hasidic." He wore a beard, but cropped it smooth.[364,365]

Although Avrum was an "Honored Guardian" of the Jewish elementary school in Radomysl, (a title which undoubtedly meant that he provided the school with considerable financial support),[366] Kiev was the center of Avrum's life. Like his father, he paid the large annual fee that entitled him to the special privileges of a Kiev Merchant of the 1st Guild.[367] He was living in Kiev by 1875; by 1881, Avrum and his family had moved into the elegant Kiev Horenstein residence.

His timing could have been better. On the first of March of that year, Czar Alexander II was assassinated by members of *Narodnaya Volya*, a terrorist organization. As a result, his son, Alexander III, ascended to the throne on May 27, 1881. His coronation was quickly followed by the outbreak of a violent anti-Semitic pogrom in Kiev, supported by the Governor-General. An angry mob broke into the Horenstein residence at 12 Bibikovski. They threw "furniture, the grand piano, dishes … from the windows and balconies, and then torched the house."[368]

"Assault on Jews in Kiev," Illustrated London News, 4 June 1881

Avrum continued to live in Kiev despite the danger of further pogroms. By 1887, he had shifted his 1st Guild merchant status to Moscow,[369] apparently because he had obtained contracts from both the Moscow City Council and the Gubernia Administrative Committee to supply the Russian army with a large amount of wood from the family's forests.

He stored the wood in Obolon, just across the Dnieper River from Kiev to the south. This created a problem for him during the long Russian winter, when the

125

Dnieper regularly flooded the area, especially as the army needed the lumber for firewood to heat its buildings.

Avrum came up with a creative solution: He obtained permission from the Kiev City Council to temporarily store the firewood in private homes located close to where the troops were stationed.[370]

By 1895, his Kiev businesses also included a grocery which he apparently ran with his brother Shmuel.[371] His primary investments, however, were in sugar beet farms and refineries. As of 1900, Avrum owned five sugar refineries in various towns,[g] including the Karwice sugar refinery in Mizoch.[372]

---

[g] The names and locations of Avrum Horenstein's several sugar refineries are not entirely certain. One source states that "after his marriage (probably his first marriage - to Rachel Zeitzef) he lived in Vikhnotshka in the province of Vohlin, where he had a sugar factory" (Lieberman, Yosef. Shalshelet HaYuchasin. Jerusalem, 1977-8). Another source states that he had five sugar refineries: Karwice in Mizoch (30 km from Rovno), Krzanosiółka (location unknown), Steblów (possibly located in Steblëv, Kiev gubernia), Łoźny (possibly located in Łozna (Lyëzna), Mogilev, Belarus), and Aleksandrówka (one of several Polish towns with that name) (Kiev. Kraj, nr.9, 1900, str. 17). Only the Mizoch location of the Karwice refinery has been confirmed (Asher Ben-Oni, Ed. Mizoch – Sefer Iskor. Tel Aviv, Y. Nediv, 1961).

The Karwice sugar beet refinery, Mizoch

Shown in a postcard photo mailed from Mizoch in 1932 by Arik Goldbarg,
2nd great grandson of Feiga Bluma (sister of Yakov Yosef and Naftali).

A *Hasid* like his father, Avrum founded a small *Boyaner* synagogue in Kiev which he attended regularly.[373,374] During the week, he would dress as a Western gentleman. Each Saturday, dressed in a cap and an elegant, short coat, he would walk from his expansive Kiev home on the wide, poplar-lined Bibikovski Boulevard ...

Bibikovski Boulevard, Kiev

through Kretschatik, an expensive downtown area ...

Krestschatik Street, Kiev; ca. 1910

to the relatively poor, largely Jewish, Podil section of the city, the location of the *Boyaner shtiebel* (small synagogue).

View of Podil, Kiev, ca. 1900-1920

Once he arrived at his *shul* (synagogue), he would take off his short coat and roll down his long satin *kapote* (long coat), which was crumpled under his broad silken *gartel* (a type of belt worn by *Hasidim* during prayer), and became a "real" *Hasid* in proper costume.

He then would pray with dedication and Hasidic fervor. [375,376] Not content with simply praying with the congregation, he would often appear there as the cantor.[h] Avrum was a "singer of distinction," so every time he served as the

------

[h] *Cantor:* The synagogue official who chants liturgical music and leads the choir in prayer.

cantor, it was an event which attracted large audiences of "lovers of good syna-gogue music."[377]

When his first wife, Rachel Zeitzef, died about 1886,[378] he married Berta Te-omim a younger wife.

Berta Teomim Horenstein

In 1897, after this marriage ended in divorce, he married Marija Jekeles, a still younger woman.

Marija Jekeles Horenstein

While his wives were becoming younger, his sugar factories were becoming old and decrepit.[379] Soon after he married his third wife, Baruch Esman, another wealthy Kiev resident, said to him:

"You should be buying new factories and taking on old wives. Now, that would last! But, your taking on young wives and buying up old factories scares me!"[380,381]

That same year Dr. Theodor Herzl published an article titled "The Jewish Colonial Trust" in the weekly magazine of the Zionist movement. In it he argued that the movement was badly in need of financial institutions to support the Jewish settlers in Palestine.

The following year, at the Second Zionist Congress in Basal, The Jewish Colonial Trust was established. It was incorporated in London in 1899 with the intention of raising capital and credit to help attain a charter for Palestine.

Its officers were primarily from Europe. Doctor Herzl was one of the 23 Council members, while Avrum was selected to be one of its three Governors. For their London meetings, he was represented by his attorney.[382]

Officers of the Jewish Colonial Trust

At the height of his fortune, Avrum lived with his family in opulence. They moved from their rooms at the Tereshchenko mansion into a larger 21-room apartment at 35 Aleksandrovski. We get some idea of the grandness of their living quarters from the fact that their apartment contained three pianos. The staff consisted of 16 servants who had their own personal cook. There was a tutor and a governess for every two of his younger children. For travel within the city and beyond, the family rode in a four-horse carriage.[383,384]

As Baruch Esman had predicted, Avrum's businesses did not go well.[385] By the end of the 19th century, too many sugar factories had been built compared to the demand for sugar, causing the owners to be close to bankruptcy. Indeed, Avrum had to apply for bankruptcy several times, but each time his brothers bailed him out.

Many sugar factories failed, but Avrum was successful in selling his Karwice factory in Mizoch, as well as his factory in Aleksandriya, to Lazar Brodsky, the "sugar king," whose consortium had been managing these factories and was large enough to make the purchases worthwhile.[386]

Jewish life in Kiev was shaken again by a second pogrom in October of 1905 in which perhaps 100 Jews were massacred, at least 300 were seriously injured, and considerable property was destroyed. Soon afterward, he and his family finally left Russia and moved to Königsberg, Prussia.[387] Along with them came one

134

of the two butlers, one of the three maids, one of the two cooks, one of the two boy waiters, and all three governesses: one Russian, one German and one French.[388]

Avrum owned a 3,000-acre working ranch, with farm animals and 40 horses, a three-hour horse ride from the city. Most of the acreage (2,500 acres) was forest land and Avrum apparently harvested trees from the forest for sale. He and his family would spend much of their time there. [389]

In 1911, Avrum's declining financial assets caused him to move his family to Vienna where he bought a three-story house in an expensive neighborhood. They lived on one-story and rented out the rest.[390]

Avraham HaKohen Horenstein – late in life

World War I erupted in the summer of 1914, and life became increasingly difficult for foreigners living in Vienna.[391] In Russia, meanwhile, Avrum lost the employees of his sugar beet farms to the army.[392] Soon after, in 1917, Russia exploded with the Bolshevik Revolution. It was not long before the Bolsheviks confiscated his sugar beet farms and refineries.[393]

Avrum's fortune had now evaporated. When he could no longer afford his four-horse carriage, he reduced the carriage to one horse. Embarrassed, his wife refused to ride in it when they promenaded in the Vienna Prater[i] on Sundays.[394]

Avrum spent his final years in an apartment, living quietly and waiting for the Russian tumult to die down.[395] He died in Vienna on June 3, 1919.

SON #4: Rabbi Dov Ber HaKohen Horenstein ("Berko")

Born Aleksandriya, 1845-1846; died Frankfurt, 1918

Naftali's son Berko became the family's German emissary at a young age when his father began to send him there to negotiate with local merchants. It was said that, not only did he learn to speak the language, but he learned to behave like a German.[396]

Berko became a Kiev Merchant of the 1st Guild.[397] In Radomysl, he was considered a "famous Radomysl capitalist."[398]

He was an investor in a large cloth factory in the area along with his brothers Evel and Gur-arye.[j,399,400,401] The factory, built around 1903 on the eve of the Russo-Japanese War,[k,402,403] produced a coarse cloth for mass sale, as well as blankets and uniforms for the military.[404] As many as 120 workers were employed there.[405]

The factory gave Hasidic employees an apartment with a garden, as well as provided a kindergarten for their children.[406,407] Worker's salaries were low, however, usually only 40 rubles a week for a 12- to 14-hour work day,[408,409] causing angry workers to hold a strike in February of 1905 which forced the Horenstein brothers to raise their salaries.[410]

---

[i] *Prater*: A large public park in Leopoldstadt, Vienna's 2nd district.

[j] Located near to an iron foundry in Mykgorod or Mychesk ("Myk").

[k] As of 1913, the factory had 56 employees (All Russia. 1912; Plants and Factories of All Russia. 1913). At one time it produced products worth 164,500 rubles (Zwik, Gennady. The History of Radomyshl. Zhytomir, Polissya, 2002) (in Ukrainian).

Chimneys of the Horenstein Clothing Factory (in the background)
seen from the Teterev River

Berko also had other business interests. He was a major promoter of the Radomysl Mutual Credit Association, the biggest bank in the district, whose charter was adopted in 1907.[411] As of 1909, he was the director of a paper mill in nearby Malyn.[412] By 1913, Berko was a co-owner (with his brothers Gur-arye, Evel and Shmuel) of two saw mills.[413]

In 1908, Berko funded a group of religious structures in Jerusalem which still remain. Known as *Batei Horenstein* ("Horenstein houses"), this is a complex of 30 apartments together with a *beit midrash* and *mikveh* in the Geula neighborhood of central Jerusalem next to *Zichron Moshe*.[414]

There is a tale told about Berko's donation:

"*Childless himself, Berko Horenstein used some of his wealth to support children of poor families so that they could continue their torah studies. When the time came for one of the students he supported to marry, Berko provided the money for the wedding. On the wedding day everyone gathered in the place where the ceremony was to be held and waited for Berko and his wife, the guests of honor, to arrive. They waited and waited.*

"*After some time they realized he wasn't going to appear, so everyone, the bride and groom and their families, the Rabbi, the musicians and the guests, took the chuppa[l] through the streets of the town to Berko's house to fetch him. As the happy procession reached the house, they saw some people running in the opposite direction. They entered the house and found it in a mess, Berko and his wife tied up in a corner, and sacks filled with the family's valuables lying about. It became clear that the robbers had been disturbed by the noise of the procession, so they dropped everything and ran.*

"*The groom's party untied the hapless couple, and soon proceeded with the marriage ceremony with the Horensteins in attendance.*

"*Realizing that he had been saved by a miracle, Berko went to the Rebbe, the Pachad Yitzhak (Yitzchok Friedman), to tell the story and ask for advice. The Rebbe suggested that, since he was childless, he should build a memorial in recognition of the just transpired miracle, so he did so by funding Batei Horenstein. To pay for this project, Berko donated all the valuables that the robbers had left behind.*"[415,m]

When living in Radomysl became dangerous, Berko, the son who had served as the family's "ambassador" to Germany, decided to move to Germany to live.[416] By 1913, he had turned at least one of his houses on Prisutstvena Street into rental apartments.[417]

He died in Frankfurt on March 31, 1918.

---

[l] *Chuppa: A canopy beneath which Jewish marriage ceremonies are performed.*

[m] The assertion that the *Pachad Yitzchok* (*Rebbe* Yitzchok Friedman) was instrumental in setting up Botei Horenstein by advising Berko, because he had no children, to build the houses as a memorial to himself is repeated in The Golden Dynasty by Yisroel Friedman
(http://www.nishmas.org/gdynasty/chapt5.htm).

SON #5: **Rabbi Yoel HaKohen Horenstein ("Evel")**

Born Aleksandriya, 1846–1848; died Kiev, after 1925

Evel, like his brothers, grew up in Aleksandriya. He moved to Radomysl with his family late in his childhood. Around 1870, he married Royza Hirsh Horowitz who came from a famous rabbinical family.

Following Naftali's demise in 1899, he remained in Radomysl along with some of his brothers. A devout *Hasid*, Evel co-owned with his brothers Berko and Gur-arye a large cloth factory in the Radomysl area which he probably operated himself.

Mother to 14 children, his wife, known as "Reizel," was a very busy woman, but that did not stop her from taking on management responsibilities at the clothing factory, or from assisting Hasidic families in need. The great granddaughter of a woman who was a recipient of her generosity has written about her:

Royza Hirsh Horowitz Horenstein

"In Radomysl, ... my great grandmother was born in 1860 ... and became a widow when she was young. She had three children and was under the guardianship of Reizel Horenstein, ... a Hasid and the owner of a fabric factory. She contributed to charity, provided meals to poor Hasidim and made arrangements for their children: helping girls to get married and young men to get a job....

"My [grandparents] had a traditional Jewish wedding under a chuppa in the synagogue. Reizel Horenstein ... paid all the wedding expenses. She even bought the wedding dress and wedding gifts.

"She also arranged for a job for [my grandfather] in her cloth factory...."[418]

Later, ownership of the factory was passed down to Evel and Reizel's son, Yosef Yitzchok (Ossia).[419] While no records are available, this fact, along with the active involvement of Reizel, Evel's wife, in the factory's operations, suggest that Evel had been the primary owner and factory operator among the three Horenstein brothers.

Around 1900, Fanya (Evel's youngest child) married Pinchas Trachtenberg of the wealthy Berdichev Trachtenberg family. They lived in Malyn where he managed his father's factories.[420]

In 1907, Evel was listed as a registered voter for the election of the Kiev gubernia duma. By 1913, Evel, together with his brothers Gur-arye, Berko and Shmuel, owned two sawmills as described earlier.[421]

The date and location of Evel's death are not known. However, in 1925, he was approaching the age of 80 and living in Kiev,[422] so he probably died there.

SON #6: Rabbi Gur-arye HaKohenHornstein

Born Aleksandriya, 1856; died Vienna, 1928

Gur-arye HaKohen Horenstein

Gur-arye, Naftali's youngest son, was named after his paternal grandfather. He married Taube Horowitz, daughter of Rabbi Levi Isaac Horowitz of Bolekhiv and a descendant of the *"Shelah HaKadosh,"* Rabbi Isaiah Horowitz (ca. 1555-1630), as well as of the beloved Rabbi Levi Isaac of Berdichev (1740-1810).

During the early part of their marriage, the couple lived in Tauba's home town of Bolekhiv, but they eventually moved to Radomysl to join other Horenstein family members. In Radomysl, he appears that he became the most prominent of Naftali's sons, as well as one of the town's most distinguished residents.[423]

Like his father, Gur-arye had the reputation of being a devout *Hasid* of exceptional wealth. He was considered the town's richest factory owner.[424,425] A Kiev Merchant of the 1st Guild, his factories also included a paper mill, a tannery[426] and a beet-sugar refinery.

Gur-arye had inherited the tannery, located on Sukhark farm, from his father; it became the most important tannery in the entire district and employed 41 workers, of which 30 were local. He also owned a small steam mill at the same location which processed the tree bark needed for leather tanning; it employed five workers. [427]

In 1887 he built a luxurious home. The building, which is still standing, functions today as part of the Radomyshl district polyclinic.[428,429]

Photos by Nicole Gordon, a descendant of Avrum Horenstein,
Gur-arye Horenstein's brother

When Gur-arye built his house, the exterior was magnificent. Beautiful decorations in the form of flowers and grapes gave it a festive elegance. The exterior walls had a pinkish color, as blood and animal fats were mixed into the paint to give it better water repellency. Today the beautiful carved doors with a dramatic marquee jutting out above them remain, as well as parts of the plaster molding and cornices. Also, there are remains of a forged fence around the property, the same fencing, forged locally, which had once surrounded all of the Horenstein homes in Radomysl. [430]

The interior of his home was just as exceptional. The rooms were, of course, spacious. Gur-arye imported Italian artisans to do the décor. Floors were covered with an artistically patterned parquet, and there were beautiful paintings on the ceilings.[431]

When the Horensteins were living there, guests would gather during the long winter evenings to listen to music. In a spacious hall, a fire would be made in the fireplace, then a special feature of the house, lined with imported tiles decorated with fanciful miniature images.[432,433]

Gur-arye's house was one of five Horenstein family houses in Radomysl, three of which, including his house, were situated on beautiful Prisutstvena Street near the Town Council and the very center of town, with two of them facing the third from across the street. All were lavishly built in pre-Revolutionary Romanov style. Inside all were richly finished with gorgeous tile fireplaces, wooden fretwork,[n] plaster castings, and beautifully painted walls and ceilings.[434,435] Only Gur-arye's house remains standing today.

In 1890, Gur-arye opened an overcoat factory which, as of 1900, was the largest industrial facility in the town.[436]

That same year, Gur-arye was listed as owner of one of the three Radomysl tanneries; his tannery employed a manager and 41 workers.[437,o] He was also an investor in Radomysl's Horenstein cloth factory along with his brothers Berko and Evel.

In July 1903, the first bank in Radomysl was founded. Working capital was 10,000 rubles, some of which came from Gur-arye. In May 1907, the "Radomysl Mutual Credit Society" was opened, with Gur-arye as one of the two co-founders. The bank became the largest and most famous in the district.[438]

By 1911, Gur-arye was listed as owner of a paper mill in Berdichev.[439,p] By 1912, Gur-arye had passed the ownership of his tannery, which now had 63 employees, on to his heirs.[440,441] They decided to sell it immediately to Georgy Nikolay Garbarev who already owned one or the other two tanneries in Radomysl.[442] Two years later, it was listed as one of the biggest tanneries in the Radomysl area, with 65 employees and a yearly income of 200,000 rubles.[443,444]

---

[n] Fretwork: Ornamental design in wood, typically openwork in geometric patterns, usually done with a fretsaw.

[o] Located in the Rudnya area, it was probably inherited from his father.

[p] The mill was built by the Berdichev Trachtenbergs (Personal communication: Harry Sapir, Naftali's 2nd great grandson).

The following year, Gur-arye, together with his brothers Berko, Evel and Shmuel, were listed as owners of two saw mills as previously described.[445] Gur-arye also owned a sugar refinery, located in Sklov, which his son Avraham Yosef later inherited.[446]

Gur-arye's wealth did not protect him from the horrors of the Bolshevik Revolution. Like many other family members, he eventually had to flee to Vienna. When he died there on March 10, 1928, he was given a high honor for a Boyaner: he was buried next to the grave of Rebbe Yitzchok Friedman, the first Boyaner *rebbe*.[447] Here is an extract from his death notice in a Frankfurt Jewish newspaper:

"Gur-arye Hornstein[q] – May he Rest in Peace"

"A silent hero; an almost legendary figure was buried in Vienna last Sunday. Ukraine, the cradle of Hasidism, was also the cradle of the world-famous Hornstein family, who because of their piety and erudition, because of their wealth and sacrifice, but especially because of their attachment to the "Ruzhiner" (Rabbi Isaac Friedman ...) and his successors far beyond Russia, have earned themselves a good name....

"The Deceased ... was the last representative of a time that was completely immersed in Chassidism. Even in his younger years he withdrew from his business and devoted himself entirely to pious works. In his heavy fateful hours in exile, freed from the splendor and glory of the old, peaceful Russian homeland, where he was a leader in Russian Judaism, he carried his many sufferings with pious heroism.... Day and night he filled in quiet times with good deeds....

"The funeral took place with the great participation of the Orthodox Jews of Vienna....

"Gur-arye Hornstein ... who reached the age of 72, was the last of his equally famous brother[s], and with him [ends] a blessed and meritorious generation...."

Rabbi Avraham Yosef HaKohen Hornstein (b. Bolekhiv (1876; d. Tel Aviv 1958)

Gur-arye's 2nd son, Avraham Yosef married Rachel Trachtenberg of the Berdichev Trachtenbergs and, by late in the century, the young couple was living in Berdichev where Gur-arye owned the paper mill started by Avraham Yosef's

---

[q] Gur-arye changed his family's name to Hornstein.

father-in-law. Avraham Yosef apparently managed the paper mill, and eventually Gur-arye gave him ownership of the mill.[r,448] Gur-arye also gave him ownership of his sugar refinery in Sklov.[449]

As conditions worsened, Avraham Yosef and his family moved to St. Petersburg, Russia in 1919 and then to Vienna the following year.[450] That same year, his own son Chaim (Munia) was married in Kosice, Austria. Several of Gur-arye's descendants attended the happy event.

Times had been difficult for the Horenstein family, as the world they had known was crumbling and those who could leave had fled to Europe with whatever assets they could still gather. This wedding echoed the grand events at Naftali's Zavod estate only two decades earlier, but in a different part of the world and in a different climate. Not only had they lost much of their fortune, but they no longer dressed as Hasidic Jews. It was indeed an expected new world for them, but one with hope for the future.

---

[r] As of 1918, Avraham Yosef owned stock valued at 400,000 rubles in the large Kondrovskaya paper factory which specialized in producing writing paper. Possibly this mill was first owned by the Berdichev Trachtenbergs and the stock (which later became worthless) had been passed on to Avraham Yosef (their son-in-law) and their daughter Rachel. (Personal communication: Ittai Hershmann, great grandson of Avraham Yosef and Rachel.)

Wedding of Chaim HaKohen ("Munia") Hornstein to
Margit ("Madi") Ratzesdorfer

Kosice, Austria (1920)

Photograph taken in front of the Kosice Synagogue.

Mordechai (Marcus) Hornstein (born Radomsyl 1886; died Tiberias 1969)

Marcus, Gur-arye's 5th son, initially worked as a banker in Kiev with his father's older brother Shmuel.[451] In 1905 or 1906, he married his cousin Golda, Shmuel Horenstein's daughter.

The young couple initially lived in Shmuel's home, managing his business affairs and dealing with the needs of the Jewish community such as the *Linat HaTzedek* (hostels for the poor) institutions, and *Bikur Holim*.[452]

They eventually returned to Radomysl where he built a house on Bolshaya Kievskaya Street. It was not an average house, but an exact copy of the house which his father had built earlier. (Beside's Gur-arye's house, this is the only other of the five Horenstein houses that we know anything about.)

Home of Marcus Hornstein, son of Gur-arye

Marcus was an investor in the district's newspaper, "Radomysylian," which commenced publication in 1912 and lasted for five years, with its lifetime undoubtedly cut short by the Bolshevik Revolution. The paper was designed to inform all the district's residents, whether Jewish or Christian. In addition to "highlighting the facts of local life," it sought to consolidate Radomysl's charitable institutions as well as to promulgate the ideology of religious Zionism (which advocated the return of religious Jews to the Land of Israel).[453]

Editorial Offices of the Radomyslyanin
(Note the similarity of the marquee to those of the Horenstein houses.)

Masthead of the newspaper "Radomysylyanin," January 1, 1914

During the First World War, Marcus was chairman of the local Assistance Council for the War-injured as well as a member of the All-Ukraine Central Council. Together with the rabbi of Kiev, he worked to free rabbis from Galicia who had been taken hostage by the Russian army administration during the Galician occupation and were about to be sent to Siberia. By offering Naftali, his only son, as a guarantee, he succeeded in convincing the Russian authorities to permit these rabbis to remain in Radomysl during the Passover holiday before returning to their imprisonment.[454]

In 1916, Marcus moved to Kiev where he opened his own private bank. He donated 10,000 rubles to help supply the pharmacy next to the *Bikur Holim* office. In 1918, he participated in the convention of Ukrainian Jews in Kiev, representing "*Achdut*," the religious faction.[455]

In 1921, he immigrated to Vienna, and then to Berlin. There, he managed buildings belonging to Swiss capitalists and represented the interests of the state-owned "Eidgenossen Bank" of Zürich. He also became a leader of the eastern European Jewish and Hasidic communities, maintaining his contacts with the *rebbes* who descended from Rabbi Yisroel of Ruzhin.

He founded a prayer house for the Boyaner *Hasidim* and did a great deal of charity work, including providing support for charitable institutions in Jerusalem.[456]. In addition, he was elected to be the representative of the eastern European Jews to the Great Community Council.[457]

About 1933, Marcus made *aliyah* (immigrated) to Israel and settled in Tel Aviv where he continued the family's tradition of supporting the Hasidic community from the Volhynia province in Ukraine. He also supported industries in the new *yishuv* (area of Jewish settlement) as well as the Zionist movement. His support of these causes was not just monetary as he was elected to the National Council of the *Mizrachi* (Religious Zionist) Organization.[458]

His house in Radomysl remained standing until the autumn of 1943 when, during the liberation of the city by Soviet troops, it was destroyed by fire.[459]

POGROMS AND REVOLUTION

Starting with the Kiev pogrom, the assassination of Czar Alexander III in March of 1881 ignited a wave of pogroms throughout the country. The situation for Jews living in Ukraine gradually deteriorated afterwards. In October of 1905, when Kiev experienced its second pogrom, it was one of 160 pogroms in various locations in southern Russia. Neither the army nor the police controlled the rioters, who ran amok unhindered for three days.

These pogroms were only the beginning. In February of 1917 a revolution overthrew the Tzarist autocracy and the establishment of a provisional government. That summer, soldiers fleeing from the front murdered and robbed Jews in various areas of Volhynia.

The situation further deteriorated the next year in the wake of hostilities between the Ukrainians and the Bolsheviks.[460] This was followed in October by another revolution, led by the Bolsheviks. In January of 1918, the Ukrainian National Council (the *Rada*) proclaimed the separation of Ukraine from Russia, but by August of 1920, the Red Army had completed its conquest of Ukraine and assumed control.

From 1919 to 1920, disorder in Volhynia reached its climax in a series of pogroms directed against the Jews by armed bands with frequent regime changes.[461] During the Polish-Soviet war of 1920, the Jews of Volhynia suffered at the hands of both sides. For a brief period, Volhynia was split between Poland and the Soviets, but soon the whole of the gubernia was annexed by the Soviet Union and a policy of liquidation of the Jewish parties, organizations and institutions was pursued.[462]

Radomysl, like the rest of the province, was in turmoil during this period. The political situation was so unstable that the group in power within the town changed 14 times between 1918 and 1921.[463] A series of pogroms began there in the spring of 1919. The first two, in February and March, were arranged by military units, while a third was conducted by a band of peasants under the hetman Sokolovski. Hundreds of Jews were massacred and many others fled to the big cities.

The Bolsheviks began to confiscate Horenstein family holdings shortly after they gained power. Many family members lost everything. Those who could escape did so, usually with at least some of their financial assets. They fanned out to a large area of eastern Europe, including Warsaw, Berlin, and Vienna as well as to Copot, which was then in the Free City of Danzig. [5,464,465,466] Those who remained lived in Kiev and Berdichev, as well as in Czernowitz and Odessa.

At the start of 1926, this is what one writer wrote about how the catastrophic events of the 20th century had affected the Radomysl Horenstein family:

"They are no longer the wealthy people they once were. But, there still lies within them till this day that splendor and glory, that majestic appearance of yesteryear.

"And, if you were to walk the streets of Warsaw or Vienna, Danzig, or of Berlin, and you encounter a tall, robust man with an attractive beard - a blonde one, or yellow or light-brown - wearing gold-brimmed spectacles, walking with a proud gait, noble-mannered, and manifesting a pedigree, you ought to know that he is a Horenstein, a Radomysl Horenstein, who has ended up there, torn away from his life and his roots."[467]

Due to the catastrophes they had befallen them, some family members

---

[5] Copot, a neighborhood in northwest Gdańsk, Poland, on the Baltic coast, pronounced "Tsopot" or "Sopot."

became impoverished. In March of 1936, the second Boyaner *rebbe*, Reb Menachem Nuchem of Boyan Chernovitz, exchanged letters with the directors of the Volhynia *Kollel*[t] in Jerusalem. Following the original construction of *Batei Horenstein*, a *mikveh* had been built which was not part of the original contract. The *rebbe* asked that the income from this *mikveh* be sent back to members of the Horenstein family

> *"who have suffered a reversal of fortune and . . . some of whom are on the verge of hunger, G-d forbid!"*[468]

The *rebbe*'s order was never carried out, however. Over the years several members of the family tried unsuccessfully to take possession of the *mikveh*, but without success.[469]

While Horenstein family members were now scattered, those who continued to be followers of the Boyaner *rebbe* retained a special tie to the region. Some even made occasional trips to visit Reb Menachem Nuchem of Boyan Chernovitz before his demise in 1936.[470] In fact, Yosef Yitzchok Horenstein (born after 1880; died 1953), one of Naftali's grandsons, was both editor and publisher of the *rebbe*'s book, *Tiferet Menachem*.[471]

THE HOLOCAUST

---

[t] *Kollel*: Full-time institute for advanced adult students of Talmud and rabbinic literature.

The Russian Revolution, as terrible as it was for most Russian Jews, was only the first of two massive waves of destruction which were to envelop the descendants of the Radomsyl Horensteins. In the 1930s, many family members who had escaped to Eastern Europe found themselves victimized again as the Nazis rose to power in Germany.

Now the lives of the Horensteins in Europe were just as endangered as the lives of their relatives who had remained in the Ukraine. In 1941, the Nazis attacked the Soviet Union and the extermination of the Jews of Volhynia began.[472] Any Horenstein family members who had remained behind died in the Nazi death camps.

Menachem Mendel HaKohen Horenstein, son of Moshe (born Bianoshpoli, Poland, 23 April 1905; died Treblinka, Poland, 5 November 1942)

In Poland, the most famous Horensteins to be murdered by the Nazis were Rabbi Menachem Mendel HaKohen Horenstein (son of Moshe HaKohen Horenstein and Sheina Bracha Schneerson) and his wife Sheindel, daughter of the sixth Lubavitcher *rebbe*, Yosef Yitzchok Schneerson (see page 107).

When the moment came for Rabbi Schneerson to leave Polish territory, he was determined to take along his daughter and son-in-law, but their Polish nationality precluded it. Subsequently, their departure was held up by the illness of Moshe Horenstein, Menachem Mendel's father, who remained bedridden until his passing in 1941. Menachem Mendel tended to his needs and refused to abandon him. After Moshe's passing, all the borders had already been sealed, so it was no longer possible for the young couple to make their escape.

In 1942, Menachem Mendel and Sheindel perished in the gas chambers of Treblinka. The Lubavicher movement commemorates their deaths each year on the anniversary of their murders.[473]

Yakov ("Jascha") Horenstein, son of Avrum (born Kiev, 1898; died London, 1973)

Jascha Horenstein and his sister 5 (1917)

One Horenstein family member not only survived the oppression suffered by the family in the early 20th century, but became world-famous. So as not to end the chapter on a tragic note, it seems fitting to close this part of the Horenstein saga with his story.

Jascha Horenstein is considered by many to be one of the greatest orchestral conductors of the 20th century. Born in Kiev, Jascha was the 13th of Avrum's 16 children, but the first-born son of Avrum's 3rd wife, Marija Jekeles. His red hair was inherited from Avrum who, in turn, had inherited it from Naftali.[474]

As a boy, music was an important part of his life. His family attended many Hasidic gatherings that were filled with music. Avrum, you may remember, had become known in Kiev for his cantorial singing and Jascha's first music lessons came from none other than his mother. Soon Jascha became a student of Max Brode, a famous violinist and conductor.

He was still a child when his father moved the family to Vienna where they joined other Horenstein family members who had made the exodus from Russia.[475]

Starting in 1916, he studied at the Vienna Academy of Music.[476] He moved to Berlin in 1920. In the 1920s, he conducted both the Vienna Symphony Orchestra and the Berlin Philharmonic Orchestra. He became principal conductor of the Düsseldorf Opera in 1928, and its music director the following year.[477]

The rise of the Nazi Party forced his resignation in 1933. He then moved to Paris and traveled extensively, conducting in Brussels, Vienna, and the USSR, visiting Scandinavia with the *Ballets Russe*, and touring Australia and New Zealand.[478]

In 1939, he emigrated to the United States where he became an American citizen. While living in New York City, he taught at the New School for Social Research,[479] also touring as a guest conductor for major orchestras worldwide, but never accepting a permanent position as principal conductor.

After the Second World War, Jascha returned to Europe and lived in Lausanne, Switzerland. He introduced Berg's opera Wozzeck in 1950 in Paris. In 1959, his performance of Mahler's Eighth Symphony for the BBC did much to stimulate a Mahler revival in Britain. After 1964, he gave many concerts in London with the London Symphony Orchestra. In his later years, he appeared frequently at London's Covent Garden.

Jascha Horenstein died in London in 1973 at the age of 74. Although his repertory was quite wide, he is particularly remembered as a champion of modern music,[480] and was especially known for his advocacy and interpretation of the music of Mahler and Bruckner, and was considered almost unrivaled in the "strength, integrity, and sincerity of his approach" to their compositions.[481] His many early recordings of their works were instrumental in bringing about their current popularity.[482]

Jascha was intolerant of routine performances, even from the greatest orchestras.[483] Viewed today as as "an intellectual and philosophical conductor of a sort not much encountered any more,"[484] he leaves a legacy of numerous great performances recorded on many of the leading labels of the time.

An article in The New York Times reviewed his life and contributions in 1994, 21 years after his death. Noting that there has been "tremendous cult interest" in him since his demise, the writer believes that there are two reasons why he had not been fully appreciated as a "major musician" during his lifetime. One was because he deliberately avoided a permanent appointment as conductor of a major orchestra; the other was because the modern repertory most important to him was unfashionable until late in his life.[485]

Even several decades after his demise, classic Horenstein recordings are treasured by connoisseurs of great classical music. These recordings ensure that his fame as one of the most outstanding conductors of his century will continue.

COMMENTS

The business success of the Horenstein brothers was part of larger changes in the economics of the Jewish population of Ukraine's Volhynia gubernia in the 2nd half of the 19th century. Decline of the estates of the Polish nobility, railroad construction and the creation of direct lines of communication with the large commercial centers impoverished the Jewish masses by depriving them of traditional sources of livelihood. Conversely, these changes prompted the development of industry,[486] which opened up new possibilities for the accumulation of wealth by the small number of Jews who could afford to invest in it.

Of the 123 large factories situated in Volhynia in the late 1870s, 118 were owned by Jews. In 1885 there were 113 1st and 2nd guild merchants in Volhynia province; all were Jewish. As to 3rd guild merchants, 3,749 were Jewish compared to only 56 who were Christian.[487]

Of the 1st guild merchants, Yakov Yosef, Naftali and Naftali's sons were among the richest, well known, and celebrated within the Jewish world of the Ukraine. From late in the 19th century until early in the 20th, millions of Jews living in Ukraine, as well as those living in Galicia and Bukovina, delighted in exchanging tales about this wealthy Hasidic family.

Then came the unraveling of the Russian government which was to lead to the collapse of the financial empire which the Horenstein brothers had so carefully built. Some family members made it out of Russia to Eastern Europe where, for a while, they could continue their lifestyle as wealthy and charitable members of the Jewish community. That was before Hitler took power.

Today their descendants are widely dispersed, with family members residing in Europe, the United States and Israel. Little remains of the characteristics for which Yakov Yosef and Naftali were known within the Jewish community. Not only is the family fortune long gone, but the family's historic tie to Hasidism has disappeared, and few descendants today are religiously observant.

In the middle of World War II (1943), Nachman Mayzel, a famous Yiddish newspaper writer and critic, noted that:

"The Radomysler Horenstein estate battled outside influences for quite a while, trying to shield its sons and grandchildren from the surrounding world; marriages were arranged only within their circle, with nephews and nieces, but to no avail - time played its role and broke through the Great Wall they attempted to build around their estate and family."[488]

Another writer reminded his readers of what the family had achieved at its height:

"Who the Horensteins are, anyone in the Ukraine, Galicia, or Bukovina can tell you. The Horensteins are the

Ukrainian Rothschilds,

the singing millionaires,

the great Hasidim.

"Above all, they were the "lords of Radomysl."[489]

Special thanks to my Horenstein cousins for sharing family memories and for assisting me with the historical research for this chapter. They include:

Hanna Cohen, Moshe Dagan (deceased), George Goldner, Nicole Gordon, Ittai Hershman, Avrom Horenstein, Lipa Horenstein (deceased), Misha Horenstein, Arnold Kremenstein, Eli Kronstein, Menachim Nahir, George Rosenwald, Harry Sapir, Galia Sartiel, Yael Sofer, and Ora Zadik.

A very early version of this chapter was published in *Sharsheret HaDorot*, the Journal of the Israeli Genealogical Society (vol. 20, #4, 2006).

PART II

EARLY ANCESTRY OF THE
HORENSTEIN BROTHERS

Part II: Chapter One

THE QUESTION OF DAVIDIC DESCENT

King David (reigned ca. 1010 - 970 BCE)

The youngest son of Jesse, a respected elder of Bethlehem with considerable wealth, David went his own way early in life and eventually became a commander in King Saul's army. His popularity threatened the King, but before Saul could capture him, David escaped to the rugged Judean wilderness where he became chief of a band of outlaws and fugitives.

Intelligent, ambitious and ruthless, he gradually gained control of part of the Negev and Judah. He assassinated the Calebite chief "Nabal" and assumed his wealth and status, thus bringing most of Judah under his control. After the elders of Judah anointed him king, he combined the clan of Judah with others to form what would become the nation of Judah.

A rival to Saul, David joined forces with the Philistines and eventually succeeded in causing Saul's downfall and, perhaps, engineered Saul's death. He then provoked war with Ishba'al, Saul's successor, and made a treaty with Abner to bring the army of Israel over to his side. By arranging for the assassinations of both Ishba'al and Abner, the elders of Israel had to declare David as their new king.

David consolidated power by defeating the Philistines, destroying Saul's heirs, and enhancing the unity between Israel and Judah by establishing a single capital in Jerusalem and giving the Ark of the Covenant, Israel's principal religious artifact, a new home there.

He maintained power by continuing to remove anyone who was in his way, including his two eldest sons. At the end of his life, it was his son Solomon who, using contrived orders from him, launched a coup against David's presumed successor, a coup which Bathsheba, David's favorite wife, may have even orchestrated.[490]

W̲e will start our discussion of the known origins of the Horenstein ancestry with a review of King David and his central importance to Jewish genealogy. In the biblical account of his life, legend is so mixed with reality that it is difficult to separate out the real David. The short biography above, derived from a recent reconstruction of David's life,[491] is closer to the truth as it attempts to present David devoid of the fictional distortions in the Biblical account which were due to both religious and political motivations.

The Biblical King David

Biblical scholars speak of David's life as described in the Bible as part of "The Deuteronomistic History," since various parts of a single narrative not only appear in the Book of Deuteronomy, but also in Joshua, Judges, 1-2 Samuel, and 1-2 Kings.[a]

There is a strong argument that David is the main character of this history.[492] His life and times take up 42 chapters compared to only 34 chapters on Moses and the law. He is the standard by which later kings are judged. Judah and Jerusalem lasted as long as they did because of him, and he became a model for restoring Israel to its former greatness. Even Judaism's focus on Jerusalem we owe to King David.

Insights from Archeology

We have learned a great deal from archeology about Judah and Jerusalem during David's lifetime as well as during the centuries afterwards. The story of David's life, stripped away as much as possible from what Biblical scholars view as its

---

[a] Specifically, the rise and reign of King David is in 1 Samuel 16 to 2 Samuel 24, while 1 Kings 1-11 describes David's death and the reign of Solomon.

later embellishments, reveals an underlying core much closer to the reality. Archeologists have done even better as they have found enough "hard" evidence to establish with reasonable certainty many aspects of life in the region during that time period.

We now know that the Kingdom of Judah was sparsely inhabited in the 10th century BCE, with few permanent settlements and a population that primarily earned its living by raising livestock. King Saul (whose existence has yet to be confirmed by archeological evidence) controlled the highlands north of Judah and west of the Jordan River, with an extension across the river to Gilead to the east. This region was more densely settled; not only were there many more settlements, but also many of these settlements were larger than those in Judah.[493]

In stark contrast to the biblical account, the evidence that has been found concerning Jerusalem at roughly the time of King David suggests that it was little more than a village. David's Jerusalem was a small, relatively poor, unfortified, hill country town, no larger than three to four acres in size.[494] According to Israel Finkelstein, Professor of Archeology at Tel Aviv University, King David, rather than a mighty king controlling distant lands, appears to have been a chieftain of a small but ambitious tribe.[495]

Did King David Really Exist?

Undoubtedly, King David is one of the most important figures in the entire expanse of Jewish history. What makes him unique is his position in that history. Not only is David's reign pivotal to the formation of the Jewish people, but his life is at the crossroads between the Biblical stories of the ancient past, accepted almost entirely on the basis of faith, and later Biblical stories for which there are often bits of scholarly confirmation. Before him, we have so little factual data outside of the Bible that the picture is usually too blurry to identify the difference between truth and legend.

There are no specific references to King David in Egyptian, Syrian or Assyrian documents of the time, and extensive archeological digs within Jerusalem's "City of David" have failed to discover any mention of David's name,[496] although this failure could well be because writing did not appear to begin in Judah before around 800 BCE, two centuries after David's death.[497]

However, the Biblical scribes have provided us with detailed accounts of his life, and these accounts agree with other sources of the time. Thus, there is no doubt that a historical King David did exist.[498]

Nothing yet unearthed refers directly to David, but there is slim archeological evidence of his existence. The strongest piece of this evidence is the Tel Dan stele, the only non-biblical source that refers to the House of David.

The stele is a broken stone fragment found between 1993 and 1994 during excavations at Tel Dan in northern Israel. It consists of several inscribed fragments making up part of a triumphal inscription in Aramaic which is thought to date from the second half of the 9th century BCE, about a century after David had ruled. It boasts of an unnamed king's victories over the king of Israel and his ally, the king of the "House of David." Most likely, the reference is to the deaths of King Jehoram of Israel and of King Ahaziah of the "House of David."[499]

While there is some disagreement, experts widely accept the Tel Dan stele as containing the first known reference to King David in his role as the founder of a politically organized unit for the Kingdom of Judah[b] outside of the Hebrew bible.[500]

The "Throne of Israel" and Davidic Descent

In the Bible, God repeatedly promises that David's descendants will "sit on the throne of Israel" forever.

- In the Book of Samuel, He states:

    "When your days are over and you rest with your ancestors, I will raise up your offspring to succeed you, your own flesh and blood, and I will establish his kingdom. He is the one who will build a house for my Name, and I will establish the throne of his kingdom forever."[501]

- Similarly, in the Book of Jeremiah, He states:

    "For this is what the Lord says: 'David will never fail to have a man to sit on the throne of Israel...'"[502]

God also repeats His pledge to David's son, Solomon:

- In the Book of Kings:

    "I will establish your royal throne over Israel forever, as I promised David your father when I said, 'You shall never fail to have a successor on the throne of Israel.'"[503]

- In the Book of Chronicles:

    "As for you, if you walk before me faithfully as David your father did, and do all I command, and observe my decrees and laws, I will establish your royal throne, as I covenanted with David your father when I said, 'You shall never fail to have a successor to rule over Israel.'"[504]

---

[b] composed of the tribes of Judah and Benjamin.

In accordance with the customs of the time, the privileges of Davidic descent usually applied only to his purely male descent line. While David had several sons, God states in the Bible that only Solomon qualified as successor to the throne of David. Thus, in general, only male descendants of King Solomon were considered by the Jewish leadership to be of royal lineage and claimants to the throne.[c]

After the destruction of the Second Temple, Davidic descent was often a necessary precondition for men to rise to certain prestigious positions within the Jewish community. Sextus Julius Africanus (160-240 CE), a Christian traveler and historian, wrote that King Herod, in order to conceal the defects in his own pedigree, ordered the genealogies of ancient Jewish families to be destroyed.[505] Since genealogies of the priests were preserved in the Temple archives, the rebuilding of the Temple would have given Herod the opportunity to burn them. However, the pedigrees possessed by individual families would have been carefully concealed to prevent their destruction.[506]

Josephus (37 – ca. 100 CE), a 1st-century Romano-Jewish historian born in Jerusalem, states that he was able to find his own genealogy in the public records. He describes the great care that was being taken to preserve the pedigrees of the priests, not merely in Judea, but in Babylon, Egypt and anywhere else "our priests are scattered."[507] Thus these genealogies apparently remained available for some time longer.

In Jewish culture, Davidic descent was also a necessary attribute of the Messiah. God describes the Messiah's identity in the Book of Isaiah as follows:

"A shoot will come up from the stump of Jesse [David's father];
from his roots a Branch will bear fruit."[508]

In the Roman Period (63 BCE - 313 CE), the Messiah came to refer to a future Jewish king of Davidic descent who would be anointed with holy oil and rule the Jewish people during the Messianic Age. God would raise him up to break the yoke of the heathen and to reign over a restored kingdom of Israel to which all the Jews of the Exile would return.[509] Whenever the conditions of Jews in the exiled lands became onerous, the desire and hope for the Messiah to appear rose among the people.

---

[c] There were rare occasions in which, based on Mosaic law, a woman could be a Davidic heiress. However, she must have been able to satisfy one condition: for an only daughter to have the right of inheritance, she must marry or be married to a member of her "father's house" (a scion of the "Davidic Dynasty") (Numbers 36:8).

Do the Horensteins descend from King David?

After researching this question extensively, I have failed to find convincing evidence that the Horensteins are of Davidic descent. They may well have claimed Davidic ancestry via a family line that descends from Rashi, the great French Talmudic scholar who lived from 1040 to 1105.[d] As one of the most famous rabbis of all time, many Jews have sought to claim Rashi as their ancestor, making Davidic lineage through him arguably the most common ancestral line for Davidic descent claims.

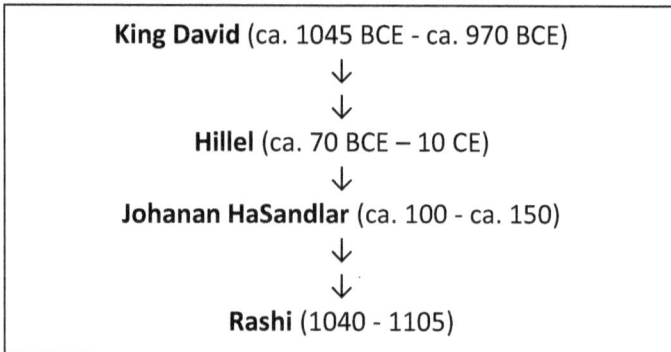

King David (ca. 1045 BCE - ca. 970 BCE)
↓
↓
Hillel (ca. 70 BCE – 10 CE)
↓
Johanan HaSandlar (ca. 100 - ca. 150)
↓
↓
Rashi (1040 - 1105)

What is the basis for modern families claiming Davidic descent via Rashi? Let's start by reviewing the sources for the claim that Rashi descends from Johanan HaSandlar (ca. 100 CE – ca. 150 CE), a famous 2nd-century *tannah*.[e] The main source for this assertion is Solomon Luria (1510 - 1573).[510] Writing more than four centuries after the great rabbi's death, Luria claimed that Rashi descends from Johanan HaSandlar, but failed to provide any evidence of the validity of his claim by naming the people in the ancestral line during the many centuries between the lives of the two rabbis.[511]

There are also secondary sources from the 16th century and later which repeated the assertion that Rashi descends from Johanan HaSandlar, but also added that Johanan HaSandlar (and Rashi, in turn) descends from the great sage Hillel (ca. 70 BCE – ca. 10 CE), who was born four generations earlier.[512] Once again, no information was provided concerning the identities of ancestors in the many intervening generations.

---

[d] Perhaps the name "Gur-arye," i.e. "cub of the lion," first given to my 3rd great grandfather, was meant as a reference to descent from King David who is often represented as a lion.

[e] *Tannah*: A sage from the time of Hillel until the compilation of the *Mishnah* in the first and second centuries CE.

Does Hillel really descend from King David? Rabbi Levi, a third-century sage, stated that

"they found a genealogical scroll in Jerusalem, and in it was written, 'Hillel is from David.' "[513]

Rabbi Levi did not report *how* Hillel (ca. 70 BCE - ca. 10 CE), one of the most important rabbis in Jewish history, descended from King David, perhaps because the scroll itself failed to give specifics. Missing is reasonably contemporaneous documentation of ancestral names after Shephatiah (King David's son) (born ca. 1020 BCE) all the way until Hezekiah (born ca. 95 BCE).[f]

There is some reliable data when we look at the generations of the Jerusalem patriarchy who claimed that they originated with Hillel.[g] However, David Goodblatt has concluded that the patriarchy's claim of Davidic descent - which first arose in the second half of the 2nd century - was most likely a fabrication designed to enhance its political influence.[514]

Two centuries ago a somewhat more detailed ancestral line for Rashi was proposed by Ephraim Zalman Margolit (1762-1828).[515] The lineage he proposed is largely unverified by any historical source, highly inaccurate according to experts, and possibly fabricated. Most importantly, it suffers from a multi-century gap between, roughly, the middle of the 3rd and the middle of the 10th centuries. If we allot 25 years for a generation, then we have no information for about 26 generations in a row! That is, we don't know any names of Rashi's putative ancestors, let alone any information about their lives.

It is also notable that, despite his voluminous writings, Rashi himself never claimed descent from either Johanan HaSandlar or King David, nor did several generations of his descendants.[516,517]

Over a century ago, Israel Lévi reviewed all the evidence concerning whether Hillel, supposedly Rashi's ancestor, was actually descended from King David. His conclusion: the claim of Hillel's Davidic descent – which first arose almost 200 years after his death - has no basis in reality.[518]

We thus have no choice but to conclude that the traditional claim of Rashi's ancestral connection to King David via Johanan HaSandlar and Hillel is mere speculation. Even if the Horensteins descend from Rashi, descent from Rashi is not a legitimate basis for a claim of Davidic descent.

---

[f] The only exceptions are Elnathan and his wife Shelomith (both born ca. 540 BCE). Their existence has been confirmed by the recent finding of a late 6th century Judean seal (https://jwa.org/encyclopedia/article/shelomith-2-bible).

[g] The patriarchy continued through Gamaliel VI who died around 425 CE. This "House of Gamaliel," a lay monarchy, passed from father to son, and led the Jewish population of Judea.

Part II: Chapter Two

THE HORENSTEINS' ASHKENAZIC GENEALOGY: AN INTRODUCTION

The Horensteins are *Askenazim* (from the Hebrew *Ashkenaz* = Germany); that is, they belong to the large group of Jews who lived in the Rhineland valley and neighboring France before migrating eastward to Slavic lands, such as Poland, Lithuania and Russia, following the Crusades of the 11th to 13th centuries.

Surviving records usually fail to reveal when these families left the land of Israel, where they fled to when the Kingdom of Israel was conquered, or when they arrived in Europe. We know that Jews were living in Europe during the Roman Empire, but have little knowledge of when specific early families arrived.

Over the centuries, certain Ashkenazic Jewish families rose to prominence and adopted family names by which to identify themselves. We cannot assume that these names were simply passed from father to son as sometimes, due to the prestige of a family whose daughter a man was marrying, the new son-in-law would adopt his father-in-law's family name, thus creating a puzzle for future genealogists to try to unravel.

While the ancestral roots of the Horenstein family can be traced back many centuries, their family name is a surname of fairly recent origin, chosen early in the 19th century when the Czar forced Jews to adopt surnames as a means of identification. Before that time, many of the Horensteins' ancestors bore the names of a number of notable Jewish families.

The commonalities of their ancestral families are striking. Many were families with considerable wealth. Through the centuries, the men were rabbis, often leaders of the Jewish community and sometimes known for their scholarship. Many were *Av Beit Din*, and quite a few served as *Av Beit Din* of the largest European Jewish communities.

Here, in alphabetical order, are some of the most prominent ancestral families from whom the Horensteins descend:[a]

---

[a] A sample descent line from each of these families to the Horenstein brothers is shown in Appendix Three, starting on page 290.

Babad

The founder of the line was Isaac Krakover, *Av Beit Din* of the city of Brody from about the year 1690. "Babad," an acronym for *Benei Av Beit Din* (children of the *Av Beit Din*), was first added by his children to their signatures and then became their surname. Many family members of this leading rabbinical family served as *Av beit din* of their respective communities, and many family members were wealthy merchants. When they were not rabbinical leaders, they often held positions of communal leadership.

Eberles

The rabbinical Eberles family is a prominent family which has a tradition of descent from Rashi, but without any evidence to substantiate the claim. Their known ancestry starts with the "Pious of Provence" who, following their expulsion from Provence, France in 1306, settled in Prague where the earliest identified family member is Abraham Eber (or Eberles) who was born about 1460.[519]

Abraham, a member of an extremely wealthy family, financed the construction of a new Prague synagogue in which stones that the family had brought from their synagogue in Provence were incorporated into the walls. As the synagogue was named the Tall Synagogue, to commemorate its construction, Abraham changed his family name to Altschuler, the Hebrew equivalent of the synagogue's name.[520] Subsequently his progeny returned to the Eberles name.

Heilprin (Halperin)

The Heilprin family name first appears in the middle of the 16th century.[521] Its origin is thought to derive from the town of Heilbronn, Germany.[522] This important Jewish family has four distinct branches. The Horensteins descend from Eliezer Zevulun Heilprin, the progenitor of the oldest branch, who was born about 1525.

Horowitz

The Horowitz name originated in Bohemia and was derived from the name of the town of Hořovice, which translates as Horowitz in both German and Yiddish. This Levite family is considered one of the most illustrious rabbinic families in Jewish history.[523] Its earlier origin is uncertain, but it is said that the family came from Spain.[b]

---

[b] See Appendix Four (which starts on page 303) for a discussion concerning the family's earlier origins.

Kalonymos

This large, prosperous, scholarly family, located primarily in Germany, France and Italy, played an important role in its communities and beyond throughout the Middle Ages. Many of its members were learned rabbis, liturgical poets, and philosophers.

The family's origin is murky. "Kalonymos" is a Greek word, meaning "good name," which suggests that the family had earlier lived in Greece, but we have no other substantiation of a Greek past.[524]

Despite the lack of solid evidence, the family has long been recognized by Jews as directly descended from King David.[525] One theory is that the family descends from Rabbi Makhir, a Babylonian scholar who himself came from a family of ex-ilarchs.[c]

Our primary source for this theory is the Chronicle of Narbonne, an anonymous document which was found inserted into a single copy of Abraham ibn Daud's *Sefer HaKabbalah*, a work written around 1160. According to the Chronicle, Makhir, who lived in Baghdad, was sent by the Caliph of Bagdad to King Charles (or King Pepin) in the mid-8th century who settled him in Narbonne.

"Then King Charles sent to the King of Baghdad [the Caliph] requesting that he dispatch one of his Jews of the seed of royalty of the House of David. He hearkened and sent him one from there, a magnate and sage, Rabbi Makhir by name. And [Charles] settled him in Narbonne, the capital city, and planted him there, and gave him a great possession there at the time he captured it from the Ishmaelites [Arabs].

"And he [Makhir] took to wife a woman from among the magnates of the town; … and the King made him a nobleman and designed, out of love for [Makhir], good statutes for the benefit of all the Jews dwelling in the city….

"The Prince Makhir became chieftain there. He and his descendants were close [inter-related] with the King and all his descendants."

This document was written at least three centuries after the events it reported. Just the lapse in time alone between the events and the document's authorship makes its accuracy highly questionable.

We also have a first-person account of the Jews of Narbonne, written just about the same time as the Chronicle, by Benjamin of Tudela, a Jewish traveler who visited Narbonne in 1165:

---

[c] Exilarch: The leader of the Babylonian Jews following their exile from Israel.

"Narbonne, a place of eminence in consequence of the studies carried on there. From thence the study of the law spreads over all countries. This city contains many very wise and noble men. At their head is R. Kalonymos son of the great and noble R. Theodoros [Todros], of blessed memory, a descendant of the house of David, whose pedigree is established. He holds landed property from the sovereign of the country, of which nobody can deprive him by force."[526,527]

Assuming that, indeed, the Kalonymos family of Narbonne descends from Makhir, roughly 13 generations had passed between Makhir and this late Rabbi Todros of the Narbonne Kalonymos family. We know nothing about the identities, families, locations, or activities of the missing generations except that they were clearly wealthy landowners and most likely also scholars.[d]

Shown below is the 14th century armorial seal of Kalonymos ben Todros of Narbonne which features a shield charged with a lion rampant, a symbol of his proud Davidic ancestry.

In 1972, Professor Arthur J. Zuckerman of Columbia University published a scholarly book entitled "A Jewish Princedom in Feudal France, 768-900."[528] Most academic books attempt to synthesize the literature on the subject while

---

[d] Arye Graboïs, professor at Haifa University, suggests that Makhir's descendants were Narbonnese who studied in Spain and founded an academy after returning home. This academy became notable towards the end of the 10th century and famous in the 11th (Graboïs, Arye. The "Jewish King" of Narbonne, in *Annales du Midi: revue archéologique, historique et philologique de la France méridionale*, Tome 109, N°218, 1997, pp. 165-188).

maintaining a neutral position. Instead, Zuckerman's book is a meticulously re-searched defense of the highly controversial thesis that a Jewish principality once existed in feudal France. Since publication, most scholars have dismissed his the-sis.[529,530]

Zuckerman elaborates on the description of Rabbi Makhir in the Chronicle, scouring the literature for additional sources. He points to the common use of the name Todros among the Narbonne (but not the Lucca) Kalonymides and sug-gests that it is a Hebraized form of Theodoric, a distinguished Frank name given by King Pepin to Makhir upon admitting him to the Frank aristocracy.[531] He is unable to prove, however, that the Narbonne Kalonymos family descends from Makhir.

The earliest known record of a member of the Kalonymos family is not a rec-ord of the Narbonnese Kalonymides, but of the Italian Kalonymos family who we first learn about in the 8th century – around the same time as Makhir may have arrived in Narbonne. By then, this family had established itself in Lucca in the central Italian region of Tuscany, then part of Lombardia. Earlier, they are thought to have lived – not closer to Narbonne - but still further south on the Italian peninsula.[532] It is this Kalonymos family, probably related to the Kalonymos family of Narbonne, from which the Horensteins descend.[e]

Although not all scholars agree, the Kalonymos family of Lucca moved from central Italy to Germany, especially to the cities near the Rhine River, roughly in the late 9th century.[533] Here the family flourished and produced, not only numer-ous rabbis, but poets, teachers, authors, moralists, and theologians.[534]

Not many people associate Rashi's ancestry with the Kalonymos family. In fact, he descends from the Italian Kalonymos through his mother and even mar-ried a woman who descends from that branch.

The two Kalonymos families probably shared a common ancestor, but we know of no early connection between them. Thus, although Rashi is clearly de-scended from the Italian Kalonymos family, we cannot clearly connect him with the Kalonymos family of Narbonne or, for that matter, with Rabbi Makhir and his Babylonian origin.

What we can state, however, is still something extraordinary about the Kalo-nymides: Through the 13th century, most prominent Jewish communal leaders belonged to one branch or another of this exceptional family.[535]

Katz

Katz, an acronym for *Kohen Tzedek* = righteous Kohan, is believed to be the oldest surname in the world as it originated with Moses' brother Aaron, the first high priest of the Jewish people.

---

[e] Eleazar HaKatan ben Judah of Worms, himself a Kalonymos from the Lucca descent line, is an early source for the Italian group. Writing about 1220, he lists their patriarch as Judah, father of Rabbi Kalonymos, who was born about 700 CE.

This family claims to descend from Aaron, via his son Ithamar and Ithamar's son Eli, the High Priest of Judea.[536] There is no surviving record, however, to validate their story,[537]

The first identified family member of this esteemed rabbinical family is Akiva the Elder Kohen-Tzedek, *Av Beit Din* of Salonika, born about 1360. The earliest known tombstone bearing the family name is dated 1536 and can still be seen in the Prague cemetery.

Katzenellenbogen

The Katzenellenbogen rabbinical family derives its name from the locality of Katzenellenbogen in the Prussian province of Hesse-Nassau. Starting with the First Crusade in 1096, the Jews endured centuries of murders, property destruction and expulsions. In 1312 Count Diether of Katzenellenbogen received permission from Emperor Henry VII to keep 12 Jews at Katzenellenbogen. Then, in 1330, Ludwig the Bavarian permitted Count Wilhelm and his heirs to keep 24 Jews in their dominions.[538]

Soon Jewish residents of the town began to affix the town's name after their own to identify their location. This evolved over time into use of Katzenellenbogen as a family name. Notable rabbis with this name start to appear in the 15th century with Meir ben Isaac Katzenellenbogen (1473-1565), head of the Padua Yeshiva.

The family became so famous that men who married Katenellenbogen daughters took their wife's family name.[539] While the family was widely disbursed, its unity was maintained through meticulously kept family records.[540]

Due to frequent intermarriages, the Horensteins descend from multiple Katzenellenbogen family lines. The record number of descent lines from a single family member is Rabbi Meir Katzenellenbogen, the "MaHaRam of Padua," (1482-1565) as the brothers descend from one of his sons, Rabbi Samuel Judah, the "MaHaRSHIK," (ca. 1521, Padua – 1597, Venice), as well as from four of his daughters.

Loew

This well-known and respected family name is derived from the German Löwe which means "lion." It is a *kinnui*[f] for the Hebrew "Judah" referring to the tribe of Judah, the ancient Jewish tribe which is traditionally associated with a lion.

---

[f] *Kinnui*: A "nickname," consisting of a man's Hebrew name followed by the same name in the local language.

The most famous family member is Yehudah Loew ben Betzalel, the MaHaRaL of Prague who, like Rashi, is considered one of the greatest rabbis of all times.

Luria

The prominent Luria rabbinical family claims to descend from King David.

"Among families which claim descent from biblical King David, probably the one with most authenticity is that of the Luria family...."

Rosenstein, Neil. The Lurie Legacy. Bergenfield, NJ, Avotaynu, 2004, p. xxi

"The Luria family is the most ancient of all families of note that we know of."

Epstein, Abraham. *Mishmachat Luria*. Vienna, 1901

Unfortunately, the identities of the earliest Luria ancestors were lost centuries ago. Before his death, Rabbi Jechiel Luria told his nephew, Moses Enosh, that he used to possess a *yichus* brief showing the Luria Davidic line, but the brief was stolen by a robber during the Swiss War of the late 15th century.[541,542] It will never be known if this brief included the missing names of Rashi's putative Davidic ancestors.

Roughly a century later, Rabbi Solomon Luria (who died in 1593) wrote that his family goes back to Rashi.[543] However, he was unable to provide a complete list of the names of his ancestors back to Rashi due to the loss of the *yichus* brief.[544,545]

We do have information from another *yichus* brief which was in the possession of Rabbi Jechiel Heilprin (1660-1746), known as an expert in Talmud as well as a scholar and historian. Heilprin only referred to it briefly in his book, *Seder HaDorot*, but a more complete transcription eventually appeared in *Ma'alot HaYochasin*, published 1900 in Lvov, in which the editor transcribed it "letter for letter."[546] (This latter source is questionable at best.)

The transcription is imperfect. Because of age and wear-and-tear, some words have become illegible. To make matters worse, the editor misread some of the unclear words so that, according to the genealogist and author Dr. Neil Rosenstein, they lost their true meaning.[547]

There is enough information in the transcription to enable us to connect the Luria family with Rashi's paternal ancestors. The common ancestor of both appears to be Yose of Constantinople who lived around the middle of the 10th century.[g]

Margoliot (Margolies)

The name Margola means "pearl" or "precious stone." The origin of the name of this Polish family of Talmudic scholars is attributed to Rabbi Jacob ben Moses Jaffe (1430-1490), *Av Beit Din* of Nuremberg, whose mother's name was Margola. Rabbi Jacob is said to have added Margoliot to his name to honor his mother's piety.[548] Soon his descendants dropped Jaffe from their name.

The Jewish Encyclopedia of 1906 disagrees with this story, and states that the first known Margoliot was Rabbi Samuel (1512-1585) who married Jutta, Rabbi Jacob ben Moses Jaffe's great granddaughter.[549] Perhaps Rabbi Samuel simply adopted the name of Jutta's prestigious family, a common practice at the time.

Spira (Shapira)

The city of Speyer in the Rhineland was known as "Spira" as early as the 5th century. It was the location of the founding patriarchs of the rabbinical Spira (Shapira/Shapiro) family and the origin of their name.[550]

Despite the custom of not educating women, Miriam Spira Luria of Germany (ca. 1403 to 1452) became a Talmudic scholar who was allowed to teach specially gifted yeshiva students – although only from behind a curtain and while sitting with them in a tent outside of the yeshiva's building.[551]

Trèves

The rabbinical Trèves family probably derived its name from the Prussian city of Trier, known in French as Trèves. As early as the 14th and 15th centuries, they were already scattered over Germany, Italy, southern France, Greece, Poland and Russia.[552]

---

[g] Elyakim, one of Yose's sons, was Rashi's great grandfather, while Abraham, another of his sons, was the father of Aaron, a physician said to have been sent to Rome by the Byzantine Emperor Constantine X to minister to Pope Urban II. One of Aaron's four sons (we don't know which one) was the 2nd great grandfather of Mar Isaac (born ca. 1175), considered to be the progenitor of the Luria family.

Part II: Chapter Three

A SEPHARDIC ROOT

Spain, at least according to legend, is the biblical Sepharad in which Jews settled ever since the period of destruction of the First Temple (586 BCE). We know that Jews were there in the 1st century CE and data starting in the 3rd century suggest that by then they were already a well-established community.

מכל הכבוד וכו ביתו שאומרי ה זק ציב

Miniature from the Sister Haggadah
Barcelona, 1350

After the fall of the Roman Empire in 476 CE, Jews were well treated by the Visigoth rulers who initially followed an Arian form of Christianity. When, however, the Visigoths embraced Catholicism in 589, the situation changed.

From 612 onward, Jews suffered from relentless persecution. For much of the time, the practice of Judaism was completely prohibited.[553] By the time of the Muslim invasion in 711, the Jews had become alienated and embittered by Catholic rule.[554] They welcomed and, at times, even assisted their new Muslim rulers who freed them from oppression.

Due to the unifying influence of the Islamic Empire, Spanish Jews quickly developed ties with their Babylonian brothers which can be traced as far back as the end of the 8th century, when the Exilarch Natronai b. Havivai, after being deposed from office, migrated to Spain where he was received with great honors.[555] For the Babylonian Jews, the ties were far stronger than those which existed with any closer part of mainland Europe, as these lands remained under Christian rule.[556]

More than 90% of world Jewry dwelt in the areas conquered by the Arabs between 632 and 711, giving Jews a single communications network and external system of government as well as relative ease of movement within the territory.[557]

Spain was the most successful area of Jewish settlement from the 8th to the 11th centuries, and it soon became one of the greatest centers of Jewish life.[558] By the 9th century, Spanish cities like Lucerna were almost entirely Jewish.

Although Islamic law prescribed rigid anti-Jewish discrimination, some Jews were able to rise to positions of great influence in the state. Hebrew literature began to flourish, largely based on Arab models – especially as to poetry and philosophy – and Spanish Jewry served as a channel through which classical science reached Christian Europe.[559] In fact, as late as the 12th century, Sephardim still made up over 90% of the world Jewish population.[560]

While the more recent ancestors of the Horenstein family saw themselves, and lived the lifestyle of, Ashkenazic Jews, the Katz family, one of their major family lines, traces back to the Sephardic Jews of Spain.

The Katz Family

The rabbinical Katz[a] family is a Horenstein ancestral line with a Sephardic heritage. The family's earliest documented ancestor is Rabbi Akiva the Elder Kohan-Zedek, referred to as a *sephardi tahor*,[b] who was born somewhere in Spain[561]

---

[a] Katz (more properly Ka"tz) is a contraction of *Kohan-Tzedek* which means "righteous Kohan."

[b] *Sephardi Tahor*: A Hebrew term, abbreviated as ס"ט, used to indicate a 'pure' lineage. (For a discussion, see: http://onthemainline.blogspot.com/2011/05/some-additional-notes-on-elusive-st.html.)

about 1340. Rabbi Akiva was reputed to possess the genealogical record of his early ancestry.[562,563] Like many other Spanish Jews, increasing persecution caused him to flee the country, probably at the time of the anti-Jewish riots of 1391.[564]

Slaughter of Jews in Barcelona in 1391 by Josep Segrelles, ca. 1910

He settled in the town of Salonika in Macedonia. Although far from Spain, Salonika had a small Jewish community that spoke Judeo-Spanish.[565] There Rabbi Akiva was appointed *Av Beit Din*.[566] He died in Salonika, probably about 1400.

Isaac Katz, Rabbi Akiva's son, was also a rabbi. Like his father, he was forced to leave his home for other lands, in his case after the Ottoman Turks captured Salonika in 1430, defeating the Byzantine and Venetian forces that had been in control. The victors decided to move the local Jews to Edirne, a city in northwest Turkey which was the imperial capital at the time, to help develop it.[567]

Faced with the necessity of resettlement, Isaac Katz left the region and moved instead to Oben (now part of Budapest) in Hungary. Then in 1453, Constantinople, capital of the Byzantine Empire, fell to the Ottomans, marking the end of the empire. Isaac decided to move there where he became *Av Beit Din* for two of the city's districts, Pera and Galata.[568] He died in Constantinople around 1460.

The Horowitz Family

The Horensteins also descend from the Horowitz family, a prestigious Levite family believed by some to have had roots in Spain before they arrived in Bohemia and adopted the Horowitz name. Specifically, the family maintains a tradition of descent from the HaLevi HaYitzhari family of Spain.

The HaLevi HaYitzharis claim descent from Yitzhar (ca. 1725 BCE), great grandson of the biblical Jacob, as suggested by the name of their first documented ancestor, namely Isaac Solomon HaLevi HaYitzhari, born about 1005 in Tortosa, Catalonia, Spain.[c] His son, Shem Tov, has explained that the family descends from Yitzhar (grandson of Levi and son of Jacob) via Yitzhar's descendant, the prophet Samuel.[569]

The Bible includes the Yitzharis as one of the Levite families,[570] but there is no known evidence to support Shem Tov's claim of descent from Samuel. In fact, according to the first Book of Samuel:

"When Samuel grew old, he appointed his sons as Israel's leaders.

"2 The name of his firstborn was Joel and the name of his second was Abijah, and they served at Beersheba.

"3 But his sons did not follow his ways. They turned aside after dishonest gain and accepted bribes and perverted justice."[571]

The Bible tells us nothing further about his sons after that indictment of their behavior. If they had progeny, biblical texts and other known sources do not provide those names, making it impossible to trace a descent line from there.[572]

The HaLevi HaYitzharis continued to live in the Catalonia region of Spain until, in the 13th century, the political situation for Spanish Jews began to deteriorate as the Catholic clergy worked to marginalize them. Jews were forced to wear yellow badges to keep them from associating with Catholics, supposedly for their

---

[c] There is some controversy as to whether "HaYitzhari" refers to the biblical Yitzhar or a place where the family came from. Since, in the Bible, Yitzhar means "oil," their name could even indicate that they had been an "oil family" perhaps associated with some aspect of olive oil production.

own safety. In 1250, Pope Innocent IV issued a papal bull which prevented Jews from building synagogues without special permission, made it illegal to proselytize under pain of death, and prohibited association with Catholics.[573] The situation worsened considerably in the second half of the 14th century, leading to the massacres and forced mass conversions of 1391. This was less than a century before the Catholic Monarchs Ferdinand II of Aragon and Isabella I of Castile were to establish the Tribunal of the Holy Office of the Inquisition to deal with heretics.

There is no surviving record of what happened to the HaLevi HaYitzhari family during this terrifying period. Perhaps they perished, or perhaps they capitulated to the pressure to convert to Christianity, as there appear to be no later records of a family using that name or claiming descent from Yitzhar.

Despite the lack of evidence, the HaYitzharis are frequently considered to be ancestors of the Horowitz family. There does not appear to be any justification for this claim, which merges the HaYitzhari descent line with a branch of the Benveniste HaLevi family, a well-known Sephardic family first mentioned in 1079 in documents from Barcelona.[574]

This conclusion is reinforced when we examine the names used in the two families in terms of traditional Jewish naming customs. So long as the HaYitzhari name was used, chosen names are repeated as would be expected, but there are no Benveniste HaLevis. About 1125, when the first Benveniste appears, the HaYitzhari name disappears, and the naming pattern switches to one that is typical of the Benveniste family.

(If you wish to review the actual name sequences, see Appendix Four which starts on page 303.)

Possibly the most detailed and accurate account of the Horowitz ancestral line comes from a chart drawn by the late Michael Honey, a meticulous researcher.[575] Here is an account of the Horowitz ancestry utilizing his findings:

Rabbi Isaiah HaLevi (ca. 1465-1517) is considered to be the family's progenitor. A wealthy man who came from Provence (France), Isaiah bought the Arenda of Hořovice, located half-way between the town of Pilsen and Prague, the country's capital. Later he moved to Prague where he became the Chief Rabbi, and added "Ish Horowitz" ("a man from Horovice") to his name.

While an earlier location for Isaiah's family line is not known, Rabbi Yosef HaLevi, probably Isaiah's great uncle, may have been born in Italy,[576] raising the question of whether this HaLevi family was living earlier in Italy, then moved north to Provence before moving still further north to Bohemia.

There is yet another reason to doubt the tradition of Spanish forebearers. In a detailed review of early sources, Rabbi Avrohom Marmorstein failed to find any contemporary written claim of Spanish roots for the Bohemia Horowitz family.[577]

The claim was first made in the late 19th century, several hundred years after the family was said to move from Spain to Bohemia. When this connection was first suggested in writing, it was usually prefaced with "as has been told" or "they tell in our family."[578] As HaLevi was a common name, an error like this could easily occur; thus the Levite Horowitz family could well have descended from any of numerous HaLevi families in Spain or elsewhere.

Itzhak Epstein, considered an expert genealogist, found the same problem when he tried to document the Epstein family's legendary Spanish ancestry. Both the Epstein and Horowitz families were thought to share a line of descent from the same Benveniste family. The two lines separated in the early 13th century, as each family descended from a different son of Joseph HaLevi ben Benveniste. While the Horowitz family moved to Hořovice, Bohemia, the Epstein family moved to Eppstein, Germany.

Epstein was also unable to document a connection between his putative Benveniste ancestors and his Epstein family in Spain. The earliest he could document his ancestors reasonably well was in 1392 when Epsteins were living in Frankfurt-am-Main. His conclusion:

> "The Spanish connection [between the Benvenistes and the Epsteins] is a real myth."[579]

DNA testing has also failed to support the theory that the Horowitz and Epstein families are both direct male offspring of the Benvenistes, as the core Horowitz haplogroup differs from the core Epstein haplogroup, suggesting that – at least in regard to direct paternal descent – the families did not share a common Benveniste ancestor.[d,580] In other words, for either the Horowitz family, the Epstein family, or more likely for both, DNA analysis fails to support a basis for a claim to this Benveniste descent line.

---

[d] The core Horowitz haplogroup is R1a1, while the core Epstein haplogroup is R1b1a2a1a1b3c.

Part II: Chapter Four

JEWS OF THE GALLIC REGION: 5TH TO 10TH CENTURIES

The next four chapters will examine the lives of the most famous of the Horenstein brothers' earlier Ashkenazic ancestors, placing them within the framework of the events of their times. While the specifics of the descent lines from each ancestor to the Horensteins are too detailed to present here, some of these lines, in an abbreviated form, will be shown to illustrate one route by which that ancestor connects to the Horensteins.

We shall start by reviewing the history of the Jewish presence in Europe, including the Horenstein family's earliest documented European origins, and finish by reviewing the life and times of Rabbi Naftali Katz, the *Smichat Chachamim*, last of the great rabbinical scholars in the family's ancestry.

G aul was a large region of Western Europe during the Iron Age that was inhabited by Celtic tribes. The region encompassed present-day France, Luxembourg, Belgium, most of Switzerland, Northern Italy, as well as the parts of the Netherlands and Germany on the west bank of the Rhine.

Gaul on the eve of the Gallic Wars (58 to 50 BCE)

Image by Feitscherg

While the origins of Jewish European settlements are murky, they began very early. The First Book of Maccabees, written prior to 63 BCE, provides a list of Jewish colonies scattered throughout the Mediterranean basin.[581] In the early years of the Roman empire, Jewish communities existed as far north as Lyons, Bonn and Cologne, and as far west as Cadiz and Toledo.[582]

These populations were small and widely scattered. During the 2nd and 1st centuries BCE, Gaul fell under Roman rule which lasted for five centuries. *Gallia* remained the conventional name of the territory throughout the Early Middle

Ages, until it acquired a new identity as the Capetian Kingdom of France in the high medieval period (ca. 11th to 13th centuries).

The Moslem conquest of Spain in the 8th century made the country the primary destination for Jews leaving Babylonia, while in the rest of Western Europe these conquests probably stimulated Jews located along the northern shores of the Mediterranean to move further north to areas no longer under Christian control. Thus, the Rhine basin became a central location for Western European Jews with links from there to the South.[583]

Then, starting in the 12th century, Christians began to reconquer Spain which forced Sephardic Jews to seek another home. They scattered widely, some moving north to Gaul which, over time, became the center of Ashkenazic Jewish culture, particularly in the part of its vast territory that now consists of northern France and western Germany.[a] The Yiddish language originated here, probably in the 9th and 10th centuries, as part of the developing Ashkenazic cultural tradition.[584]

The Middle Ages

For European Jews, the Middle Ages began when the Roman Emperor Constantine the Great came to power in 306 CE. Jews living in the Roman Empire had been declared citizens in 212, but by the time of Constantine, Christianity had become so influential that the Emperor acceded to the Christian masses and began to issue laws which radically limited the rights of its Jewish citizens.

The 5th Century

The Franks moved south into Gaul at the start of the century, establishing a dynasty known as the Merovingians. In 496, the Merovingian king Clovis I accepted Roman Christianity. The Franks then proceeded to conquer the rest of Gaul.[585]

The 6th Century

The second-class status of Jews was crystallized in 534 by the imperial laws of the Justinian Code. Moreover, Roman Law in regard to Jews set a tone that continued to influence both Christian and Moslem legislation long after the Roman Empire ceased to exist in the latter part of the 5th century.[586] (The Eastern Roman Empire endured for another millennium.)

---

[a] The word "Ashkenaz" appears several times in the bible, where it seems to refer to a land bordering on the upper Euphrates and Armenia. No one knows how and when it began to refer to the Jewish community of Germany and northern France.

The 7th Century

By the 7th century, the middle class and the towns in which they lived had disappeared due to the economic decline caused by the conquest of Gaul by the Franks. No more than 3% of the population lived in urban areas, and towns with a population of 2000 were rare.[587]

About 60% of the population consisted of serfs under the control of warring lords. There were no local clergy; once a year a priest would visit to administer the sacraments. Religious life was dominated by local superstitions which focused on controlling the demonic powers of the forces of nature.[588]

The 8th Century

Charlemagne became King of the Franks in 768, King of the Lombards in 774, and Emperor of the Romans in 800. The first emperor in Western Europe since the fall of the Roman Empire three centuries earlier, he founded the Carolingian Empire. Not only did he reunify most of Western Europe, but he united parts of Europe that had never been under Roman rule.

The 9th Century

When Charlemagne died in 814, his son Louis succeeded him as the sole ruler of the Franks. As emperor he included his adult sons, Louis, Lothair, and Pepin, in the government and sought to establish a suitable division of the realm among them. In the 830s his empire was torn by civil war between his sons. Louis's attempts to include his son Charles by his second wife in the succession plans only exacerbated the situation.

After several years of struggle, the matter was settled in 843 by the Treaty of Verdun, the first of the treaties that divided the Carolingian Empire into three kingdoms among the three surviving sons:

- Louis "the German" received East Francia which eventually became the High Medieval Kingdom of Germany, the largest component of the Holy Roman Empire.

- Lohair I received Middle Francia which included the Low Countries,[b] Lorraine, Alsace, Burgundy, Provence and the Kingdom of Italy (which covered the northern half of the Italian Peninsula). He also received the two imperial cities, Aachen and Rome. (This "middle kingdom" encompassed many cities with large Jewish communities, including Mainz, Rheims, Troyes, Lyons, and Arles.)

---

[b] Low Countries: A coastal region in Western Europe, consisting especially of the Netherlands and Belgium, and the low-lying delta of the Rhine, Meuse, Scheldt, and Ems rivers where much of the land is at or below sea level.

- Charles "the Bald" received the West Francia portion of the empire, which later became the Kingdom of France.

The 10th Century

By the 10th century, there were in effect only two territories. One would become Germany, the other, France. It was a politically unstable time, with invasions of the Vikings from Scandinavia, Magyar warriors from what is now Hungary, and North African Muslims raiding the Mediterranean region.[589]

We do not know how these events directly affected the Jewish population, but merchants must have suffered heavy losses, while local residents were sometimes accused of assisting the Viking and Muslim invaders in their assaults on Christian towns.[590]

The Jewish population of the Ashkenaz region (roughly what is now Northwestern Europe) was about 20,000 to 25,000 late in the century, only a small percentage of the world Jewish population; most were living in Spain and in lands bordering on the eastern Mediterranean. They were influential well beyond their numbers because of their concentration in urban areas at a time when major urban centers were no larger than small towns today. Many were merchants and thus widely known by the local Christian majority.[591]

Feudalism was starting to develop within Western Europe. Central to feudal society was each baron's ownership of local land. The society was authoritarian and hierarchical. In return for the military support of his knights, the baron granted them their own land along with a modest share of his wealth and prestige.[592]

This was in stark contrast to Jewish society; it existed in a world of urban communities which regularly interacted with one another and were at least nominally egalitarian. Scholarship and commercial success constituted their sources of authority and prestige. Heavily dependent upon Christian lords, they were, at best, tolerated.[593]

The Horensteins' Famous 10th Century Ancestors

Moses Kalonymos HaZaken (The Elder) (Lucca, ca. 825 – Mainz, ca. 915)

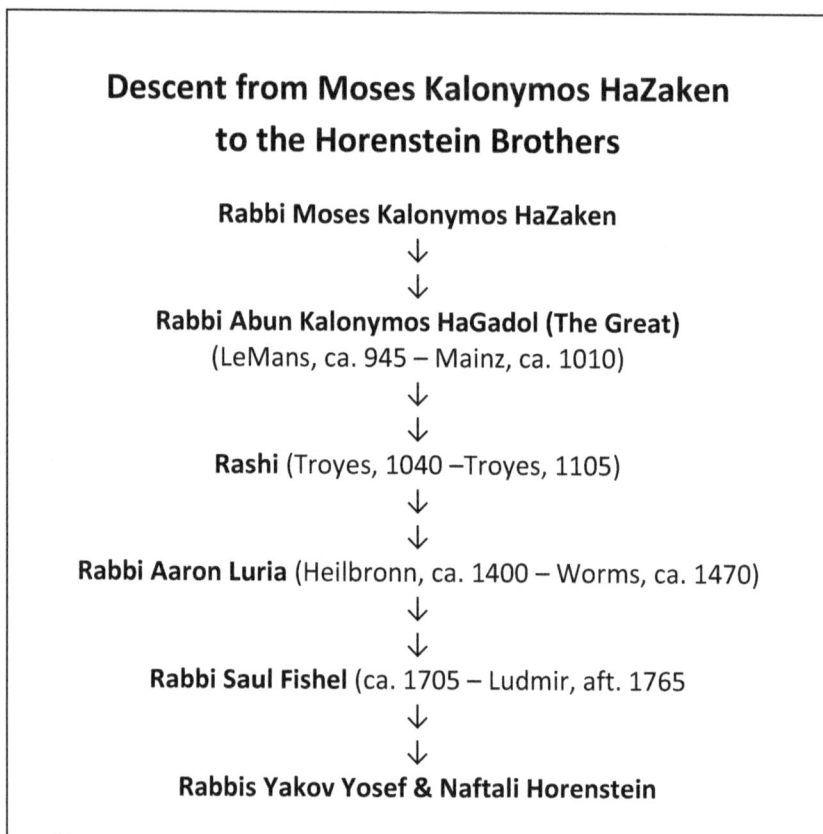

Descent from Moses Kalonymos HaZaken
to the Horenstein Brothers

Rabbi Moses Kalonymos HaZaken
↓
↓
Rabbi Abun Kalonymos HaGadol (The Great)
(LeMans, ca. 945 – Mainz, ca. 1010)
↓
↓
Rashi (Troyes, 1040 –Troyes, 1105)
↓
↓
Rabbi Aaron Luria (Heilbronn, ca. 1400 – Worms, ca. 1470)
↓
↓
Rabbi Saul Fishel (ca. 1705 – Ludmir, aft. 1765
↓
↓
Rabbis Yakov Yosef & Naftali Horenstein

In the previous century, some family members had migrated to Mainz and Speyer in Germany.[594] Rabbi Moses Kalonymos HaZaken left Lombardy to move to Mainz. A specialist in Talmudic jurisprudence, Rabbi Moses was especially renowned for his liturgical songs,[595] and it is said that he brought the art and music of liturgical singing to German Jewry.[596]

Other Kalonymos family members who migrated to Germany served as heads of the Mainz community for several generations. They were also were among the main spokespersons of the Jewish community in Speyer.[597]

Meshulam ben Kalonymos HaGadol (The Great) (Lucca, ca. 930 – Mainz, ca. 1020)

Descent from Meshulam ben Kalonymos HaGadol to the Horenstein Brothers

Rabbi Meshulam ben Kalonymos HaGadol
↓
↓
Rabbi Judah Sir Leon (Paris, ca. 1165 – Paris, ca. 1224)
↓
↓
Rabbi Eliezer II Trèves (Neuss-on-the-Rhine, 1495 – Frankfurt, 1566)
↓
↓
Rabbi Betzalel HaKohen Katz (ca. 1680 – Ostroh, 1717)
↓
↓
Rabbis Yakov Yosef & Naftali Horenstein

Perhaps the most distinguished of the Horenstein's European ancestors in this century for whom we have abundant information was Rabbi Meshulam ben Kalonymos HaZaken. Born in Lucca, Italy, he moved to Provence and eventually settled in Mainz, Germany where he brought the knowledge of the Babylonian Talmudic academies together with the knowledge of Italian Jewry.[598]

Meshulam is believed to have had a decisive influence on the development of Ashkenazic worship.[599] Like his father and grandfather, he was a talented liturgical poet, with numerous prayers attributed to him. He is also known by his halakhic decisions, especially those regarding trade between families or communities.[600]

He died in 1020. His tombstone in Mainz is the oldest identified tombstone of the Jews of that city.[601]

Rabbi Abun Kalonymos HaGadol (The Great) (Le Mans, ca. 945 –Mainz, ca. 1010)

According to some scholars, Rabbi Abun Kalonymos HaGadol, son of Rabbi Meshulam Kalonymos HaGadol, was a wealthy physician who became director of a school of medicine in Narbonne, France.[602] Others state that he was the director of the Narbonne yeshiva.[603] Six centuries later, Rabbi Solomon Luria remarked that

"Rabbi Abun was great in Torah, wisdom and wealth...."[604]

Rabbi Shimon Kalonymos HaGadol (the Great) (Mainz, ca. 975 – Mainz, ca. 1020)

The grandson of Rabbi Abun Kalonymos HaGadol, many of his liturgical compositions have become part of the High Holiday prayer book as well as other parts of Jewish prayer. After he successfully persuaded King Henrich II to rescind an order expelling the Jews of Germany, local Jewish communities thanked him by inserting special prayers into the religious service on his behalf.[605]

One day, Elchanan, Rabbi Shimon's son, was kidnapped by Christians while still a child. The captors baptized him and raised him as a Christian. Distraught and heartbroken, the Rabbi never gave up hope of finding his son and restoring him to Judaism.According to folklore, many years later, Rabbi Shimon gained an audience with the Pope to plead for the relaxation of Catholic decrees against the Jews. When they met, both were shocked to discover that they were father and son. In one version of the tale, Rabbi Shimon proved his fatherhood by describing his son's own birthmarks to him.

Illustration in *Jewish Fairy Tales and Legends* (1919)

An echo of the Rabbi's pain 11 centuries ago has come down to us. On the second day of Rosh Hashanah, observant Ashkenazic Jews recite a *piyut* (prayer poem) during the *Shacharit* (morning) prayer service, a piyyut written a thousand years ago by Elchanan's grieving father.

The prayer consists of an acrostic which begs God that:

"my son, Elchanan, may live into the eternal world."

Part II: Chapter Five

JEWS OF THE GALLIC REGION: 11ᵀᴴ TO 15ᵀᴴ CENTURIES

The 11th Century

The First Crusade (1096)

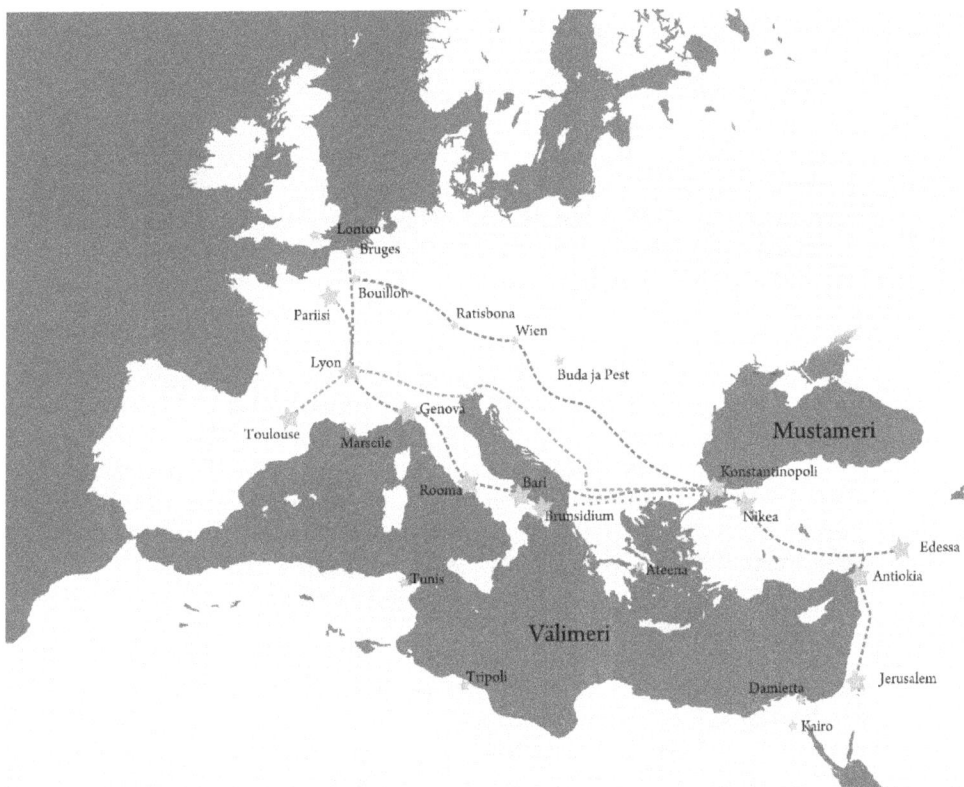

map by QWerk

Jerusalem had been under the rule of Shiite Muslims when, in 1071, a band of Seljuk Turks overran the city and much of the Land of Israel. For the next 20 years, Byzantines, Turks, and Shiites fought over the entire region with little to show for it. Then, in 1095, the Byzantine emperor appealed to Pope Urban II for aid against the enemies of Christendom. The pope agreed to call upon the knights and clergymen of his native France to embark on a holy war of liberation. He found his countrymen to be eager for battle.[606]

The goal of the crusaders was to defeat the enemies of Christendom in Jerusalem. It would be a long and difficult journey, making it tempting to punctuate the monotony by attacking the Jewish non-believers along their route.

By December, the Jews of France, gripped by fear, were sending letters to the Jewish communities of the Rhineland, warning that armies were assembling that may soon head in their direction on the way to Jerusalem. French Jews were relatively fortunate as each region was controlled by a powerful duke or count who could monitor the transient armies and see that they maintained discipline while in their territory.

The situation in Germany was different as only the emperor had the power to enforce discipline over the transients. He happened to be out of the country when the crusaders arrived.[607]

The assembled armies were led by powerful dukes and counts, and traveled mostly through Italy rather than Germany. They were well disciplined and did not harass Jews. However, an assortment of haphazardly assembled bands of untrained, ordinary folk, eager for the excitement of an adventure, gathered under lesser barons. These were the people who attacked the Jews of the Rhineland.

With inadequate provisions for the journey, they obtained needed supplies by pillage. They would never make it as far as Jerusalem. If they didn't drop out, they died along the way, often when the people they plundered defended themselves.[608]

One of these ragtag groups, under the leadership of a charlatan named Emicho who probably proclaimed that he had been divinely appointed to lead the charge, attacked the Jews of Speyer, then the Jews of Worms. After having massacred some 800 people, the group proceeded to Mainz where the Jewish community was led by Rabbi Kalonymos ben Meshulam, son of the Horenstein brothers' ancestor. In return for money, the archbishop granted the Jews refuge in his palace and Emicho promised not to attack; yet, when the town gates were opened to his mob, they headed directly to the archbishop's palace, hungry for slaughter.[609]

When the massacre was over, the foremost Jewish community of the Rhineland had been all but destroyed. Emicho now headed to Cologne, exactly in the opposite direction of Jerusalem, where he directed yet another massacre. After rampaging in five other villages, Emicho, who by now had virtually eliminated the Jewish population in his own region, headed to Hungary where, in battles with Hungarian forces, his entire band was eliminated.[610]

Not all the murders took place in the Rhineland. Attacked by other crusader armies, many Jews in the Moselle valley region, particularly in Trier and Metz, were killed, although some converted in order to be spared. There were also mass murders in both Prague and Regensburg, Germany.[611]

Most members of the German branch of the Kalonymos family perished during the First Crusade.[612] Chances of survival depended upon their location.

Despite extensive rights granted by Emperor Henry IV, crusaders and burghers attacked the Jews of both Worms and Mainz during the 1096 campaign and devastated the community.[613]

In the words of one Kalonymos family member:

"... in Mainz ... family members multiplied and flourished very much; until God's fury hit all the holy communities in 1096. And then we were all lost, all perished, except very few who were left from our kinsmen."[614]

Fortunately, Kalonymos family members from Mainz had escaped to Speyer in the 1070s where they were followed later by others fleeing the Mainz riots of 1084. The refugees were invited to live in Altspeyer under the protection of the Bishop and to build a wall around their settlement. Also, they were given land for a cemetery and accorded the privilege of unrestricted trade and moneylending activities.

In 1090, these rights were confirmed and expanded by Henry IV, and they were accorded civil rights *(Buergerrecht)* in the city as permanent residents along with the right to acquire land.

The Horensteins' Famous 11th Century Ancestor

Rashi (Troyes, 1040 – Troyes, 1105)

Solomon ben Yitzchok, the man the Jewish world would remember by the acronym "Rashi" (= **RA**bbi **SH**lomo **I**tzhaki) is one of the most illustrious figures in Jewish history. Also referred to as Solomon Tzarfati,[a] he was born in Troyes, France on February 22, 1040. At about 20 years of age, he left France to study in the Yeshiva of Mainz; later he moved to Worms for further study. When he returned to Troyes ten years later, he founded a Yeshiva and became a community leader.

As his writings spread throughout the Jewish world, he became widely acclaimed for his exceptional ability to present the basic meaning of the Bible and the Talmud in a concise, but also lucid, manner. To quote the 1906 version of the Jewish Encyclopedia:

"Their primary quality is perfect clearness: Rashi's explanations always seem adequate. He manifests also a remarkable facility in the elucidation of obscure or disputed points, recurring, whenever he finds it necessary, to schemata. His

---

[a] Tzarfati: A derivative of *"Tsarefat,"* originally designating a Phoenician city on the Eastern shore of the Mediterranean. Among Jews, the name initially indicated that the family had migrated from France.

language is not only clear, but precise, taking into consideration the actual context and the probable meaning and reproducing every varying shade of thought and signification. Yet it is never diffuse; its terseness is universally conceded. A single word frequently suffices to summarize a remark or anticipate a question."[615]

תמונת רבינו שלמה יצחקי זל, רשי
נולד ד תשטו נפטר ד תתניג לבע

R. SALOMO JIZCHAKI

R. Kunstadt Wien

The analysis of the Talmud by this remarkable man was so exceptional that, to this day, all printed versions of the Talmud include Rashi's commentary on the inside column of each page, next to the binding.

His writings also show him to have been a modest, humble and kind man with a great love of people. Always willing to admit his mistakes, he had no sense of pride or arrogance. These characteristics of his personality, as much as the clarity and insight of his written words, made him such an important spiritual leader.

Rashi had no sons and three daughters. He lived in an age when a family's heritage was passed down through the male line, while daughters were poorly educated and even forbidden to study sacred texts.

Going against custom, he appears to have educated his daughters himself. Evidence for this comes from one of his later responsum[b] in which he writes that, because he is too weak to write down his words, he is dictating to his daughter - so she must have been capable of writing down complicated legal terminology in Hebrew.

Descent from Rashi to the Horenstein Brothers
via his daughter Miriam

(They also descend from his daughter Yocheved.)

Rabbi Solomon Tzarfati (RASHI)
↓
Miriam (b. Troyes ca. 1065)
m. **Rabbi Judah Azriel (RiBaN)**, (Mainz, ca. 1065 -Paris, ca. 1105)
↓
Rabbi Yom Tov of Falaise (Falaise, ca. 1100 – Paris, ca. 1140)
↓
↓
Rabbi Judah Sir Leon of Paris (Paris, ca. 1166 – Paris, ca. 1224)
↓
↓
Rabbi Matityahu Trevès (Marseille, ca. 1323 – Paris, ca. 1386)
↓
↓
Rabbi Eliezer Treves (Neuss-on-the-Rhine, 1495 – Frankfurt, 1566)
↓
↓
Rabbi Betzalel HaKohen Katz (ca. 1680 – Ostroh, 1717)
↓
↓
Rabbis Yakov Yosef & Naftali Horenstein

---

[b] Responsa: A written reply by a rabbi or scholar to an inquiry concerning Jewish law.

Toward the end of his life, he was living in Troyes when he was informed of the loss of relatives and friends who were victims of the First Crusade (1096) and expressed his shock in some of his commentaries as well as in several poems.

He died on July 13, 1105 at the age of 65.

The 12th Century

This century, at the outset of the high Middle Ages, was a period of social, political and economic transformations, as well the intellectual revitalization of Western Europe, and of Christian renewal. These dynamic changes have earned it the title of the "renaissance of the 12th century."[616]

Yet France and Germany remained feudal societies in which residents were forced to submit to the authority of a regional ruler with virtually unlimited power. Most importantly for Jews, this was the century when the Church became the dominant center of power.

Most towns remained small, with only a few thousand inhabitants, but many more of the townspeople had become merchants, and many towns were becoming centers of commerce with commercial fairs.[617] Most Jewish communities still only numbered a hundred or so individuals, although Jews were also found in the major population centers, such as Paris, Orléans, Cologne and Mainz where they lived in tightly organized communities.[618,619]

Literacy increased everywhere and people began to write about issues beyond those of religion. For the 1st half of the century, intellectual life centered on the monasteries but by mid-century, the precursors of modern universities began to develop in the growing urban centers. Their focus was on theology but, rather than merely accepting an author's assertions, scholars now examined and debated their value and meaning in "disputations" during which both the pros and the cons of statements were presented followed by a resolution.[620]

Jewish intellectual achievements paralleled those of the Christian world. Outstanding scholars, some descendants of Rashi, developed a method of biblical and Talmudic scholarship similar to that of their Christian counterparts, but outside of the universities.

Despite these achievements, negative changes in the attitude of the Christian world towards Jews led to a gradual decline in their status. Earlier, Jews had received charters on the assumption that they were independent and thus free to decide where they lived and on what terms. Now, as their social standing fell, they became needy of protection and obliged to please their protectors.[621]

Jews and Moneylending

Central to their decline was pressure from the Christian world for them to confine their incomes to moneylending. According to an edict issued in Charlemagne's time, "lending" meant giving something and requiring only that it be returned later, while "usury" meant claiming a return greater than the original loan.[622] Strictly speaking, even buying and selling merchandise for profit was unacceptable for a Christian, as was a "mortgage," a common arrangement at that time in which the creditor received temporary usage of an estate, including its produce and income, until the loan was repaid.[623]

This woodcut, from a book published in Nuremberg, Germany in 1491, shows a Jewish moneylender, his wife and child in the background, negotiating with a peasant and a townsman. (Foltz, *Die Rechnung Kolpergers von dem Gesuch der Juden.* Nuremberg.)

The tradition of denigrating the charging of interest for loans goes back to the Gospel of Luke in which Jesus tells his disciples to give freely for

> *"If you do good to those who do good to you, what credit is that to you? Even sinners do the same. And if you lend to those from whom you expect repayment, what credit is that to you? But love your enemies, do good to them, and lend to them, expecting nothing in return. Then your reward will be great, and you will be sons of the Most High."*[624]

Although a Germanic "gift economy" had developed earlier based on personal relationships and reciprocity, it was unsustainable in the new commercial economy.;[625] thus moneylending became an increasingly important aspect of the economy.

Despite its rising importance, the Church's disapproval of the practice among Christians gradually shifted them away from the activity. Many Christians, including the clergy, turned to Jews for loans because of the paucity of Christian moneylenders. Also, Jewish moneylenders had an advantage for them over fellow Christians, as they would have trouble in gaining support from the authorities when debtors failed to repay.[626]

The Second Crusade (1146-1147)

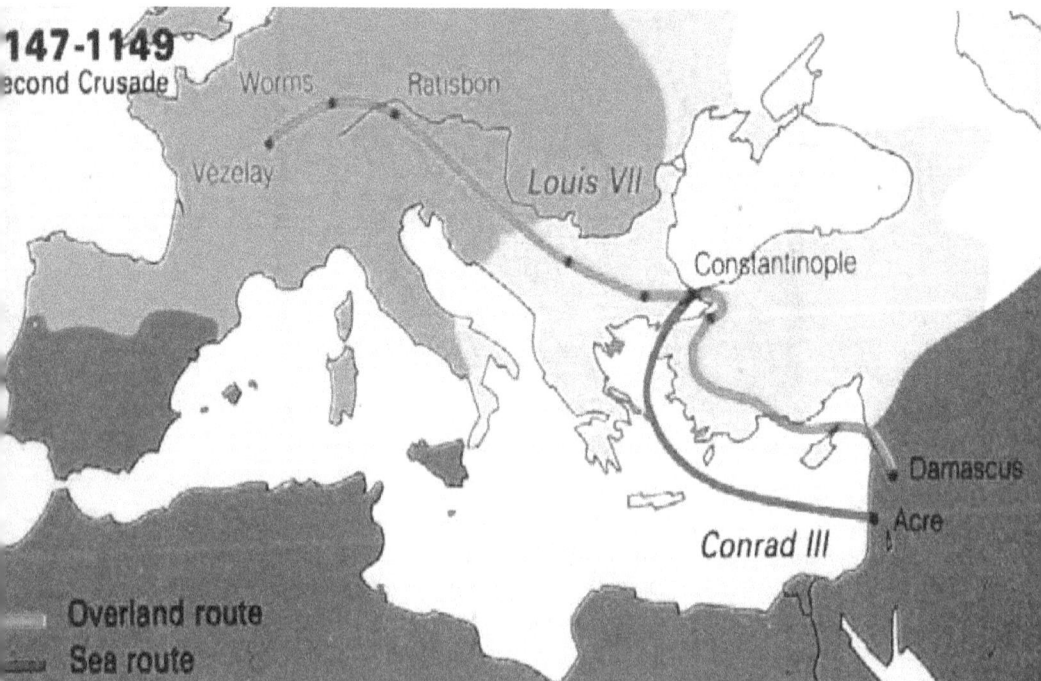

147-1149
econd Crusade
Worms
Ratisbon
Vézelay
Louis VII
Constantinople
Damascus
Acre
Conrad III
Overland route
Sea route

In the summer of 1145, word reached Europe that a Muslim army had captured the capital city of Edessa, a large territory in what is now southeastern Turkey, and overrun the entire area, making them well situated for assaults on the neighboring crusader states, including Jerusalem. On December 1st, the pope addressed a letter to King Louis VII of France, calling for a new crusade, promising not only remission of all sins but also remission of all interest on debts and postponement of payment until the crusaders returned.[627]

As enthusiasm for a new crusade mounted, Rhineland Jews – and probably Jews in northern France as well – were subject to repeated episodes of violent assaults. After the crusaders departed for Jerusalem in May and June of 1147, the situation calmed down.[628] The attacks differed from those of the First Crusade in that most of the assaults were perpetrated by individuals or small bands, so they were substantially less devastating.[629]

By the second half of the century, Jews were being falsely accused of murdering Christians. Usually the accusation started with the discovery of a corpse which was soon followed with groundless charges against the local Jewish community which could do little to properly defend itself.[630]

The Expulsion of the Jews from France

Philip Augustus became the French monarch in 1179 at the age of 15. In order to fight the powerful feudal barons and strengthen his hold on the throne, he needed money, and one way to obtain that money that appealed to him was to confiscate Jewish wealth. By such a move, he would also gain the goodwill of the Church.

All Jews residing in his lands were imprisoned in 1180. Only after they paid a heavy ransom were they released. The following year he annulled all loans made by Christians to Jews and took 20% of those funds for himself. The year after that he confiscated all Jewish lands and buildings and drove them out of the lands that he governed directly. (At that time, the royal domain was a relatively small region of what would become modern France.) Most moved no further than to neighboring regions, especially to Champagne.

A miniature from *Grandes Chroniques de France*
depicting the expulsion of Jews from France in 1182

Sixteen years later, however, many of the same barons who had accepted them into their territories decided to repudiate half of all the debts owed to the Jews and to expel them.[631] Philip Augustus then decided to readmit the Jews – although it seriously marred his reputation. This was not an act of kindness. Through taxes and duties, he made large profits from their ongoing banking business.[632,633]

German Jewry under Frederick I

The situation for German Jews at this time, while not good, was far better than that of their French counterparts due, primarily, to the difference in the monarchs. Frederick – king of Germany and Holy Roman Emperor - ruled, at least theoretically, over a high territory that included German lands from the Rhineland to Bohemia as well as much of Burgundy and Italy.

In 1182, he issued a charter for the Jews in Regensburg. He renewed the charter granted by Henry IV in 1097, immediately after the assaults of the First Crusade, which ensured that they could live and work there in safety, and guaranteed Jews the right to pursue their commercial interests "in the ancient manner."[634]

The attitude of the Christian population was another matter, and that differed little from that of the French, resulting in repeated episodes of sudden violence directed against the local Jewish population without due cause.

In 1188, as the Third Crusade approached, German Jews fasted and mourned, expecting the worst. In March, Jews from Mainz joined their brethren in Speyer and Worms and fled to nearby villages and fortifications. An attack upon the remaining Jews of Mainz was thwarted by the marshal, and soon Frederick issued a decree promising prompt punishment for offenders harming a Jew. Of course, he was gratified to receive a large tribute from the Jewish community in return, a tribute which he needed to finance the crusade.

This difference between the French and German monarchs continued even after Frederick's rule. However, the hostility of the population towards the Jews, who had become an alien and despised minority within a Christian society increasingly under the influence of the Church, was no different.[635]

Pope Innocent III and the Jews

The papacy had reached the height of its power when Innocent became Pope in 1198. He refused to grant Jews any privileges not previously granted by Church authorities and scrupulously observed the anti-Jewish legislation previously enacted. By expanding and enforcing decrees already in effect, especially in the matter of dress, he increased the social isolation of the Jews, thus reinforcing the social and political decline of Jewry, especially in Western and Central Europe.[636]

The Horensteins' Famous 12th Century Ancestors

Rabbi Eliezer ben Nathan of Mainz (RaBaN) (ca. 1065 – ca. 1125)

The great grandson of Abun Kalonymos HaGadol, Rabbi Eliezer was another member of the scholarly Kalonymos family who became an outstanding Jewish leader. Known as RaBaN, he was a leading rabbinic authority of his century as well as a liturgical poet.

Eliezer studied in Mainz, then lived for a while in Slavic countries and possibly in Russia before returning to Mainz. Greatly respected by his contemporaries in both Germany and France, he was in contact with all the major Jewish communities of his time.[637]

His great work (*Sefer ha-Raban*), which he called *Even haEzer* ("Stone of Help"), contributed much to our knowledge of the way of life of the Jews of France and Germany in the 12th century. Among his other contributions, the horrors of the First Crusade form the theme of some of his *piyyutim.[c]* He also wrote a booklet describing the massacres in detail.[638]

Rabbi Tam (Jacob Kalonymos) (1096-1171)

Grandson of Rashi, and considered, even in his lifetime, to be the greatest Talmudic authority in France and Germany. A wealthy man favored by the King of France, his chief work, *Sefer haYashar*, only remains in a version written by a relative, although with great precision and faithfulness to the original. His contributions to Hebrew poetry were also substantial, as was his work as a grammarian.[639]

Rabbi Judah "HaHasid" of Regensburg (ca. 1150 - 1217)

Rabbi Judah, great grandson of Rashi and the 2nd great grandson of Eliezer ben Nathan of Mainz, wrote *Sefer Hasidim* ("the Book of the Righteous"), the most popular and widely-read book of Jewish ethics during the Middle Ages. His book fostered a new movement, the *Hasidei Ashkenaz* ("the Righteous of Germany"), which set new standards for a properly led Jewish life (piety, asceticism, self-denial, and humility), paralleling a similar trend within Christianity. Although a scholar and head of the *beit midrash* of Speyer, Rabbi Judah stressed that faith, good conduct and prayer were more important than study.[640]

---

[c] *Piyyut*: A liturgical composition written in a poetic form. Based on some type of poetic metrical rhyming scheme or word pattern, authors usually wrote their compositions as alphabetical acrostics or embedded a name in the text. Many became standard in prayer books and continue to be recited today in synagogue services, such as *Ein Keloheinu, Yigdal, Adon Olam* and *L'kha Dodi*.

He was said to often remove his rabbinical garb, dress in the clothes of a beggar, and travel around the countryside in disguise to experience the humiliations and trials that afflict the poor and homeless.[641]

While he was born in the small town of Speyer, he left due to an "accident" - probably a false accusation of participation in the ritual murder of a Christian - and settled in Regensburg in 1195, 13 years after the local Jews had been granted their first official privileges in a charter.

He apparently chose Regensburg because the town treated its Jews more humanely – even though the Jewish community there had suffered in the First Crusade. He founded a very successful yeshivah, some of whose students became widely known, and soon became the most famous Jewish resident in the history of the town.[642]

While known mainly for his writings on ethics, he was extremely knowledgeable about Jewish law. His many contributions to the *Siddur* (Jewish prayer book) are still recited today.[643] In addition to his academic activities, Judah is said to have maintained a social relationship with the Bishop of Salzburg and to have acted as seer for the Duke of Regensburg.[644]

Rabbi Meshulam ben Jacob de Lunel (Lunel, ca. 1130 – Lunel, 1170)

Descent from Meshulam de Lunel
to the Horenstein Brothers

Rabbi Meshulam de Lunel
↓
↓
Rabbi Pinchas HaLevi Horowitz (Prague, 1535 – Kraków, 1618)
↓
↓
Rabbi Saul Brody Katzenellenbogen
(Chelm, 1617 – Pinczów or Brody, 1691)
↓
↓
Rabbi Saul Fishel (ca. 1705- Ludmir, aft. 1765)
↓
↓
Rabbis Yakov Yosef & Naftali Horenstein

A French Talmudist believed to descend from King David,[645] he directed a Talmudic school which produced several famous scholars. He was a man of considerable wealth with a large library, known for his philanthropy. Together with his sons, he provided for the support and maintenance of the disciples and scholars who attended his *beit midrash*. The town of Lunel, due to his influence, became an important center for Jewish study, and many of his students were among the great scholars of the time.[646]

Jewish scholars living in Christian countries had customarily restricted their interest to the Talmud. Meshulam, by contrast, was also distinguished in other fields of study, and was known for his zeal in investigating various branches of knowledge. He sponsored the translation of books on grammar, theology, rhetoric, ethics, and parables. He also wrote several works dealing with moral philosophy.[647]

Rabbi Judah Sir Leon (Paris, ca. 1166 – Paris, ca. 1224)

Considered one of the most illustrious French rabbis of the Middle Ages, Judah left Paris, the city of his birth, in 1182, when the Jews were expelled from the French king's dominions, and returned in 1198 when he founded an important school of tosafists (Talmud commentators). Like many other Jewish scholars, he also wrote several poems.

The 13th Century

In 1215, shortly before his demise, Innocent III convened the Fourth Lateran Council, charged with the task of creating a unified, orthodox and obedient Christendom. One of its five edicts concerning Jews was the first effort by the Church to make Jews more readily identifiable, decreeing that

> *"these people of both sexes, in all Christian provinces and at all times, shall be readily distinguishable from everyone else by their type of clothing."*[648]

Since the priests of the Lateran Council felt the need to issue this edict, we can assume that, up to this time, Jews were not distinguished from others by their clothing. Now it became mandatory for Jews to look different from the Christian population.

By 1217, the Jews of Paris were required to wear badges. By 1270, the Jews of the German empire, required to wear distinguishing clothing, began to wear the pointed cap, a unique hat which they continued to wear for several centuries.

(The 1483 woodcut on the left, by Johannes Schnitzer of Armsheim, shows five Jews, wearing their required clothing, disputing an issue in a book, probably the Talmud.)

In France, the kings following Philip Augustus were no better to the Jews. By the middle of the 13th century, Jews were routinely subjected to a hostile king and his barons. While judged to be a despicable people, they were also seen as necessary for commerce.[649]

Persecutions and restrictions mounted still further in the latter half of the century. Under Louis IX (1226-1270) and his immediate successors, France evolved from a confederation of feudal territories into a true country with a centralized government and a sense of national identity as the feudal social order was slowly replaced by commercial enterprises focused on production for sale and export. These new businesses were controlled by increasingly powerful urban merchants. With their own capital, they did not need to resort to the Jewish moneylenders.[650]

German Jews suffered a similar decline as anti-Jewish riots became common and they found that they could no longer count on the royalty for protection. Following the death of Frederick II in 1250, Germany entered a multi-century period of dissolution and decentralization. Lords ruled independently over their territories despite nominally remaining loyal to the king. Their real competition was the local bishops as well as the emerging class of wealthy burghers who insisted on controlling their own towns.[651]

Rudolph I, emperor from 1250 to 1273, claimed that he owned the Jews of the realm, although relatively few were under his actual control. Those Jews, like those under the control of French kings, were treated as transferable property. In 1284, Rudolph levied so heavy a tax on the Jewish communities under his jurisdiction that many Jews fled the country. Since, according to the king, they left the country without legal permission, all their remaining property was put into the imperial treasury.[652]

Conditions continued to worsen for the Jews who remained. The lack of support from the central governments assured local townspeople that they could assault Jews with relative impunity. Jewish communities knew that, at any time, they could be accused of fabricated charges of ritual murder or Host desecration[d]

---

[d] Host desecration: A form of sacrilege in Christianity involving the mistreatment or malicious use of a consecrated host—the sacred bread used in the Eucharistic service of the Divine Liturgy or Mass. In Catholicism, where the host is held to have

which would then justify vicious persecutions, usually resulting in deaths and the destruction of properties. Sometimes martyrdom became their best option: Jews would kill one another and commit suicide rather than being faced with the choice of forced conversion of death at the hands of the mob.[653]

By the end of the 13th century, the development of mercantilism had rendered the Jews superfluous to the economy, leaving them with nothing to warrant tolerance for their heresy.[654] All of Europe was now considered to be a single community of faithful Christians presided by a pope who was not under the command of any earthly ruler.

For centuries, Jews had been granted conditional acceptance as bearers of the "Old Testament." The problem for the Christian world was with the Hebrew Scriptures written since then, especially the Talmud, a work whose interpretation of the Pentateuch (the "five books of Moses") was considered blasphemous.

Jews burned alive during the southern German pogroms of 1298.
(Woodcut by Hartmann Schedel, "Chronicle of the World," 1493)

Since Jews were heretics, they needed to be eliminated, ideally by conversion into Christians. Thus, Christian society expended increasing energy in convincing Jews to convert, sometimes by enticements, other times by threats. Those who

---

been transubstantiated into the body of Jesus Christ, host desecration is among the gravest of sins.

211

refused conversion were believed to deserve harsh punishment, ranging from fines to death.[655]

The Horensteins' Famous 13th Century Ancestors

Abba Mari de Lunel (Perpignan, ca. 1220 – Perpignan, ca. 1310)

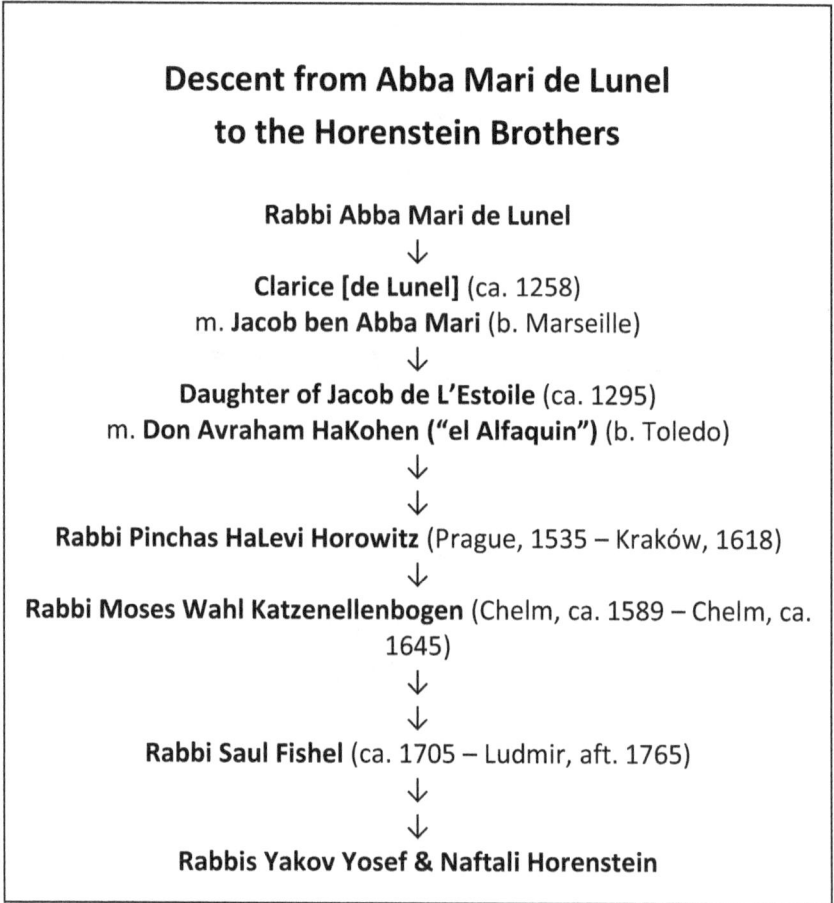

Descent from Abba Mari de Lunel
to the Horenstein Brothers

Rabbi Abba Mari de Lunel
↓
Clarice [de Lunel] (ca. 1258)
m. **Jacob ben Abba Mari** (b. Marseille)
↓
Daughter of Jacob de L'Estoile (ca. 1295)
m. **Don Avraham HaKohen ("el Alfaquin")** (b. Toledo)
↓
↓
Rabbi Pinchas HaLevi Horowitz (Prague, 1535 – Kraków, 1618)
↓
Rabbi Moses Wahl Katzenellenbogen (Chelm, ca. 1589 – Chelm, ca. 1645)
↓
↓
Rabbi Saul Fishel (ca. 1705 – Ludmir, aft. 1765)
↓
↓
Rabbis Yakov Yosef & Naftali Horenstein

Opponent of the "extreme" rationalism of the philosophical approach to Bible study, Abba Mari, like his grandfather Meshulum and father Asher, was highly respected for both his general erudition and his rabbinical knowledge.

Born in Lunel, he moved to Montpellier where he was dismayed to find that the youth focused their studies on science and philosophy, while neglecting the traditional study of rabbinical lore. Such studies, he was convinced, undermined religious belief.[656]

He therefore appealed to Solomon ben Adret of Barcelona, the most influential rabbi of the time, to use his authority to combat this "evil" by railing against both the study of philosophy and allegorical interpretations of the Bible (which did away with all belief in miracles.)

In 1305, following three years of negotiations, the synagogue of Barcelona issued a 50-year ban against all those who, before their 25th birthday, engaged in the study of science or of metaphysics.[657] The following year, however, the ban came to an abrupt end when Phillip the Fair expelled the Jews from France.

The 14th Century

The situation reached a new low when, by the start of the 14th century, the nobility started to treat Jews as "movable property." By the end of the century, this had become routine practice.

France

When it seemed that conditions could not get much worse, King Phillip IV, without warning, issued an edit in 1306 expelling all 125,000 Jews from France. He also ordered that their entire property be sold at public auction, with the proceeds to go to the royal treasury.[658]

Phillip died eight years later. The following year, Louis X, his son and successor, readmitted a small number of Jews who were granted a charter that gave them limited and conditional rights. Most who returned were moneylenders and were persecuted from the start.

When Charles IV assumed the throne in 1322, one of his first acts was to once again expel all Jews from France.[659] The great centers of Jewish life in northern France disappeared, although a few communities remained in Provence and in the eastern border regions.[660]

In the middle of the century, after repeated incidents of torture, murder and dispossession of property by the authorities, French Jews of the province of Vienne appealed, not to the French King, but to the pope. He was sympathetic, and responded with letters of reprimand, demanding the release of imprisoned Jews and the return of confiscated property.[661]

The final decree of expulsion from France came in 1394, after which Jews remained only in peripheral lands not under direct royal control. Most of the refugees moved eastward.[662]

Germany

For German Jews, there was another massacre from 1336 to 1339 led by bands of peasants whose leaders claimed to have received divine messages. They attacked about 120 Jewish communities and murdered thousands of residents.

In some towns, townspeople successfully protected local Jews, but in many other towns, the townspeople joined in the massacre.[663]

Around the middle of the century, the Black Plague, carried from the Orient by infected rats and fleas, struck Europe with ferocity. Blame for the disaster, which would eventually kill one-third of the population, increasingly fell on the Jews. Jewish massacres began in 1349 involving a number of towns in Provence.

Soon they spread everywhere. Throughout the Rhineland, townspeople attacked their Jewish populations. Local authorities often tried to discourage the riots, but were overridden by merchants and artisans who wanted to get rid of their Jewish neighbors. More than 300 Jewish communities were destroyed and countless thousands were killed, even though the pope spoke out against the accusation and urged against physically abusing the Jews.[664]

The Horensteins' Famous 14th Century Ancestor

Matityahu Ashkenazi Trèves of Provence (Marseille, ca. 1323 – Paris, ca. 1386)

French scholar and Chief Rabbi of France (by Royal degree)

Son of the rabbi of Marseilles, Rabbi Matityahu was born in France about 1323. After Charles IV forced the Jews to leave France, he studied for a while in various locations in Spain.

He moved to Paris following repeal of the Edict of Expulsion in 1361. There he found only a few Jews who were well-versed in the Talmud. This was because all manuscripts of the Talmud had been burned in 1244 when the famous Yeshiva of Paris with several hundred of its students were transferred to Acre in Palestine.[665]

He therefore founded a new yeshiva where many students came to study under him. The King, Charles V the Wise, appointed him Chief Rabbi of Paris and of all of the newly organized communities of France. While Charles had decreed that all Jews must wear a Jewish badge,[e] Matityahu and his family were exempted.[666]

Matityahu had eight children, In one of the many examples of endogamy[f] among the Horensteins' ancestors, they descend from four of his children.

---

[e] Jewish badge in Medieval Catholic Europe: The fourth Lateran Council had ruled in 1215 that Jews must wear distinguishable dress. For French Jews in the mid-14th century, a "distinguishing mark" was required which usually consisted of a badge which looked like a ring of white or yellow. Married women were often required to wear two bands of blue on their veil or head-scarf (Yellow badge. Wikipedia.org).

[f] Endogamy: The practice of marrying within your own ethnic group. As to the Horensteins' descent from multiple children of the same parents, a descendant of each

---

**Descent from Matityahu Ashkenazi Trèves of Provence
to the Horenstein Brothers**

Rabbi Matityahu (III) Ashkenazi Trèves
↓
Rabbi Eliezer Trèves (ca. 1460 – Sélestat, Alsace, 1490)
↓
Rabbi Shmuel Trèves (Italy, ca. 1440 – Alsace, after 1490)
↓
↓
Rabbi Eliezer III Ashkenazi Trèves (born ca. 1540)
↓
↓
Rabbi Naftali Hirsh II Katz (*"Smichat Chachamim"*)
(1645, Stepan – 1719, Constantinople)
↓
↓
Rabbis Yakov Yosef & Naftali Horenstein

The 15ᵗʰ Century

The Jews of Provence (now in the South of France), who had fared better than their brethren to the North, continued to enjoy a relatively benign environment. In 1423, Queen Yolanda issued a statute granting Jews basic freedoms and protection. This policy was confirmed by her successor, King René, but after his death most of Provence was ceded to the French crown. Without royal protection, their situation quickly deteriorated and soon they found themselves persecuted. By 1500, they were expelled from essentially all of Provence.[667]

In Germany, following the devastation of the Black Death, some Jewish communities remained, but only with provisional charters granting a degree of tolerance in return for large payments. Expulsions had become commonplace everywhere. Sometimes the provisional charter was not renewed, but other times it was the usual libels that led to a massacre, with an expulsion not long afterwards.[668]

The devastating medieval phase of Jewish history, shared by both France and Germany, had essentially ended by mid-century. Eastward migration had begun

---

would eventually marry a spouse from a descendant of another child, thus bringing two descent lines together.

which, over the next century, would shift the center of Ashkenazic life to Poland and Lithuania.

The Horensteins' Famous 15th Century Ancestors

Josef ben Solomon Colon ("Maharik") (Chambéry, ca. 1420 – Padua, 1480)

ספר
שאלות ותשובות
מהרי"ק
לרבינו מוה יוסף קולון זל.

In the 15th century, Italy, with a long tradition of Jewish learning and Talmudic studies, was a center for Talmudic study of almost equal rank with France and Germany.[669]

The foremost Talmudist of Italy in the second half of the century was Josef Colon. Moreover, for the final third of the century, he was the dominant Ashkenazic rabbinic figure in all of Europe.[670]

Colon was born in Chambéry, Savoy, France about 1420. Trabotto, the family surname, is derived from Trévou, a town in Burgundy where his family must have moved after the Jews were expelled from Chambéry. The Trévou Jews were subsequently expelled in 1429 which forced the family's move to Italy.[671]

Colon left home at an early age and wandered for some time while making his living by teaching children. About 1469 he obtained his first rabbinical appointment. Soon he became the Rabbi of Bologna, then the Rabbi of Mantua. Eventually he was appointed the Rabbi of Padua.[672]

At the time, the rabbinic academy at Padua was second to none, and many Italian rabbis were among the leading authorities of their time.[673] His reputation quickly spread well beyond Italy, and his decisions in both civil and religious questions were sought from as far away as Constantinople.[674]

Colon's responsa were highly influential on the development of rabbinical law. Not only did he endeavor to decide the case in hand, but he also sought to establish general principles for deciding related cases in the future. His knowledge of rabbinical literature was enormous, and he showed remarkable critical insight in regard to the Talmud.[675] With a strong sense of justice, he spoke out courageously against decisions that he deemed unjust, but were widely accepted at the time.[676]

He remained in Padua for the rest of his life, and died there in 1480.

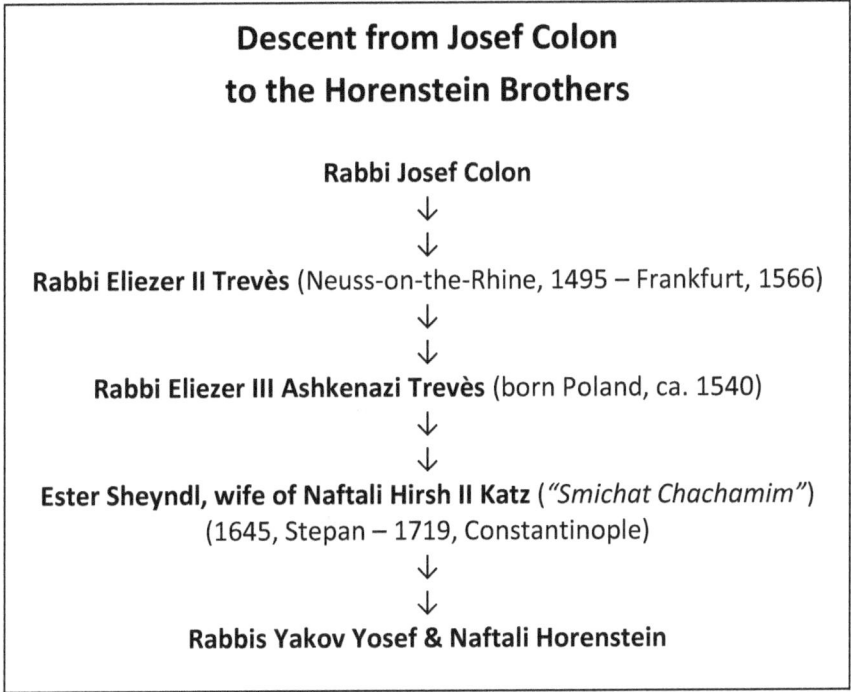

Descent from Josef Colon
to the Horenstein Brothers

Rabbi Josef Colon
↓
↓
Rabbi Eliezer II Trevès (Neuss-on-the-Rhine, 1495 – Frankfurt, 1566)
↓
↓
Rabbi Eliezer III Ashkenazi Trevès (born Poland, ca. 1540)
↓
↓
Ester Sheyndl, wife of Naftali Hirsh II Katz (*"Smichat Chachamim"*)
(1645, Stepan – 1719, Constantinople)
↓
↓
Rabbis Yakov Yosef & Naftali Horenstein

Jacob Jaffe Margoliot of Nuremberg (Lucca, 1430 – Worms, 1491)

The *Av Beit Din* of Nuremburg, Germany, he was considered by his contemporaries to be one of the greatest rabbis of his time.

In an unusual move, he added a second surname (Margoliot) to the family's paternal surname of Jaffe, supposedly in order to honor his mother (Margola = Pearl) for her piety (see page 178).

As the years passed, the Margoliot family became one of the most highly respected of the Ashkenazic rabbinical families.

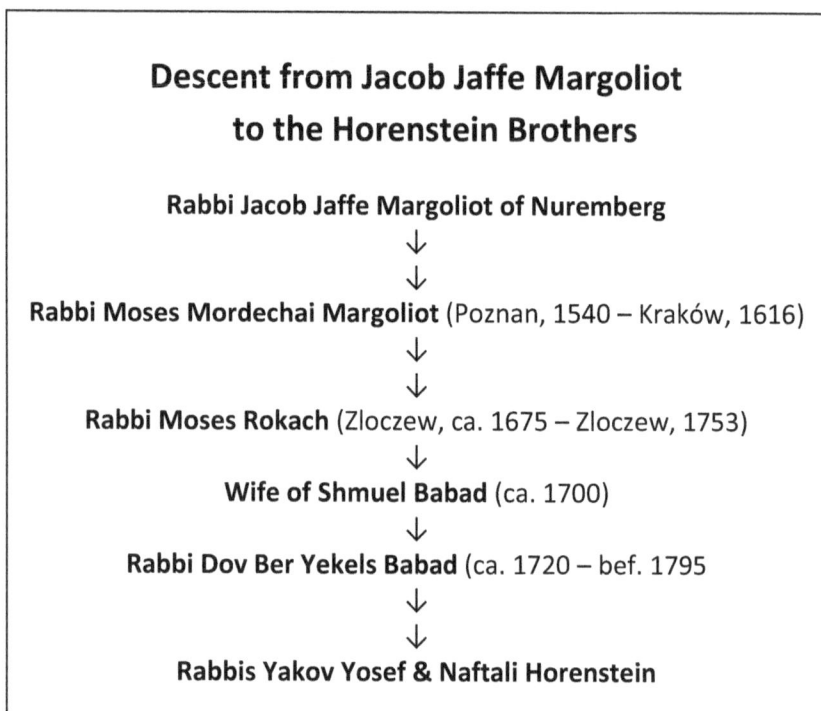

Descent from Jacob Jaffe Margoliot
to the Horenstein Brothers

Rabbi Jacob Jaffe Margoliot of Nuremberg
↓
↓
Rabbi Moses Mordechai Margoliot (Poznan, 1540 – Kraków, 1616)
↓
↓
Rabbi Moses Rokach (Zloczew, ca. 1675 – Zloczew, 1753)
↓
Wife of Shmuel Babad (ca. 1700)
↓
Rabbi Dov Ber Yekels Babad (ca. 1720 – bef. 1795
↓
↓
Rabbis Yakov Yosef & Naftali Horenstein

Miriam Spira (Konstanz, ca. 1403 – Worms, 1452)

The daughter of Rabbi Solomon Spira of Speyer, Germany, the *Av Beit Din* of Heilbron and Landau, Miriam became known for her scholarship and wisdom. While Jewish women of the time received only a minimal religious education, she became so knowledgeable that she taught advanced courses in Jewish law to young men. She did so while sitting in front of a curtain to preserve her modesty. The students heard her voice, but could not see her face.[677]

With her marriage to Rabbi Aaron Luria, the *Av Beit Din* of Heilbronn, the Spira rabbinical family merged into the Luria line.

Descent from Miriam Spira
to the Horenstein Brothers

Miriam Spira
m. **Rabbi Aaron Luria** (Heilbronn, ca. 1400 – Worms, ca. 1470)
↓
Rabbi Jechiel Luria of Brest-Litovsk (Heilbronn – Brest-Litovsk)
↓
↓
Hinde [HaLevi Horowitz] (ca. 1560 – ca. 1617)
m. **Rabbi Meir Wahl Katzenellenbogen** (born & died: Brest-Litovsk)
↓
Rabbi Moses Wahl Katzenellenbogen (Chelm, 1590 – Chelm, ca. 1645)
↓
↓
Rabbi Saul Fishel (ca. 1705 – Ludmir, aft. 1765)
↓
↓
Rabbis Yakov Yosef & Naftali Horenstein

Judah HaLevi Mintz (Mainz, ca. 1408 – Padua, ca. 1508)

Perhaps the most prominent rabbi of his time, he belonged to a family of scholars and bankers which derived its name from the town of Mainz, Germany, where he was probably born. He most likely left Mainz in 1462 when the Jews were expulsed and settled in Padua where he founded a large yeshiva for which he served as head for 47 years. He was 100 years old at the time of his death.

Only one year later, his tombstone and almost all of his writings were destroyed during the sack of Padua. His grandson discovered 16 of his responsa which were subsequently published. Although scanty, they provide interesting information on the events and customs he observed during his many years as the head of the Padua yeshiva.[678]

Descent from Judah HaLevi Mintz
to the Horenstein Brothers

Rabbi Judah HaLevi Mintz
↓
Rabbi Abraham HaLevi Mintz (Padua, ca. 1440 – Padua, 1530)
↓
↓
Feigela [Katzenellenbogen] (ca. 1525 – Prague)
↓
↓
Rabbi Naftali Hirsh II Katz (Stepan, 1645 – Constantinople, 1719)
↓
↓
Rabbis Yakov Yosef & Naftali Horenstein

Avraham HaLevi Mintz of Padua (Padua, ca. 1440 – Padua, 1530)

The son of Judah HaLevi Mintz, he was one of the important rabbinical scholars of his century in Italy.[679]

Abraham was appointed to succeed his father as head of the Padua yeshiva after his father's death, but six months later the Venetian authorities expulsed him for having presented a gift in the name of the Padua community to the chief of the conquering imperial German army during the sack of Padua. He subsequently became the rabbi of Mantua, while his son-in-law, Meir Katzenellenbogen, became the rabbi of Padua.[680]

THE MOVE EASTWARD: 16ᵀᴴ TO 17ᵀᴴ CENTURIES

At least since Hellenistic times, Jews were living in the Russian border territories, especially on the shores of the Black Sea. By the early Middle Ages, they were active as traders throughout much of southern Euro-Asia. Their Russian presence was cut short when Tsar Ivan IV Vasilievich (1530-1584), known as "Ivan the Terrible," ordered that Jews who refused to embrace Christianity be drowned. After that, Jews were excluded from Russian territory until the partition of Poland in the late eighteenth century.[681]

Continued oppression and persecution in France, Germany and Bohemia forced Jews to seek refuge by emigrating to the East.[682] Penetration into Russia was forbidden, so they settled in Poland, Lithuania and the Ukraine. There is evidence of Jewish communities in Poland by the early 11th century, although they may have been temporary.[683]

Jews arriving in Poland in the 13th century found a far more benign atmosphere. In 1264, Duke Bolesław the Pious of Greater Poland granted Jews the privileges of the Statute of Kalisz, creating a legal precedent for their official protection from local harassment and exclusion, and providing the foundation of future Jewish prosperity in the Polish kingdom. Jews were exempted from enslavement or serfdom and granted a broad range of freedoms of religious practices, movement, and trading. The Statute of Kalisz was later followed by many other comparable legal pronouncements.[684]

Following a series of expulsions of Jews from Western Europe, Jewish communities were established in Kraków, Kalisz and elsewhere in western and southern Poland during the century. The overwhelming majority of these new Jewish immigrants were from German and Bohemian lands west of Poland (within Ashkenaz).[685]

A liberal attitude towards Jewish settlement in Poland continued in the 14th and 15th centuries. In 1349, following an expulsion from Germany, King Casimir received the Jewish refugees.[686] During the 14th century, another series of Jewish communities were established in Poland at Lviv, Brest-Litovsk, and Grodno further east.[687]

The 16th Century

Woodcut of the blowing of the shofar in the synagogue, with women and children behind the screen in the foreground. From J. J. Pferrerkorn, *Judenbeichte*, Cologne, 1508

This was a century of dynamic changes. The growth of cities populated with a rising middle class of merchants, financiers and manufacturers was a force of sufficient magnitude to revolutionize society, causing destruction of a social equilibrium which had long been based on feudalism. Concurrently, the opening of a vast new world across the Atlantic extended the physical confines of the medieval world, while advances in science were changing man's conception of the universe and the perfection of the printing press permitted increased diffusion of knowledge.[688]

The Renaissance, with its emphasis on humanism, was the cultural expression of these changes, while interest in mysticism rose as the political and religious instabilities and the collapse of the familiar conception of the universe undermined the sense of security.[689]

These revolutionary developments clashed with the political and religious institutions within which feudal Europe had been organized. The medieval ideal of a world community, as expressed by the Holy Roman Empire on the physical plane, and by the Catholic Church on the religious plane, was shaken by the emergence of national states and national churches.[690]

The cultural transformation initially seemed to reduce the antipathy of the Christian population toward the Jews. Their traditional antagonism was questioned, while a marked interest in Jewish culture, including Hebrew, was developing. The mysticism of *Kabbalah* was studied with zeal to find guidance.[691]

As the century unfolded, however, Hebraic tendencies among the Christian humanists was denigrated by conventional Christian leaders. With the fighting between the Catholic orthodoxy and the Protestants, the Church charged the rising Protestant sects with being a "Judaizing" heresy while Protestants, to disprove the charge, accentuated their own polemic against the Jews. As nationalism rose, the Jews were increasingly viewed as an alien cultural element that disturbed the unity of the new society.[692]

While mob violence abated somewhat, Jews became increasingly subject to expulsions. Following the massive expulsion from Spain in 1492, there were a series of expulsions from various other European states throughout the century powered by the explosive force of nationalism.[693]

The situation began to improve later in the century as the power and influence of the church started to decline. Leading legal and political writers championed secular governments. Jews started to be readmitted to the very same German-speaking towns and principalities which had expelled them earlier in the century. They were, for example, readmitted to Bohemia and subsequently even given a charter of privileges. Vienna and Prague once again became lively centers of Jewish life. A reversal in the royal attitude towards Jews was so extreme that Court Jews now started to appear as financial advisors to the monarchs.[694]

The Jewish Renaissance in Prague

Predecessor of the modern Czech Republic, the Kingdom of Bohemia, with Prague as its capital, was a Central European Monarchy. Jews settled in Prague as early as the 10th century, but were persecuted starting in the late 11th century. In 1215, the Fourth Lateran Council mandated that Jews must wear distinctive clothes, were prohibited from holding public office and were limited in the amount they could charge for interest on loans. The emperor relinquished some of his power over the Jews in the first part of the 14th century and allowed others to manage Jewish affairs in return for a large sum of money, but also allowed estates to renege on loans owed to Jewish lenders.[695]

In 1389, mobs burned and pillaged the Jewish quarter. Nearly the entire Jewish community perished, while many of the remaining women and children were baptized. The Hussite Wars brought a decline in royal authority in the 15th century, with power shifting to the middle-class Burghers in the cities and landowners in the countryside. Jews were still beholden to others, however, and had to pledge allegiance to various groups and pay them money in return for protection.[696]

The 16th century was the time of the Prague Renaissance. The city's population almost doubled between 1522 and 1541 as Jews who were expelled from Moravia, Germany, Austria and Spain migrated there. Although, under the Habsburgs, they were expelled in both 1542 and 1561,[697] each time they returned and prospered.[698]

Western European Jews move to Poland

At the dawn of the 16th century, despite centuries of a benign political climate, there were still only between 20,000 and 30,000 Jews living in Poland, out of a total population of five million inhabitants. Now, however, the Jewish population began to explode. Seventy-five years later, while the total population had risen to seven million, the number of Jews had increased to 150,000, and the rate of Jewish population increase was still accelerating.[699]

In 1503, the Polish monarchy appointed Rabbi Jacob Pollack "Rabbi of Poland." This was the start of a Chief Rabbinate, backed by the crown, which allowed the Jews limited self-government for the first time since the end of the Babylonian exilarchate.[700]

The Jews themselves were electing the Chief Rabbi by 1551. He exerted wide powers over law and finances, as well as the power to appoint judges and many other officials. At times he shared power with locally-elected town councils, but only between one and five percent of Jewish householders had the right to vote.[701]

The Polish monarchy welcomed the Jews because they were a new source of revenue. Both the rabbinate and local Jewish councils were charged with raising money for taxes, and seventy percent of the money they raised was given to the crown in return for protection.[702]

Despite the benign attitude of the national government, new Jewish arrivals quickly discovered that their move did not free them from dealing with hostility from their Christian neighbors. In Kraków, for example, where the local merchant class was powerful, Jews were usually kept out.[703]

By the 1560s, Jewish pioneer settlers, with easy access to credit through Jewish firms in other countries, were playing a leading part in developing eastern Poland, the interior of Lithuania, and the Ukraine. With a rapidly expanding west European population, increasing quantities of grain were needed, so Polish landowners devoted more of their land to farming and went into partnership with Jewish entrepreneurs to move the harvests through the rivers to Baltic ports and ship them west. Jews ran the estates and owned the river boats which returned from the ports laden with goods which they sold in their shops.[704]

Jewish towns (*shtetls*) developed on lands owned by absentee Polish nobles where Jews and their shops dominated the center, while the peasants lived in the surroundings.[705] In Poland and Ukraine, Jews became agents and advisors to the Polish nobility, keeping the books, collecting their taxes, and writing their letters.[706]

In 1565, a visiting papal diplomat reported that

"... one still comes upon masses of Jews who are not disdained as much as in some other lands. They do not live here under pitiful conditions and do not engage in lowly pursuits.... But rather, they possess land, engage in commerce, and devote themselves to study, especially medicine and astrology.... They possess considerable wealth and they are not only among the respectable citizens, but occasionally even dominate them. They wear no special marks to distinguish them from Christians and are even permitted to wear the sword and to go about armed. In general, they enjoy equal rights."[707]

The process of forcibly removing Jewish residents from western Europe was almost completed by the end of the 16th century so that, in the 17th century, apart from the Ottoman Empire, the Polish-Lithuanian Kingdom was the main region inhabited by a considerable number of Jews.[708]

The Horensteins' Famous 16th Century Ancestors

The Horensteins' ancestors from France and Germany were part of the mass exodus to eastern Europe. Many of the men became rabbis of the rapidly growing Jewish communities. The dedication to scholarship and writing which their ancestors had shown in France and Germany now continued in this new land. Some were even among the most outstanding Jewish scholars of their time.

In a previous chapter, we noted how the number of the Horensteins' prominent ancestral families rapidly increased through marriages in which multiple children married into other distinguished rabbinical families. Often, within a few generations, descendants of related families married one another, thus creating an interconnected network of ancestral families.

As a result, by the 16th century, as a group, the Horensteins' ancestors in eastern Europe had become a major rabbinic and literary force within the Jewish world.

Rabbi Solomon Luria (the "MaHaRSHaL" = our teacher, Rabbi Solomon Luria) (Germany or Poland, ca. 1510 – Lublin, Poland, 1573)

One of the greatest Polish Talmudists,[709] Rabbi Luria, a descendant of Rashi, was born in 1510. He studied in the Ostroh yeshiva under Rabbi Kalonymus Kalman Haberkasten, the Horenstein brothers' 11th great grandfather, and married Rabbi Haberkasten's daughter.

When Rabbi Haberkasten moved to Brisk (Brest-Litvosk) to assume the position of yeshiva principal there, Luria succeeded him as the official rabbi of the city of Ostroh and the Ostroh region.[710] His fame brought many students to the town, leading to the founding of a widely known rabbinical seminary.[711]

By 1540, he had become the head of the yeshiva in Brest-Litvosk. A decade later was appointed *Av Beit Din* of Ostroh. Later he assumed the same position in

Lublin where the yeshiva attracted students from all over Europe. Eventually, he opened his own yeshiva in a building that remained intact until World War II.

A prolific writer, he became widely known for his work on *Halakhah* as well as for his Talmudic commentary. He was harshly critical of some of his fellow rabbis, and willing to say so in public.

> *"The ordained are many; but those who know something are few. The number of overbearing ones is steadily increasing; none of whom knows his place. As soon as they are ordained, they begin to domineer and, by means of their wealth, to gather about themselves disciples, just as lords hire slaves to run before them.*

> *"They rule over the scholars and the congregation. They excommunicate and anathematize, and they ordain pupils who did not study under them, and receive therefore money and reward. They are always seeking their own interests."*[712]

Rabbi Luria died in Lublin on November 7, 1573.

Descent from Solomon Luria to
the Horenstein Brothers

Rabbi Solomon Luria [MaHaRShal]
↓
Valentina (ca. 1530)
m. Efraim Fishel HaKohen (ca. 1530 – Jerusalem, ca. 1595)
↓
Rabbi Naftali Tzvi Hirsh Fishel HaKohen (ca. 1550 – 1626)
↓
Rabbi Efraim Fishel HaKohen (ca. 1580 – L'vov, ca. 1650)
↓
Yute (ca. 1615)
m. Rabbi Arye Leib Kloizner (Kraków, ca. 1615 – Kraków, 1671)
↓
Rabbi Efraim Fishel Kloizner (ca. 1650 – ca. 1725)
↓
Rabbi Jacob Fishel Kloizner (ca. 1690 – 1730)
↓
Rabbi Saul Fishel (ca. 1705 – Ludmir, aft. 1765)
↓
Rabbi Pinchas (Ludmir, ca. 1725 – Ostroh, 1786)
↓
Rabbi Arye Judah Leib (Ludmir, 1744 – Ostroh, after. 1805)
↓
Rabbi Shmuel Asher (1770 – Berestechko, 1840)
↓
Rabbis Yakov Yosef & Naftali Horenstein

Rabbi Judah Loew ben Betzalel ("MaHaRaL" = *moreinu* [our teacher] HaRav Rabbi Loew) (Posen 1512 – Prague 1609)

Tall and distinguished-looking, Rabbi Judah is considered to have had one of the most outstanding Jewish minds of his century. He was born in Posen, Poland in 1512 to a prominent family from Worms. At an early age, he was introduced to the study of the Talmud. He also studied the Zohar, the central book of *Kabbalah*, as well as other esoteric Jewish literature. In addition, he was an avid reader of books which covered all other branches of Jewish knowledge and wisdom, and was equally knowledgeable of Greek philosophy, physics, mathematics and astronomy.[713]

He was independently wealthy, probably due to his father's success in business. He wrote numerous books on Jewish law, philosophy, and morality. *Gur-arye*, a study of Rashi's biblical commentary, was his first work and was published in Prague in 1578. Although he wrote many other books, *Gur-arye* was to be his most famous.[714]

Rabbi Judah's career began in Nicolsberg in 1553 where, as rabbi of the province of Morovia, he assisted the Morovian Jewish community in organizing its affairs, dealing with such issues as education, elections to local offices and methods of taxation. Persecution of innocent Jews was common, and many Jews died "by fire and sword."

In 1574 he moved to Prague, probably due to family considerations as he had not been offered a rabbinical position. Also, Prague was becoming a major center of Jewish intellectual life. There he opened an academy for higher Jewish studies which invited advanced students to deepen their knowledge of Judaism.[715]

In 1584, Rabbi Judah was 71 years old and had achieved an outstanding reputation as rabbi and scholar. He was the leading candidate for Chief Rabbi of Prague, although he had gained a reputation of speaking openly against abuses which he saw around him, many of which were due to corruption in the Jewish community government.

Invited to preach the sermon on the Sabbath of Repentance, he stood on the pulpit of the main synagogue and warned that it was the duty of the community's leaders to attend to the needs of the poor and lowly, rather than to serve the interests of the wealthy.

He proceeded to denounce the practice of calling people "*nadler*," a derisive epithet suggesting illegitimate birth, which reflected on the honor of a number of leading Jewish families. Then he summoned ten leading citizens to come up to the pulpit holding Torah scrolls, and intoned the solemn formula of excommunication against the slanderers.[716]

Shortly afterwards, there was an assembly to elect the Chief Rabbi – and Rabbi Israel Hayot, Rabbi Judah's brother-in-law, won the election. Rabbi Judah thus moved to Posen where he had been invited to be rabbi.

He returned to Prague in 1588 after Rabbi Hayot resigned as Chief Rabbi. There he received a plea to protect certain distinguished families from a new variety of slander, this time the unfounded claim that they descended from oedipal marriages (i.e. between parents and their children), and joined other rabbis in issuing an edict of excommunication against those guilty of spreading this charge.[717]

In 1592, he was invited to a lengthy audience with Emperor Rudolph II, a clear indication of the fame and recognition he had obtained. However, that same year he was ignored once again by the electors for the position of Chief Rabbi (who chose instead Rabbi Mordechai Jaffe – see his biography below) and returned to his rabbinical post in Posen where he became Chief Rabbi of Poland.

Five years later, he returned to Prague once again, resigning his post in Posen. Rabbi Jaffe then resigned his post as Chief Rabbi and accepted a call to fill Rabbi Judah's post in Posen, leaving open the position of Chief Rabbi of Prague. This time, not surprisingly, Rabbi Judah was finally chosen to fill the position of Chief Rabbi.[718]

Ill health forced him to resign his post in 1604, when he had reached the age of 92. He lived five years longer, finally dying on August 22, 1609. As his wife died the following year, the two have a joint tombstone in Prague which is decorated with a heraldic shield showing a lion with two intertwined tails, alluding both to Rabbi Judah's first name and Bohemia, whose coat of arms shows a two-tailed lion.

The MaHaRaL's Ancestry

As in the case of Rashi, the desire of Jews to trace their ancestry to the Ma-HaRaL generated attempts of genealogists to "make it so." Moreover, there was a strong desire to claim the existence of an ancestral line from the MaHaRaL to King David as it meant that anyone who could claim the MaHaRaL as an ancestor could also claim Davidic ancestry.

Until recently, the MaHaRaL's Davidic ancestry was generally accepted, based on the book *Megilat Yukhsin* by Meir Perels. This was hardly a genealogy claimed by the MaHaRaL himself, as Perels wrote his genealogy in 1727, 118 years after the MaHaRaL's death.

A rabbi named Judah Loew HaZaken was central to this proposed ancestral line which was based on information Perels personally found inscribed on the rabbi's tombstone in Prague. According to Perels, the tombstone states that he died in 1439-1440 (*"resh"* in Hebrew). Perels also wrote that the tombstone in-cludes the inscription "descended from Yishai," the name of King David's father; thus suggesting that this putative ancestor may have descended from King David.

Based on this evidence, Perels concluded that the MaHaRaL's grandfather, Chaim Loew-Beer, was a grandson of Judah Loew HaZaken; moreover, he believed that the descent of the MaHaRaL's family from King David was "proven" by the inscription.

We now know that Perels was mistaken. Closer inspective of the tombstone has revealed that Judah Loew HaZaken died, not in 1439-1440, but in 1539-1540 (*"shin"* in Hebrew); thus, he could not have been the MaHaRaL's ancestor. Moreover, when "Yishai" on the tombstone was examined more closely, the word that was inscribed is actually *"Khamishi,"* Hebrew for the fifth day, namely Thursday, which is followed by a Hebrew date, the 25th of *Kheshvan*.[719,720,721,722]

Another long-standing tradition is that the MaHaRaL descends from King David via Judah HaNasi (135-217),[723,724] the editor of the *Mishneh*[a] in its final form. Since there is no record of the generations for the 14 centuries in between the two men, this lineage is fanciful; thus there is no evidence that the MaHaRaL was of Davidic descent.

---

[a] *Mishneh*: A redacted record of the debates of the post-temple sages (the *Tannaim*) from 70 to 120 AD which, together with the *Gemara* (rabbinic commentary on the Mishnah), is known as the Oral Torah or *Talmud*.

Rabbi Loew and the Golem

Sometime in the Middle Ages, eastern European Jews, subject to repeated acts of violence by Christians, began to believe that, with esoteric knowledge, it was possible to infuse life into a clay or wooden figure of a human being, called a "golem," which would quickly grow huge and powerful. While the golem had no mind of its own, it would carry out any order of its master.[725]

To create a golem, its master would write on a piece of paper a combination of Hebrew letters to form a "*Shem.*"[b] Then he would insert the paper either into the mouth or in the forehead of the golem, thus bringing the creature to life.[726]

The first person credited for having made a *golem*, according to legend, was Rabbi Elijah of Chelm, a contemporary of Rabbi Loew (who also happens to be a Horenstein ancestor). While his golem performed hard work for him for a long time, it continued to grow. Eventually, it became so huge that the rabbi feared it might destroy the world, so he extracted the Holy Name embedded in the golem's forehead and it instantly became dust.[727,728,729]

As an intrepid defender of people's rights, as well as a master of the mystical power of *Kabbalah*, Rabbi Judah became the perfect historical figure for the

---

[b] *Shem:* Name; here the word seems to refer to the concept of God's name in the ancient *Sefer Yetzirah* ("Book of Formation"), the earliest extant book on Jewish esotericism, which states that the creation of the world was achieved by the manipulation of the sacred letters that form the names of God (Names of God in Judaism. Wikipedia.org).

immensely popular and enduring legend which claims that he created a *golem* out of clay in order to defend the Jews of Prague from anti-Semitic attacks. Varieties of this legend began circulating in the 18th century; it was eventually given literary form by multiple writers.[730]

Descent from the MaHaRaL to the Horenstein Brothers

Rabbi Judah Loew ben Betzalel [MaHaRaL]

↓

Vögele (Prague, 1550-66 – Prague, 1629)
m. **Rabbi Yitzchok I Katz** (Vienna, ca. 1550 – Prague, 1624)

↓
↓

Rabbi Naftali Hirsh II Katz [Smichat Chachamim] (Stepan, 1645 – Constantinople, 1719)

↙ ↓ ↘

Shprintze   **Eidel**   **Rabbi Betzalel Katz**

↘ ↓ ↙

↘ ↓ ↙

Yakov Yosef & Naftali Horenstein

Rabbi Moses Isserles (the "ReMA" = acronym of Rabbi Moses Isserles) (Kraków, 1520 – Kraków, 1573)

Isserles is considered one of the greatest Jewish scholars of Poland. Born in Kraków to a very wealthy family, his father was a prominent Talmudic scholar.

A founder of rabbinic learning in both Poland and Germany, he became one of the world's greatest authorities of *Halakhah*. In fact, his rulings and customs were accepted as binding on Ashkenazic Jewry and still form the basis of Ashkenazi *Halakhah*. He was also recognized as an authority in *Kabbalah* and philosophy, and even in the secular sciences, as he had an extensive knowledge of astronomy. In addition, he had a particular liking for history and was well versed in Greek philosophy.

He was also prominent in the Council of Four Lands, which was first established during his lifetime.

Descent from Moses Isserles to the Horenstein Brothers

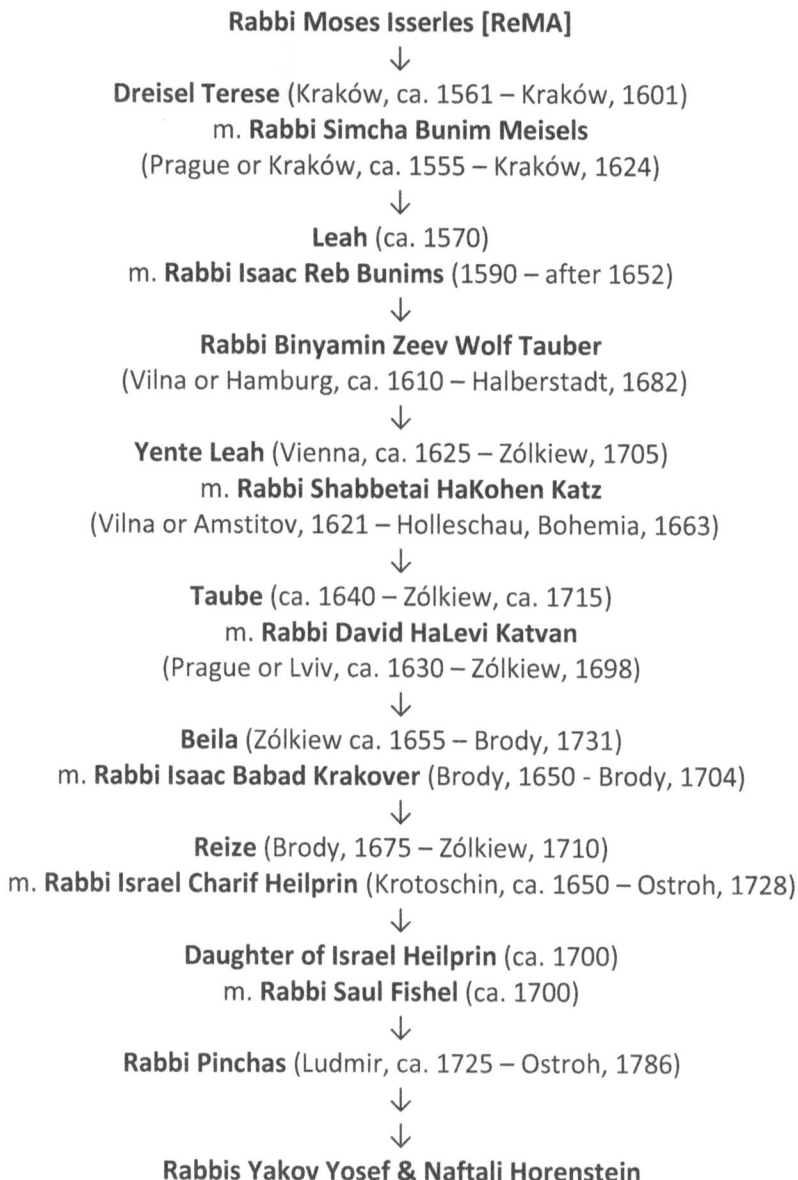

Rabbi Moses Isserles [ReMA]
↓
Dreisel Terese (Kraków, ca. 1561 – Kraków, 1601)
m. **Rabbi Simcha Bunim Meisels**
(Prague or Kraków, ca. 1555 – Kraków, 1624)
↓
Leah (ca. 1570)
m. **Rabbi Isaac Reb Bunims** (1590 – after 1652)
↓
Rabbi Binyamin Zeev Wolf Tauber
(Vilna or Hamburg, ca. 1610 – Halberstadt, 1682)
↓
Yente Leah (Vienna, ca. 1625 – Zólkiew, 1705)
m. **Rabbi Shabbetai HaKohen Katz**
(Vilna or Amstitov, 1621 – Holleschau, Bohemia, 1663)
↓
Taube (ca. 1640 – Zólkiew, ca. 1715)
m. **Rabbi David HaLevi Katvan**
(Prague or Lviv, ca. 1630 – Zólkiew, 1698)
↓
Beila (Zólkiew ca. 1655 – Brody, 1731)
m. **Rabbi Isaac Babad Krakover** (Brody, 1650 - Brody, 1704)
↓
Reize (Brody, 1675 – Zólkiew, 1710)
m. **Rabbi Israel Charif Heilprin** (Krotoschin, ca. 1650 – Ostroh, 1728)
↓
Daughter of Israel Heilprin (ca. 1700)
m. **Rabbi Saul Fishel** (ca. 1700)
↓
Rabbi Pinchas (Ludmir, ca. 1725 – Ostroh, 1786)
↓
↓
Rabbis Yakov Yosef & Naftali Horenstein

Rabbi Mordechai Jaffe (the *"Levush,"* referring to his 10-volume book *Levush Malchut* [Royal Vestments]) (Prague ca. 1540 – Posen 1612)

Descent from Mordechai Jaffe
to the Horenstein Brothers

Rabbi Mordechai Jaffe
↓
Abigail Olga (Padua, ca. 1565 – Padua, 1594)
m. **Rabbi Samuel Judah Katzenellenbogen**
(ca. 1521, Padua – 1597, Venice)
↓
Rabbi Saul Wahl Katzenellenbogen
(Padua, ca. 1543 – Brest-Litowsk, 1617)
↓
Rabbi Meir Wahl Katzenellenbogen
(Brest-Litowsk, ca. 1563 – Brest-Litowsk, ca. 1630)
↓
Rabbi Moses Wahl Katzenellenbogen
(Chelm, ca. 1590 – Chelm, ca. 1647)
↓
Rabbi Saul Brody Katzenellenbogen
(Chelm, 1617 – Pinczów or Brody, 1691)
↓
↓
Rabbi Saul Fishel (ca. 1705 – Ludmir, aft. 1765)
↓
↓
Rabbis Yakov Yosef & Naftali Horenstein

Rabbi Jaffe was born in Prague and studied under Rabbis Solomon Luria and Moses Isserles (see above). He became head of the Prague Yeshiva when, in 1561, the Emperor Ferdinand expelled the Jews from Bohemia. He then moved to Venice to study astronomy.

In 1588 he was elected rabbi of Lublin where he became a leader of the Council of Four Lands. Later, he became the rabbi of Kremenets, then rabbi of Prague and, finally, Chief Rabbi of Posen.

While still in his youth, Rabbi Jaffe decided to compile a book on *Halakhah*, especially as earlier works failed to include the customs which were accepted among the Jews of the Ashkenazic (i.e. Germanic) lands and Eastern Europe. He compiled a multi-volume book on practical law, *Levush Malchut* ("Royal Vestments"), which provided the reasons behind various Halakhic decisions, both based on his own reasoning and earlier sources.

Saul Wahl Katzenellenbogen ("King for a Day") (Padua ca. 1543 – Brest-Litowsk 1617)

Katzenellenbogen, the name of a prestigious Jewish family, was first used by Saul's grandfather Meir, a famous rabbi and Talmudic authority, who was born in Katzenellenbogen, Germany and moved to Padua, Italy. His father, Rabbi Samuel Judah, was distinguished at a young age for his scholarship and oratorical gifts.

Saul was born in Padua, but moved to Poland to study at the Brisk yeshiva, the best in Poland and Lithuania. According to historians, the story of what happened to him after that is unverified. Here is one version:

"Prince Nicholas Radziwill undertook a pilgrimage to Rome to consult the pope as to how to best do penance for the many atrocities he had committed in his youth. He took the pope's advice that he spend a few years as a wandering beggar.

"Later, when he was ready to return to his former life, he was living in Padua. He was destitute and could not find anybody who would believe his true identity.

He then decided to appeal to Saul's father, the Padua rabbi, who immediately recognized him for who he was and furnished the prince means for returning to his native country in royal style. In return, he asked the prince if he would find Saul with whom he had lost contact after Saul left for Poland years earlier. The prince agreed.

"After his return to Poland, Prince Radziwll fulfilled his promise and located the rabbi's son. He became so captivated by Saul's intellect that he took him into his castle and supplied with whatever he needed to continue his studies. As noblemen who visited the court marveled at his learning and wisdom, his fame spread throughout the country.

King Báthory by Jan Matejko

"Following the death of King Báthory in 1586, the electors of the contending parties could not agree on who to elect king. A Polish law stipulated that the throne could not remain unoccupied, so it was decided to appoint an outsider 'rex pro tempore' (temporary king). Prince Radziwell refused the honor, but he had a recommendation of someone who, despite one slight 'shortcoming', belonged to neither party and who was far superior to anyone else he knew in both wisdom and goodness. If the Diet would make his election unanimous, he would reveal his name. Accordingly, Saul's name was proposed and he was elected to this high office with great enthusiasm."

It is unclear whether he reigned for one or a few days although, at least according to Saul's grandson, he succeeded in passing several wise laws, including some that were helpful to the Polish Jews. Afterwards, the German word "wahl" meaning "election" or "chosen," was attached to his name.

According to one historian, there is a kernel of truth to this enduring legend: a prince Radziwill made a pilgrimage to Jerusalem. On his way back, he was robbed and left penniless. Everyone except one Jewish merchant, Samuel Judah Katzenellenbogen (Saul's father), ignored his pleas for help, but Samuel Judah believed his claim to be a Polish noble and provided him with funds to return to Poland.[731]

Moreover, the author of a history of the Jews in Lithuania has reproduced documents proving that King Béthori, in the 3rd year of his reign, awarded "Saul the Jew" the salt monopoly for the whole of Poland. Moreover, a proclamation issued by the king who followed Béthori states, in part:

> *"We, King of Poland, having convinced ourself of the rare zeal and distinguished ability of Saul the Jew, do herewith grant him a place among our royal officials, and that he may be assured of our favor for him we exempt him and his lands for the rest of his life from subordination to the jurisdiction … of any court in our land…"*[732]

Rabbi Shmuel Eliezer Edels ("MaHaRSHA" = acronym for: our teacher, Rabbi Shmuel Adels) (Kraków ca. 1535 – Ostroh 1631)

Descent from Shmuel Eliezer Edels to the Horenstein Brothers

Rabbi Shmuel Eliezer Edels
↓
Wife of Solomon Spira (born ca. 1555)
↓
Rabbi Natan Neta Spira (ca. 1575 – Kraków, 1633)
↓
Chava Dobrosh Freide (ca. 1595, Kraków – 1642, Kraków)
↓
Rabbi Meir Zak (ca. 1610 – 1653)
↓
Rabbi Shmuel Shmelke Zak (Ostroh, ca. 1630 – Ostroh, 1680)

Ester Sheyndl, wife of Rabbi Naftali Hirsh Katz
(Stepan, ca. 1650 – Constantinope, 1719)
↓
Shprintze (born ca. 1670)
↓
↓
Rabbis Yakov Yosef & Naftali Horenstein

Considered to be one of the foremost Talmud commentators, his commentary is still included today in almost every edition of the Talmud. He studied Torah in Posen, where he married the daughter of his uncle, the rabbi of Brisk.

In 1585 his wife's parents founded for him a large yeshiva, which was under his management until 1609. Edel, his mother-in-law, was a wealthy woman who supported him and his numerous disciples for 20 years for which he honored her by adopting her name.

In 1590, he participated at a session of the Council of Four Lands which pronounced a ban on those who purchase rabbinic office, a practice which had become commonplace. Rabbi Joel Jaffe Sirkes, himself a famous rabbi (see below), introduced him, stating

"You have in your midst the greatest man of the present generation ... with whom to consult and deliberate."[733]

He moved to Ostroh in 1615 to become head of its famous yeshiva. A modest and hospitable man, the town's residents were so impressed by him that they considered him to be the Father and Patron of the town. After his death in 1632, Ostroh Jews honored Rabbi Edels by naming the Great Maharsha Synagogue after him[734] and preserved his home for a century and a half until, in 1889, it was destroyed by fire.[735]

Edels had a positive attitude toward the secular sciences, considering them important for achieving a fuller understand of the bible. He possessed a knowledge of astronomy and especially philosophy which he studied in depth.

He was sharply critical of social evils, such as the dishonesty and egotism of some of the rich lay leaders of the Jewish community (*"parnasim"*):

"in these times, whoever possesses wealth is appointed to public office for a price and is in constant pursuit of honor."[736]

Rabbi Joel Jaffe Sirkes (the "BaCh" = acronym for his book, *Bayit Chasash* [House of the Holy]) (Lublin 1561 – Kraków 1640)

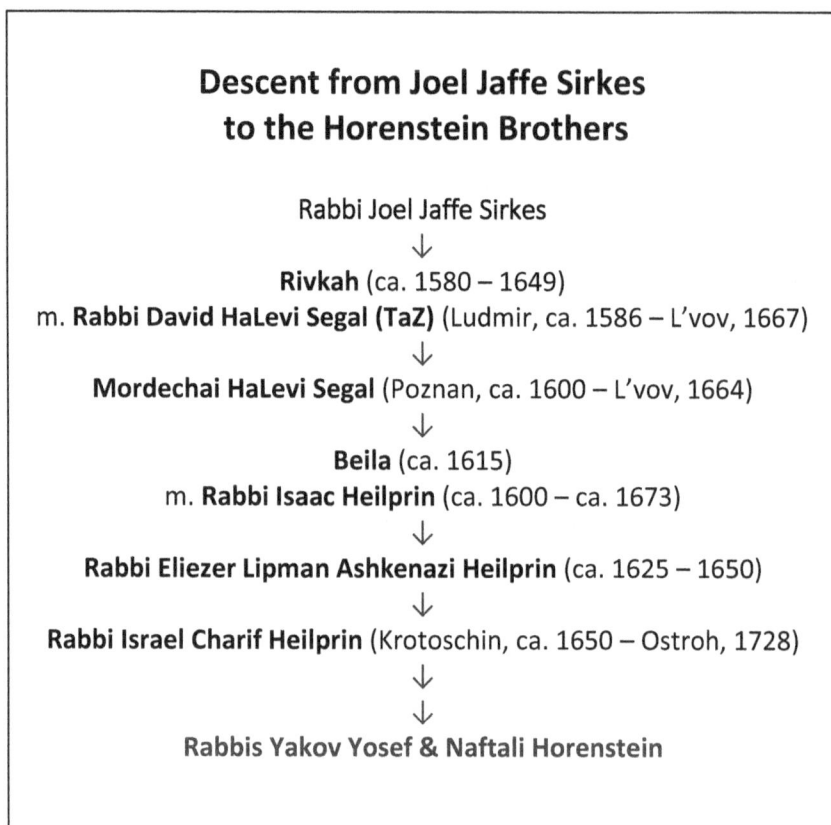

Descent from Joel Jaffe Sirkes to the Horenstein Brothers

Rabbi Joel Jaffe Sirkes
↓
Rivkah (ca. 1580 – 1649)
m. **Rabbi David HaLevi Segal (TaZ)** (Ludmir, ca. 1586 – L'vov, 1667)
↓
Mordechai HaLevi Segal (Poznan, ca. 1600 – L'vov, 1664)
↓
Beila (ca. 1615)
m. **Rabbi Isaac Heilprin** (ca. 1600 – ca. 1673)
↓
Rabbi Eliezer Lipman Ashkenazi Heilprin (ca. 1625 – 1650)
↓
Rabbi Israel Charif Heilprin (Krotoschin, ca. 1650 – Ostroh, 1728)
↓
↓
Rabbis Yakov Yosef & Naftali Horenstein

One of the foremost Talmudic scholars of Central and Eastern Europe, he was an adherent of *Kabbalah* and an opponent of *Pilpul*.[c]

His *magnum opus*, *Bayit Chadash* (House of the Holy), is a commentary on the *Arbah Turim* of Rabbi Jacob ben Asher, which presents and elucidates the fundamental legal principles of the Torah as recorded in the Mishnah, the Babylonian and Jerusalem Talmuds, and the chief codes.

After serving as Rabbi of various towns, in 1618 he was appointed Chief Rabbi of Kraków, the largest Jewish community in Poland. In 1636, he adjudicated a

---

[c] *Pilpul:* study of the Talmud through intense textual analysis.

dispute between the Jewish governing councils of Poland and Lithuania. Afterwards, he was widely acknowledged as the "Rabbi of the Diaspora."

Rabbi Yom Tov Lipman Heller (Wallerstein 1579 – Kraków 1654)

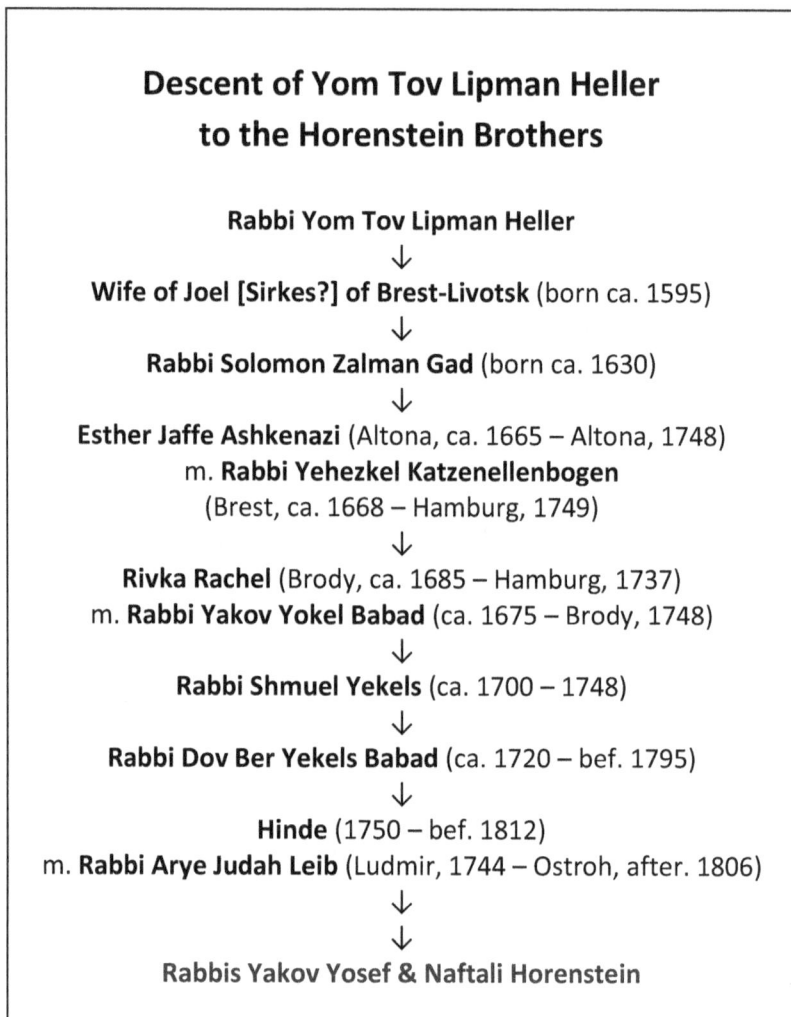

Descent of Yom Tov Lipman Heller
to the Horenstein Brothers

Rabbi Yom Tov Lipman Heller
↓
Wife of Joel [Sirkes?] of Brest-Livotsk (born ca. 1595)
↓
Rabbi Solomon Zalman Gad (born ca. 1630)
↓
Esther Jaffe Ashkenazi (Altona, ca. 1665 – Altona, 1748)
m. **Rabbi Yehezkel Katzenellenbogen**
(Brest, ca. 1668 – Hamburg, 1749)
↓
Rivka Rachel (Brody, ca. 1685 – Hamburg, 1737)
m. **Rabbi Yakov Yokel Babad** (ca. 1675 – Brody, 1748)
↓
Rabbi Shmuel Yekels (ca. 1700 – 1748)
↓
Rabbi Dov Ber Yekels Babad (ca. 1720 – bef. 1795)
↓
Hinde (1750 – bef. 1812)
m. **Rabbi Arye Judah Leib** (Ludmir, 1744 – Ostroh, after. 1806)
↓
↓
Rabbis Yakov Yosef & Naftali Horenstein

An outstanding Talmudic scholar both in Prague and in Poland, best known for writing a commentary on the *Mishneh* called the *Tosafot Yom-Tov*. In 1625, he became the Rabbi of Vienna and obtained the right for Jews to establish a central Jewish community for which he drew up the constitution.

As a youth, he became a disciple of the MaHaRaL of Prague, receiving an appointment as a *dayan* (judge in the religious court) of that city when he was only 18 years old. In 1627, he was elevated to the position of Chief Rabbi of Prague.

Falsely accused of insulting Christianity in the summer of 1629, he was arrested and imprisoned in Vienna. He mounted a spirited self-defense, but was convicted and sentenced to hard labor.

After spending more than a month in prison, an influential court Jew pleaded his case before the Holy Roman Emperor Ferdinand II. He agreed to pay for the rabbi's release, but he was only released on the condition that he resign his post and leave the country.

Rabbi Heller spent two years paying off the fine. He moved to the Ukraine (then part of the Polish-Lithuanian Commonwealth) in 1631. There he served as rabbi of Nemirov for three years before moving to the larger town of Ludmir in Volhynia province. During these years, he was among the rabbinic leaders of the Council of Four Lands.[737]

In 1643, he was elected *Av Beit Din* of Kraków and became one of the two Chief Rabbis of the city. Five years later, he also became head of the Kraków yeshiva.[738]

One of the many tales about him is the story of Yossele the Holy Miser:

"The town leaders had been upset by this rich man's lack of charity so, when he died, they directed that his body be buried in a far corner of the cemetery. A few days later, the town's poor cried out, as they were now struggling to do without Yossele's secret generosity.

"When Rabbi Heller became aware of Yossele's secret, he instructed the town leaders to bury him next to Yossele when his time came."

This story is said to explain why one of the greatest Talmudic scholars is buried in such an undistinguished section of the cemetery.[739]

Rabbi David HaLevi Segal (the "TaZ" = acronym for his book, *Turei Zahav* [Rows of Gold]) (Vladimir-Volynskiy ca. 1586 – L'vov 1667)

The rabbi was born in Vladamir-Volynskiy (Ludmir) in Volhynia gubernia of the Ukraine. His family was both wealthy and known for scholarship.

He married the daughter of Rabbi Joel Jaffe Sirkes (see above). As was customary, he lived in his father-in-law's house for several years while studying Talmud. After he went out on his own, he served as rabbi for various small towns. Those years he and his family suffered from poverty and several of his children died in infancy.

In 1641, due to the growth of his reputation, he was invited to become the Rabbi of Ostroh – which had become famous as a city of scholars. His books soon won worldwide recognition and established him as one of the greatest Talmudic scholars of all time.

This productive period of his life was suddenly interrupted by the riots of the Khmelnytsky Uprising in 1688. He was fortunate enough to flee the town with his manuscripts before the town was captured by the Cossacks. He was subsequently invited to become the Rabbi of L'vov where, only three years before his death at age 81, his two oldest sons were murdered in a pogrom.

Rabbi Abraham Joshua Heshel (Brisk, Poland 1596 – Kraków 1663)

Descent from Abraham Joshua Heshel
to the Horenstein Brothers

Rabbi Abraham Joshua Heshel
↓
Rabbi Issachar Berish (Kraków, ca. 1615 –Kraków, ca. 1700)
↓
Rabbi Isaac Heshel Babad (Brody, ca. 1650 – Brody, 1704)
↓
Reize (Brody, 1675 – Zólkiew, 1710)
m. **Rabbi Israel Charif Heilprin** (Krotoschin, ca. 1650 – Ostroh, 1728)
↓
Daughter m. **Rabbi Saul Fishel**
(ca. 1705 – Ludmir, after 1765)
↓
Rabbi Pinchas (Ludmir, ca. 1725 – Ostroh, 1786)
↓
↓
Rabbis Yakov Yosef & Naftali Horenstein

The wealthy son of the Rabbi of Lublin and head of its yeshiva, Abraham assisted his father as a teacher during his youth. When his father died in 1644, Abraham became head of the yeshiva and then Rabbi of Lublin.

In 1654, he succeeded Yom Tov Lipman Heller (see above) as head of the Kraków yeshiva. His superb reputation as a teacher attracted many students, a number of whom became famous in their own right. Also, his reputation as an authority in Jewish law caused him to receive questions from all over Europe.

Following the Khmelnytsky Uprising, he was commissioned by the Jewish communities of Poland to travel to solicit aid for the victims from the wealthy Jewish communities of Austria, Bohemia and Moravia. He was said to have been received by the emperor of Austria who accorded him great honor.

The *Ḥanukkat ha-Torah* of E. J. Ersohn (1900) contains 600 of Heschel's homilies on the Bible. Events connected with Heschel and his time are recorded in the appendix, *Kunteres Aharon*, which contains both legends and material of histori-cal value.

Rabbi Heshel descends from Rashi both via his father's parents and his mother's father.

POLAND IN THE 17TH CENTURY

By the 17th century, the Jewish community of Poland-Lithuania had become the largest in the Diaspora and was continuing to grow rapidly. Its growth rate was not due to a higher birthrate among Jews as compared to Christians, but to a lower rate of infant mortality.[740] Increasing population contributed to stimulating the movement of Jews to Ukrainian lands, especially after the Union of Lublin in 1569 led to the transfer of these territories to the Polish crown.[741]

A catastrophe was coming, however, for the Jews of south-eastern Poland and the Ukraine. The informal Jewish network that operated during the Thirty Years War (1618-1648) benefitted the Polish landlords at the expense of the Ukrainian peasants, while the Jews were caught in between. Under the arenda system, Jews leased from the Polish nobility, not only land, but all fixed assets (mills, breweries, distilleries, inns, tolls, etc.) in return for payments. The nobility raised the price of each lease each time Jews renewed it. This, in turn, made the Jews to put pressure on the Orthodox peasants, which resulted in increasing anger by the peasants towards both groups.[742]

The Khmelnytsky Uprising

As first discussed in Part One, Bohdan Khmelnytsky, aided by Dneiper Cossacks and Tartars from the Crimean, led a peasant revolt aimed at Polish rule and the Catholic church in the spring of 1648. However, since the Jews, seen as agents of their oppressors, were the people with whom they interacted daily, they received the brunt of their rage. Thousands of Jews fled to the large, fortified towns for safety, but they became death traps. The Poles, under threat themselves, abandoned their Jewish allies in order to save themselves.[743]

The number of Jews who were murdered is uncertain. Possibly as many as 100,000 died along with the destruction of 300 Jewish communities.

Shabbetai Zevi, the False Messiah (1626-1676)

The survivors, made aware once again of the fragility of their existence as a small minority group in a land overwhelmingly populated by others of a different faith, took hope with thoughts of messianic deliverance, while the mysticism of *Kabbalah* gained in stature, aided by the appearance of Shabbetai Zevi, whose agent, Nathan of Gaza, proclaimed him to be the Messiah. This claim became widely accepted until the Turkish sultan gave him the choice of converting to Islam or death - and he chose conversion along with a government pension.[744]

The Grand Duchy of Moscow and The Decline of Poland

The Grand Duchy of Moscow (or Muscovy) was a later medieval Rus' principality centered on Moscow which became the early modern Tsardom of Russia. In the 16th century, it was profoundly anti-Semitic and refused to admit Jews into the country as they regarded them as dangerous magicians and seducers. The exception was occasional visits from Jewish merchants of Poland and Lithuania to Smolensk, a border city – although Jews also illegally visited Moscow on occasion for business reasons.[745]

In 1610, an agreement between the noblemen of Moscow and Poland stipulated that

"... the Jews shall not be allowed to enter the Muscovite Empire either on business or in connection with any other affairs."

Only 40 years later, the Muscovite Empire pushed its way into Poland and Lithuania, a region heavily populated with Jews. Russian troops, allied with the Cossacks, overran White Russia, Lithuania, and the Ukraine where they discovered entire areas populated by this strange people about whom they knew nothing except that they had crucified Christ. In Vilna and Moghilev the Jews were murdered, and those who survived were expelled.

A peace conducted in 1667 between Russia and Poland permitted captive Jews to remain in Moscow, thus starting the nucleus of a small Jewish colony which grew both legally and illegally. Also, Jews who survived the massacres of the Khmelnytsky Uprising occasionally did business in the Polish section of the Ukraine.[746]

Anti-Semitic bias continued under Peter the Great (1672-1725) who, through several wars, expanded the Tsardom into a much larger empire. While he replaced some of the traditional and medieval social and political systems with modern, scientific and westernized ones, he maintained the anti-Semitic prejudice of the past:

"[The Jews] are rogues and cheats. It is my endeavor to eradicate evil and not multiply it. They shall not be allowed either to live or to trade in Russia, whatever efforts they may make, and however much they may try to bribe those near me."[747]

The Horensteins' Famous 17th Century Ancestors

Shabbetai HaKohen Katz, the SHaKH (Vilna or Amstitov, 1621 – Holleschau, 1663)

A 3rd cousin to Rabbi Abraham Joshua Heshel, Shabbetai HaKohen Katz was a noted Talmudist and Halakhist (expert in Jewish law). He was born in Vilna, Lithuania around 1621 to a well-known rabbinical family.

He began his studies with his father, who was *Av Beit Din* in Vilna and, by the age of 12, he was already fully versed in both the Talmud itself and in the vast literature that had accumulated on it. After several further years of study in various cities, he returned to Vilna where he was appointed to the *Beit Din*.[748,749]

In 1646, while in Kraków, he published his *magnum opus*, the *Siftei Kohen* (Lips of the Priest) (also called the "*Shackh*," which is an abbreviation of his name). The book is a commentary on the *Yoreh De'ah*[a] section of the *Shulchan*

---

[a] *Yoreh De'ah*: Section of the *Shulchan Aruch* that covers various aspects of Jewish law that are not pertinent to the Hebrew calendar, finance, torts, marriage, divorce, or sexual conduct.

Aruch.[b] Although he was only 24 years old, the book was approved by 18 of the greatest Polish and Lithuanian Jewish scholars as a brilliant work. Even today it is included in most editions of the *Yoreh De'ah*.[750]

When the Jewish communities of Poland were devastated by the Khmelnytsky Uprising in 1648, he wrote the following:

> *"On the same day 1,500 people were killed in the city of Human in Russia on the Sabbath. The nobles [Cossacks] with whom the wicked mob had again made an alliance chased all the Jews from the city into the fields and vineyards where the villains surrounded them in a circle, stripped them to their skin and ordered them to lie on the ground.*
>
> *"The villains spoke to the Jews with friendly and consoling words: 'Why do you want to be killed, strangled and slaughtered like an offering to your God Who poured out His anger upon you without mercy? Would it not be safer for you to worship our gods, our images and crosses and we would form one people which would unite together.'*
>
> *"But the holy and faithful people who so often allowed themselves to be murdered for the sake of the Lord, raised their voices together to the Almighty in Heaven and cried:*
>
>> *'Hear o Israel the Lord our God, the Holy One and the King of the Universe, we have been murdered for Thy sake so often already. O Lord God of Israel let us remain faithful to Thee'.*
>
> *"Afterward they recited the confession of sins and said:*
>
>> *'We are guilty and thus recognize the Divine judgment'.*
>
> *"Now the villains turned upon them and there was not one of them who did not fall victim."*[751]

In 1655, he, along with the entire Jewish community, had to flee Kraków due to fighting between Polish forces and the invading Swedish army. He subsequently received a rabbinical appointment in Holešov where he remained until his death in 1663.[752]

---

[b] *Shulchan Aruch* ('Set Table'): The most widely consulted of the various Jewish legal codes, written by Joseph Karo in 1563.

Rav Naftali Katz, the *Smichat Chachamim* (Stepan, 1645 – Constantinople, 1719)

Descent from the MaHaRaL of Prague to the *Smichat Chachamim*

Rabbi Judah Loew ben Betzalel
(Worms or Poznan, ca. 1525 – Prague, 1609)
↓
Vögele (Prague, ca. 1555 – Prague, 1629)
m. **Rabbi Yitzchok I Katz** (Vienna, ca. 1550 – Prague, 1624)
↓
Rabbi Naftali Hirsh I Katz (Prague or Frankfurt, ca. 1590 – Lublin, 1648)
↓
Rabbi Yltzchok II Katz (Prague, 1608 – Stepan, 1670)
↓
Rabbi Naftali Hirsh II Katz

He is considered one of the most interesting Jewish rabbinical figures of the 18th century.[753] A man of considerable intellect and high achievement, the story of his life is never-the-less somewhat sad.

Rabbi Katz descended from the marriage of Rabbi Akiva HaKohen Katz of Budin and Chava, granddaughter of Moshe Asher HaLevi Ish Horowitz. He was born in 1645 in the town of Stepan, located within the Volhynia province of the Ukraine. He studied in Przemysl, then Miedzyrec, and finally in Fiorda.

When he was about 18 years old, he was captured by Tatars who had invaded the country. They kept the young man in servitude for several years. Eventually, he managed to escape and return to Stepan.[754]

He later succeeded his father as the town's *Av Beit Din* and married Esther Sheindl, the daughter of Shmuel Shmelke Zak, *Av Beit Din* of Ostroh. There he headed a yeshiva which his father-in-law built for him.

צורת הגאון מ"וה נפתלי כהן ז"ל
אב"ד דק"ק פאזנן ופפ"ד רמ' ובו'

Naftali Kohen.

Oberrabbiner zu Posen, FF. a. M. etc.

Rabbi Katz was appointed *Av Beit Din* of Ostroh (1680-1689) following the death of Rabbi Shmuel. As his reputation grew, he went on to become *Av Beit Din* of Posen (1690–1704) where he was chosen to become head of the Council of Four Lands.

While living in Posen, he devoted himself to *Kabbalah* and collected a large library of Kabbalistic literature. He was a believer, not only in the mainstream tradition of Theoretical *Kabbalah*, but also in the controversial Practical *Kabbalah*, a type of magic which involves the use of amulets to control events. It was the latter belief that was to cause him grief on two different occasions.

In 1704 he accepted the prestigious position of *Av Beit Din* of Frankfurt. Several years later, on January 14, 1711, a fire broke out in his house and quickly spread. Soon it destroyed the entire Jewish quarter which consisted of several hundred homes. Four people died in the incident.

Since he was a believer in Practical *Kabbalah*, he was maliciously charged with limiting his efforts to stop the fire to attempts to harness the power of his amulets for that purpose. The Frankfurt Jews did not make this accusation as they valued the rabbi's holiness "even more than the wood and stones used to build the city."[755] He was imprisoned, however, by the local governmental authorities, and only regained his freedom in exchange for leaving Frankfurt.[756]

He initially went to Prague, where many family members lived, and stayed at the house of Rabbi David Oppenheim, the Chief Rabbi of the city. Rabbi Oppenheim's house was to be the setting for a second incident to falsely impugn his integrity, as it was there that he met the Kabbalist Nehemiah Hayon.[757] A man of scholarly mien, Hayon declared that he was a preacher, an emissary from the Land of Israel, and gained the confidence of the credulous rabbi. Hayon began to sell amulets, but the rabbi, himself a believer in Practical *Kabbalah*, saw no fault in that activity.

One day Hayon asked Rabbi Katz for an approbation (endorsement) for his mystical work *Mehemnuta de-Kula*. He submitted to him a few innocuous pages of the main text, but was careful to leave out the accompanying commentaries which, for example, professed the Catholic doctrine of the Trinity. Rabbi Katz granted his request and provided him with a glowing recommendation.

Armed with the recommendation of the former *Av Beit Din* of Frankfurt, as well with as other recommendations secured with the same duplicity, Hayon traveled throughout Moravia and Silesia, propagating his Sabbatian[c] teachings.

In 1713, Rabbi Katz was appointed Rabbi of Breslau. There, to his dismay, he learned from Zvi Ashkenazi (the *"Chacham Zvi"*), Rabbi of Amsterdam, details of the tenets of Hayon's book which the rabbinate of Rome referred to as *Minuta de-Kula* (total heresy) and the rabbinate of Ferrara as *Mebenmuta de-Kula Ra'ah* (completely evil faith).[758] When Rabbi Katz discovered that he had been deceived, he attempted, but without success, to revoke his approbation.[759]

---

[c] Sabbatianism: A popular Jewish movement which claimed that Shabbatai Tzvi (1626-1676) was the Messiah.

The rabbi admitted that:

"I did give him a haskamah (approbation; endorsement) on his heretical book. I sinned out of ignorance.... If the Av Beit Din [David Oppenheim] had been at home at the time surely he would have given zealous pursuit, but he was away, and his sons were beguiled by Havon's smooth tongue....

"The treatise called Mehemnuta de-Kola I have never seen, nor his two commentaries which frame it.... I only saw a few innocuous pages ... and now, upon reading the excerpts ... I can wrench the hair out of my head over my blunder in this matter."[760]

He immediately launched a ban against the book and its author and became one of the most zealous supporters of the rabbi of Amsterdam in his campaign against Hayon.[761]

Two years later, King Augustus of Poland rejected Rabbi Katz's application to be restored to his post as rabbi of Posen because of the opposition of community leaders. He therefore returned to Ostroh where his son Betzalel was now rabbi.

In 1719, at the age of 74, he undertook a journey to the Land of Israel but never completed his journey as he fell ill along the way. He died on December 20, 1718 in Orta Kiya, then a village near Constantinople, and now a suburb of the city. His grave, in the Ortaköy Cemetery, continues to attract many religious Jews who come to pray at it.

Rabbi Katz was not only considered to be one of the greatest Kabbalists of Poland,[762] but was also considered one of his generation's most important authorities in *Halakhah*, although his writings in this field have been lost.[763]

He had a special interest in ethical questions related to terminal illness, as well as in death customs. In *Birkat HaShem* (Blessing of the Lord), published while he was Chief Rabbi of Frankfurt, he discussed issues related to the origin and nature of death. In his Ethical Will,[d] Rabbi Naftali included detailed death rituals for when his own death will occur. Because of his fame, his Ethical Will had such wide appeal that it was printed more than 20 times in the following two centuries.[764]

In the book, he was quite clear in stating how he wished to be remembered:

---

[d] Ethical Will: The Jewish custom of sharing values and life's lessons with others through writing. It is not a legal document and does not concern the distribution of personal wealth.

"It is my order, on penalty of the ban of my fathers, that I shall not be eulogized anywhere. Letters should be sent to every place where the couriers reach, that I have ordered, on penalty of a ban, that I should not be eulogized, neither in the cemetery nor in the synagogue. Even without a eulogy, I should not be praised by any title, as righteous or pious, and so on. This is the only way I wish to be praised:

'That he was accustomed to study page by page, and was well versed even in homilies, and was close to the truth in everything.'

"This will I speak in the world of Truth, even against kings, and I will not be ashamed. What was done to me in this world of Falsehood was due to pride and jealousy."[765]

Of special interest is a leaf of the book containing a poem, written by the author and shaped like a star, relating "happenings and events" he had experienced:

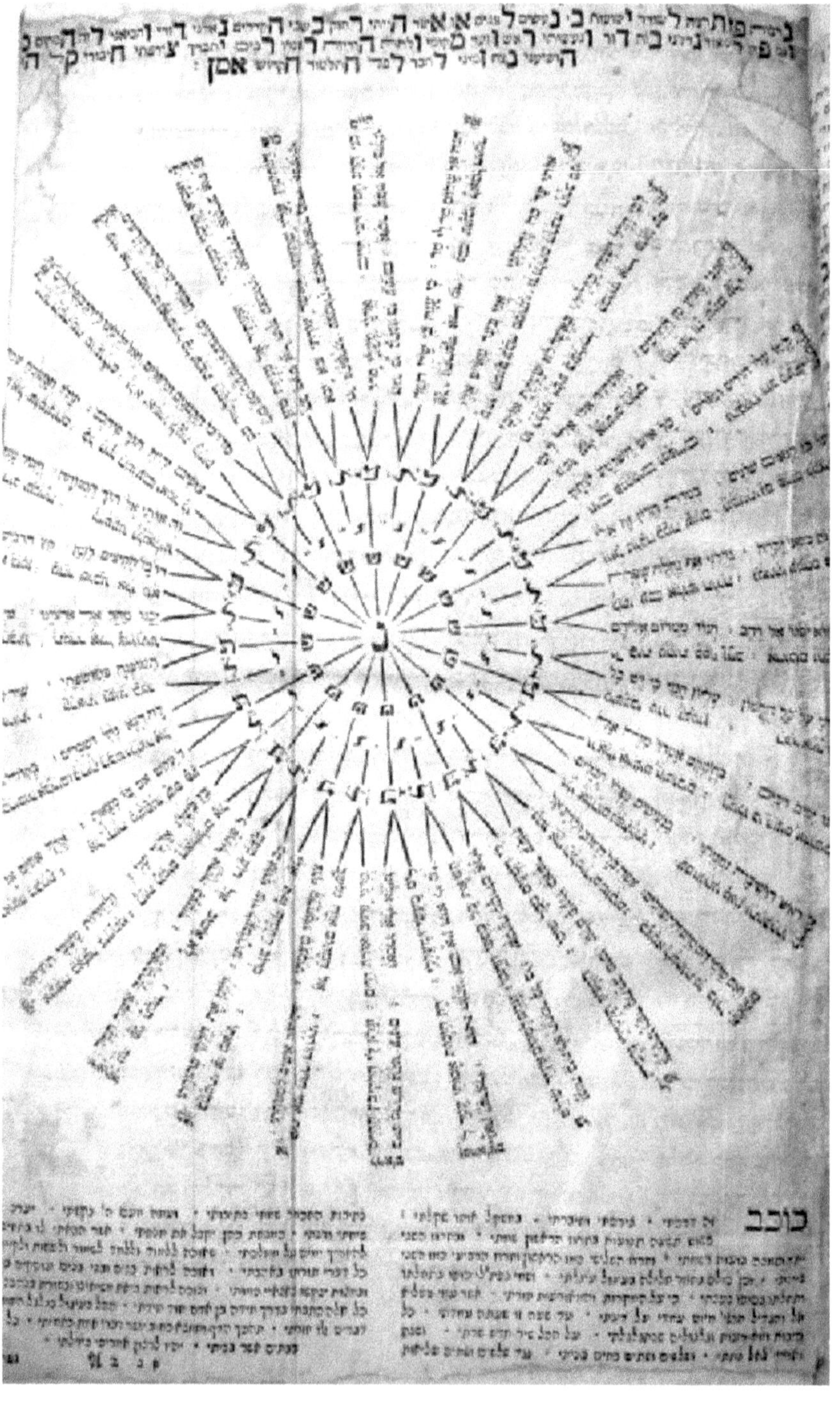
כוכב
אמן

Smichat Chachamim (Applying Intelligence) is his main book of homilies. It became so well known that, to this day, Rabbi Katz is respectfully referred to as "the *Smichat Chachamim*."

In the book, he explains the rationale behind the order of the Talmudic tractates, as well as the spiritual essence of each one, so that ordinary people would be able to review the main issues covered in the tractate on a daily basis, including on the day of their deaths.[766] His writings also include poetry and *midrash*.

The Horensteins descend from Rabbi Katz via three of his 13 children: his son, Rabbi Betzalel, and his daughters, Shprintze and Eidel.

Descent from the *Smichat Chachamim* to the Horenstein Brothers
(one of three descent lines)

Rabbi Naftali Hirsh II Katz (Stepan, 1645 – Constantinople, 1719)
↓
Rabbi Betzalel HaKohen Katz (ca. 1680 – Ostroh, 1717)
↓
Wife of Dov Ber Babad (Ostroh, ca. 1715)
↓
Hinde (1750 – bef. 1812)
m. **Arye Judah Leib** (Ludmir, 1744 – Ostroh, after 1806)
↓
Rabbi Shmuel Asher (1770 – Berestechko, 1840)
↓
Rabbi Yakov Yosef & Naftali Horenstein

Rabbi Naftali Katz was the last of the great rabbinical scholars in the Horensteins' descent line, although males in the line usually continued the long tradition of becoming rabbis. When, in the latter part of the 19th century, the wealthy Horenstein brothers achieved prominence in the Jewish communities of the Ukraine, Rabbi Naftali Katz still remained the closest ancestor claimed by the family to demonstrate their *yichus* as, a century after his demise, his name was still highly respected by the region's Jewish community.[e]

---

[e] It appears that this claim first appeared in print in 1977/8 (5738) on page 39 of *Shalshelet HaYuchasin* by Rabbi Yosef Lieberman, himself a Horenstein descendant and the 8th great grandson of Rav Naftali Katz:
"*Gur Arieh HaKohen [was]*
g) *son of the brilliant rabbi, Shmuel HaKohen; [who was]*
h) *a descendant of our master, Naftali Ka"tz, author of Semikhat Chakhamim.*"

Subsequent ancestors of the Horenstein brothers made no further contributions to Jewish scholarship, although they sometimes continued to serve Jewish communities as *Av Beth Din* and played an active role in contributing to the communities' welfare.

PART THREE

THREE PARTICULARLY FAMOUS 19TH CENTURY COUSINS

While I have focused this book on the ancestors of the Horenstein rabbinical family, I also want to mention three particularly famous Horenstein cousins out of the multitude of names found in such an extensive family tree. Not by coincidence, all three of these cousins lived in the 19th century when the great historical divide between Jewish and Christian societies eroded.

An extensive family tree such as the one we have just reviewed contains numerous ancestors, and we have reviewed some of the most outstanding. Despite their remarkable achievements, few are known outside of the Jewish world.

In the 19th century, as Jews increasingly integrated into the surrounding Christian society, they began to pursue fields of endeavor beyond those directed towards Jewish audiences. This resulted in an enormous expansion of their audience and the possibility of becoming world-famous, although often at the expense of their commitment to Judaism.

Out of the multitude of relatives found in this extensive family tree, these were the Horenstein cousins whose contributions have reverberated most strongly throughout the entire world.

They are listed in the order of their births.

Drawing by Friedrich Wilhelm Schadow

Jakob Ludwig Felix Mendelssohn Bartholdy
(1809-1847)

The Horenstein brothers' 5th cousin, 3 times removed

Widely known as Felix Mendelssohn, he was a German composer, pianist, organist and conductor of the early Romantic period of Western classical music.

A grandson of the famous Jewish philosopher Moses Mendelssohn, Felix was born into a prominent Jewish family. He was brought up without religion until the age of seven when he was baptized as a Reformed Christian.

Recognized early as a musical prodigy, he wrote symphonies, concertos, oratorios, piano and chamber music. His best-known works include his overture and incidental music for A Midsummer Night's Dream, the Italian Symphony, the Scottish Symphony, the Overture to The Hebrides, his mature Violin

Concerto, and his String Octet. His Songs Without Words are his most famous solo piano compositions.

He incorporated both Classical and Romantic sources into his own compositions in addition to influences of Italian Renaissance composers and J. S. Bach, combined with his highly original contributions. While his musical language is missing the harmonic or structural innovations on the scale of Beethoven or Wagner, his many finely-crafted works display the uniqueness of his personal style.[767]

His compositions were conservative for the time, and he was unappreciated, especially after his death, due both to anti-Semitism and to changing musical tastes in the late 19th and early 20th centuries. Now, however, his creative originality is appreciated and he is among the most popular composers of the Romantic era.[768,769] Still, however, several of his works are only now being published.

In addition, he almost singlehandedly revived the works of Johann Sebastian Bach who, due to his efforts, was reestablished at the forefront of Western music.

In some ways, his musical career resembles that of Jascha Horenstein, Mendelssohn's 5th cousin five times removed, a century later. Neither would have become world-famous if he had not broken out of the insularity of the Jewish world. Also, neither was fully appreciated until after his death.

Mendelssohn died in Leipzig on November 4, 1847, at the age of thirty-eight.

Daguerreotype by John Jabez Edwin Mayall

Karl Marx
(1818-1883)

The Horenstein brothers' 7th cousin, once removed

German philosopher, economist, historian, political theorist, sociologist, journalist and revolutionary socialist, Marx has been described as one of the most influential figures in human history.[770]

Born in Trier,[a] Prussia, the 3rd of nine children, his maternal grandfather was a Dutch rabbi, while his paternal line had supplied Trier's rabbis since 1723. His father, who had received a secular education, became a lawyer. To escape the constraints of anti-Semitic legislation, he converted to Lutheranism, changing his given name from Herschel to Heinrich.

Karl was particularly interested in studying political economy and Hegelian philosophy. He spent much of his life in London, England, where he collaborated with Friedrich Engels. His theories about society, economics and politics – called "Marxism" - hold that human societies develop through class struggle. In capitalism, this manifests itself in the conflict between the ruling classes (known as the bourgeoisie) that control the means of production and working classes (known as the proletariat) that enable these means by selling their labor power in return for wages.

He predicted that, like previous socioeconomic systems, capitalism would produce internal tensions which would lead to its self-destruction and replacement by a new system: socialism. For Marx, class antagonisms under capitalism, owing in part to its instability and crisis-prone nature, would eventuate the working class' development of class consciousness, leading to their conquest of political power and eventually the establishment of a classless, communist society constituted by a free association of producers.

Marx actively fought for the implementation of communism as he defined it, arguing that the working class should carry out organized revolutionary action to topple capitalism and bring about socio-economic emancipation. His two most well-known works are the pamphlet The Communist Manifesto and the three-volume *Das Kapital*. His work had a major influence on subsequent intellectual, economic and political history.[771]

He had no Jewish education and no interest in acquiring any, yet Paul Johnson, in A History of the Jews, states that "there can be no question about his Jewishness." Johnson backs up this assertion with several points:

- Marx's sense of history as a positive and dynamic force in human society, governed by iron laws, is profoundly Jewish as it is an "atheist's Torah."
- His concept of a Communist millennium is deeply rooted in Jewish messianic and apocalyptic ideas.
- Ruling, according to Marx, was up to the elite intelligentsia, who had studied the texts and understood the laws of history, while the proletariat, like that of the "people of the land" as described in the Jewish bible, ignorant of the laws, had the duty to obey.
- Marx's methodology was wholly rabbinical as his conclusions were entirely derived from books rather than from real-life experiences.

---

[a] Formerly Trèves, the town of origin of the Horensteins' Trèves ancestors.

- His work, while he called it "scientific," was more akin to religious theology or superstition than science, without any objective, empirical research.

Marx's anti-Semitism, according to Johnson, is typical of a person struggling to free himself from his own Jewishness.[772]

He died in London on March 14, 1883 after years in both creative and physical decline.

Photo by Max Halberstadt

Sigmund Freud
(1856-1939)

The Horenstein brothers' 5th cousin, twice removed

Born Sigismund Schlomo Freud, Freud was born to Jewish parents in the town of Freiberg, in the Austrian Empire (later Příbor, Czech Republic). His parents were from Galicia, in modern-day Ukraine. His father, Jakob Freud (1815–1896), was a struggling wool merchant.

Jakob's family were Hasidic Jews, and although Jakob himself had moved away from the tradition, he came to be known for his Torah study. Freud's mother, Amalia Nathansohn, was Jakob's third wife.

The first of eight children, Sigmund became a neurologist and was the founder of psychoanalysis, a clinical method for treating psychopathology through dialogue between a patient and a psychoanalyst. Though in overall decline in clinical practice, psychoanalysis remains influential within psychology, psychiatry, and psychotherapy, and across the humanities.

He began his study of medicine at the University of Vienna in 1873. Afterwards he collaborated with Josef Breuer in treating hysteria by having patients recall painful experiences while under hypnosis. In 1885, Freud moved to Paris where he studied neurology under Jean Charcot.

Freud began his private practice in 1886 as a specialist in nervous and brain disorders. He developed the theory that humans have an unconscious in which sexual and aggressive impulses are in perpetual conflict for supremacy with the defenses against them. "The Interpretation of Dreams," his major work, was published in 1900. In the book, he analyzed dreams as manifestations of unconscious desires. After World War One, he concentrated on the application of his theories to history, art, literature and anthropology.[773]

Freud's Jewish origins and his allegiance to his secular Jewish identity were of significant influence in the formation of his intellectual and moral outlook, especially with respect to his intellectual non-conformism, as he noted in his *Autobiographical Study*. They would also have a substantial effect on the content of psychoanalytic ideas.[774]

He was diagnosed with cancer of the jaw in 1923, and underwent over 30 operations before he finally died of cancer on September 23, 1939.

Freud's work has suffused contemporary Western thought as well as popular culture. In a poetic tribute written shortly after his death, W. H. Auden wrote:

"to us he is no more a person
Now but a whole climate of opinion
Under whom we conduct our different lives."[775]

COMMENT

While this book concerns the genealogy of a Jewish family, none of these three great men was a religious Jew; in fact, both Marx and Mendelssohn were at least nominally Christian. This is undoubtedly one of the reasons why they became so famous throughout the Christian world, in stark contrast to the Horenstein family's religious ancestors whose numerous literary, scientific and poetic contributions were directed exclusively towards the Jewish world and who were therefore essentially unknown outside of it.

You would never guess it, but both Felix Mendelssohn and Karl Marx descend from the same couple: Rabbi Meir Wahl Katzenellenbogen and Hinde Halevi Horowitz, born about 1560, each representing one of the great European Jewish rabbinical families.[b,c] (They are the Horenstein brothers' 7th great grandparents.)

Meir, known as the "MaHaRasH," was the son of Saul Wahl Katzenellenbogen, the putative "One Day King" of Poland (see Part II, Chapter 6), while Hinde was the daughter of Rabbi Pinchas HaLevi Horowitz, a distinguished rabbi who became principal of the Kraków yeshiva. He also was integral in the formation of the Council of the Land of Lithuania (the controlling legal body for Lithuanian Jews), as well as a leader of the Council of Four Lands. Meir and Hinde themselves were close cousins.

Sigmund Freud's descent line is different as he descends from the marriage of Rabbi Jacob Fishel Kloizner and Hinde Katzenellenbogen which occurred around 1700. (They are the Horenstein brothers' 4th great grandparents.)

---

[b] For Felix Mendelssohn, the line of descent is via their son, Judah Katzenellenbogen → Saul Wahl Katzenellenbogen → Bela Rachel Katzenellenbogen Wahl → Moses Mendelssohn → Abraham Bartholdy Mendelssohn → Felix Mendelssohn-Bartholdy.

[c] For Karl Marx, the line of descent is via their daughter, Nissele Wahl Katzenellenbogen → the wife of Joseph Samuel of Frankfurt → their daughter (wife of Aaron Moses Ezekiel) → Joshua Heschel Lwow → Moses Lwow → Eva, wife of Marx Levi → Herschel Levy (Heinrich Marx) → Karl Marx.

PART FOUR

A FINAL LOOK BACK

"It becomes incumbent on every head of family to prepare a yuchsin [yikhus] chart for his offspring. It is not just family pride that the yuchsin chart is to emphasize, but to teach children who their ancestors were so as to charge them to follow in their paths. On the contrary, they should feel more culpable if they failed in life having had such great parents. Why did they not emulate their good ways?"

Rabbi Sheftel (Shabtai) HaLevi Horowitz (1590-1660). *Vavei HaAmjudim*

We have now completed our virtual journey through the Horensteins' early ancestry. Along the way, we have witnessed some of the twists and turns of Jewish history, with times of plenty and times of tragedy. Looking backwards from the 21st century, a single overriding historical theme has been central to Jewish life for many centuries: After existing as an independent nation under King David and his successors, Jews lost their kingdom in battle and became a minority group living in lands ruled by other peoples, making their existence there precarious.

When conditions grew ominous, or when better opportunities presented themselves elsewhere, they often moved from the country of their birth to another, more inviting, land. Thus, many of the Horenstein ancestors were born in one country and died in another. At times their host nations attempted to convert them to the majority religion, but many Jews remained loyal to their heritage, even when this decision resulted in expulsion, or even in martyrdom.

While the laws of their host nation were primary, Jews were usually permitted limited self-government, with specific areas of independence as determined by the ruling power. Jewish self-government, based on principles first elucidated in the Torah and later expanded in the Talmud, included a comprehensive system of laws which, for the most part, functioned independently of the laws of the ruling nation. This combination of religion and law proved a formidable glue which kept the Jewish people together through repeated catastrophes, most of which were imposed by outside forces.

This same theme, begun with the Babylonian Exile in the sixth century BCE, was still playing out when, in the early 19th century, the Horenstein brothers were born. Jews in Russia constituted a visible, and largely unwelcome, minority group with a distinctive appearance, distinctive language and customs, separate religious institutions, separate communal buildings and separate communal administrations. They were foreigners, even in the land of their birth.

They were a common sight in the Pale of Settlement where they were permitted to live but, although they interacted regularly with the non-Jewish majority, their relationships with Christians were usually superficial and business-oriented, leaving their neighbors more susceptible to anti-Semitic lies. Such lies fanned the flames of bigotry and justified heinous, barbaric actions against the peaceful Jews.

While the Horenstein brothers had to grabble with these issues, the origin of their fortune may have been an exception to the rule: a generous Christian noble who decided to give his young Hasidic clerk the opportunity to achieve his wish to become wealthy.

CLOSING THOUGHTS

There are large gaps in our knowledge of the personalities of the Horenstein brothers and their progeny. By putting together what we do know, however, we can begin to compare and contrast the two of them.

Yakov Yosef and Naftali Horenstein were, in some ways, so alike that they almost seemed like twins. Both were steadfast Hasidic Jews whose dress, behavior, and basic sense of values were typical of *Hasidim*. In conformity with Hasidic norms, they displayed and enjoyed their wealth, and they were generous to the needy. Moreover, the strength of their character was never in question.

There were, however, important differences between them. The specifics are unclear, but Yakov Yosef had a psychological problem. While this problem was not serious, neither was it minor, as this problem appears to be the reason why the tension between the two brothers reached the point where Naftali had to move to another town just to minimize their direct interactions.

To guess, Yakov Yosef's problem appears to have been his underlying insecurity, insecurity that he covered up with egotistical behavior which increasingly offended Naftali and worried their *rebbe*.

Of the two brothers, Yakov Yosef was more interested in displaying his wealth to the public; even his considerable charitable donations were often made in a very public manner. Naftali lived well but more modestly than his brother, and was less concerned with such public displays.

The two brothers differed more sharply in the manner in which they raised their sons. Yakov Yosef seems to have encouraged his sons to spend as lavishly as he did and apparently failed to prepare them to take over the responsibilities of running his business enterprises. Naftali, by contrast, raised his sons to be responsible, hard-working, generous, religious young men who were fully capable of assuming control over his financial empire.

The result is hardly surprising: There is no evidence that Yakov Yosef's sons were able to manage their father's businesses; even his grand estate fell into ruins. After their father's death, Yakov Yosef's sons disappeared from our view; no documents have been found which describe their lives and progeny. The single exception is a prophetic folk tale in which Leibush, his oldest son, refuses to promise Rabbi Avraham Yakov of Sadigura that he will earn a good livelihood because he may be unable to break away from his "habits," namely a life focused on indulgence in extravagances.

Naftali's sons, by contrast, easily took over their father's business operations. They even formalized the charitable giving which had been so important to Naftali by opening up an office purely for this purpose.

All of Naftali's six sons were rabbis and all were as charitable as their father had been. Besides their many common characteristics, Radomysl Horenstein businesses were often owned by multiple partners. Thus, when discussing them, the Jewish public found it difficult to separate the six brothers out by their given names. This resulted in the unusual practice of any one of the brothers being identified simply by the family surname; the given name of the brother seemed to make little difference since he acted so much like his siblings.

Yakov Yosef and Naftali became an inspiration to the Jews of the region. Why? In part because they were so successful despite the anti-Semitic currents in Russia, yet most other wealthy Russian Jews were not the folk they were.

There appear to be at least two reasons for their popularity. The first was that, despite their wealth, they continued to act like, and dress like, *Hasidim*, rather than emulating the Christian population. The second was their personal, and often quite public, style of giving, whether the unusual manner in which Yakov Yosef chose to distribute money to the poor, or the annual Passover festivities held at Naftali's estate which were open to the entire community. Their frequent practice of throwing money to the poor from lavish horse-drawn carriages was another characteristic certain to be part of community gossip.

The two brothers remained Hasidic to the core, both in dress and behavior, showing the average Jew that, despite the difficulties, wealth and success could be achieved in Russia without having to hide your Jewish roots. They thus served as an important role model for the impoverished Jewish population, and gave people hope of a better tomorrow. That is, until the massive upheavals in the early 20th century changed everything.

Superficial, external changes in some of the men of the family could be noted even earlier. The obvious example was Avrum HaKohen Horenstein who, while remaining a loyal Boyaner, trimmed his beard and spent most of his week dressed in public as a wealthy Russian citizen.

The Radomysl Horenstein children who fled to Europe and Israel due to the Bolshevik Revolution made much greater lifestyle changes when they reached adulthood. They wore Western dress and the men usually shaved. Although some maintained ties to the Boyaner court, the Hasidic lifestyle was fading out.

The next generation in Europe further integrated into the surrounding Christian world. For example, while Jascha Horenstein, the famous conductor, initially married a Jewish woman, following her death, he married a Christian opera singer.

The Radomysl Horensteins were representative of this gradual drift away from traditional Judaism by Jews whose lives were no longer focused within their minority group, semi-isolated from the surrounding Christian world. As they became better accepted in that world, they also became more comfortable with it.

Concurrently, as the physical distances between family members grew, traditional family bonds loosened.

Today the Horensteins and their immediate cousins, located mainly in Israel and the United States, are well educated and fairly prosperous. Most remain Jewish, although they vary widely in regard to their religiosity, and none is known to claim loyalty to the Boyaner Hasidic court.

The unusual world of the fabulously wealthy Horenstein brothers has vanished, but many of their progeny, despite the vicissitudes of the 20th century, have managed to survive, and sometimes to prosper.

What has been lost is, not only their fortune, but also the family's distinctive characteristics, the stuff that generated the many folk tales. However, no matter what the characteristics of the Horensteins of the future will be, they will remain a family blessed with *yichus*.

APPENDICES

Appendix One
from Part I, Chapter Three

Issue One: Is Hinde Berkova the daughter of Berko Yekels?

Hypothesis

"Hinde Berkova," listed in the 1795 Ostroh Census as the wife of Arye Leib, is the daughter of Dov Ber (Berko) and Perl Katz Yekels - and therefore Rabbi Nachman Katz's niece.

There are several reasons to strongly suspect that Hinde Berkova is Hinde Yekels, daughter of Dov Ber (Berko) Yekels:

- The time period and location match.
- Arye Leib's 1st wife was the daughter of Nachman Katz, a fellow member of the Ostroh *chevra kadisha*. If we assume the probable scenario that Arye Leib's 1st wife died in childbirth, it would not be surprising, based on the customs of the time, for him to choose a close relative of Rabbi Katz as his 2nd wife.
- Although Nachman Katz did not have another daughter available for marriage, one of his daughters had married Dov Ber (Berko) Yekels who, like Nachman and Arye Leib, was a member of the the *chevra kadisha*.[776] I propose that this daughter and Berko Yekels were the parents of Hinde Berkova, the 2nd wife of Arye Leib.

There is further evidence that is consistent with this hypothesis:

- Menachem Mendel Biber, writing in *Mazkeret LeGedolei Ostroha* states that:

> *"Rabbi Dov Ber [Yekels] had a daughter, whose name was Sarah."*[777]

Although Biber does not mention Hinde as another daughter, it is likely that Dov Ber had other daughters because, before mentioning Sarah, he states that:

"among the sons of Rabbi Dov Ber [Berko] is Rabbi Tzvi Hirsh, a gabbai of the Ostroh chevra kadisha."[778]

Thus, as Berko had multiple sons, he probably also had multiple daughters.

• Biber's quotation indicates that Rabbi Tzvi Hirsh was another member of the *chevra kadisha*. Moreover, Berko's daughter Sarah married R. Asher Enzil Babad,[779,780] *gabbai* and *parnas* of the *chevra kadisha*. Thus, Berko would probably have wanted Hinde to marry a member of the *chevra kadisha*.

• As a previous *Av Beit Din* of Ludmir, as the treasurer of the Ostroh *chevra kadisha*, as a Merchant of the 3rd Guild, and as a man coming from a respected family, Berko would have considered Arye Leib to have had the perfect credentials to be a prospective husband for Hinde.

• In 1770, Hinde gave birth to a baby boy named Shmuel.[781] If Hinde's identity is correct, her great grandfather would have been Shmuel Babad (d. 1748).[782] Thus, the choice of Samuel for the name of her son is consistent with Jewish naming customs and adds further support to the hypothesis.

Conclusion

While the evidence is not definitive, it is highly probable that *"Hinde, daughter of Berko,"* listed in the 1795 Ostroh Census as the wife of Arye Judah Leib, refers to the daughter of Rabbi Dov Ber Yekels and niece of Rabbi Nachman Katz.

Issue Two: Is Shmuel Asher identical to Shmuel Horenstein?

Hypothesis One

"Shmuel Leibovich," listed this way in the 1795 Ostroh Census, *is* Shmuel <u>Asher</u> Leibovich, son of Aryeh Leib of Ludmir.

Review of the Evidence

• In the style that names were listed in the Census, Shmuel Asher would have been listed as *"Shmuel Leibovich."* He is the only Shmuel Leibovich (except for a 1-year-old temporary resident) to be listed in the 1795 Ostroh District Census, and Ostroh is the known location of Shmuel Asher.[783]

- The Accounts Book of the Ostroh *chevra kadisha* records the day when Rabbi Aryeh Leib, son of Rabbi Pinchas, presented his young son Shmuel to serve there when he grows up.[784]
- [Aryeh] Leib was born in 1741; his son, Shmuel Leibovich, was born in 1770.[785] While Shmuel Asher's year of birth is unknown, he first ran for election as a treasury executive of the burial society in 5554 (1793-4).[786] Assuming the two men are the same person, he would have been in his early 20s at the time, a reasonable age at which to run for such an office.
- Pinchas, Shmuel Asher's grandfather, died in Ostroh in 1786,[787] while Shmuel Leibovich had a son born in 1790 who he named Pinchas. This would be in accord with Jewish naming customs, thus confirming the hypothesis.
- Shmuel Asher's uncle, Rabbi Yoel Katz (a great grandson of the *Smichat Chachamim*), along with his wife and mother, resided in house #112 of the Old Town district of Ostroh, probably only six doors away from the home of Shmuel Leibovich.[788] This apparent physical closeness of their homes increases the likelihood that the two Shmuels are identical.

[Note: The above identification of Rabbi Yoel Katz in the 1795 Ostroh Census is definitive: he is listed as the son of Nachman, and his mother, listed as "Zolda Khaimovna," is known from rabbinical genealogies to be Zelda, the daughter of Chaim Rapaport.]

Conflicting Evidence

Shmuel Asher is listed as having being born in 1770,[789] while Shmuel Horenstein was listed a half century later as having being born in 1778.[790] This difference, while troublesome, is common enough in such records to be insufficient to indicate that the two Shmuels were different men. For example, it could have been due to a scribal error, an unclear notation of the last digit causing it to be misread by the transcriber, or Shmuel's decision to change his official year of birth for personal reasons.

Hypothesis Two

Later in life, Shmuel Asher Leibovich adopted the Horenstein surname to become Shmuel Leibovich Horenstein.

Review of the Evidence

• The last known listing of Shmuel Asher was between 1800 and 1801 (i.e. 5561 on the Hebrew calendar),[791] shortly before surnames became mandatory in 1804. By the time of 1816 Census, he would probably have been listed with his new surname. ("Asher," an appellation, would likely have been replaced by the surname.)

• The descendants of Shmuel Leibovich Horenstein claim descent from Rav Naftali Katz, the *Smichat Chachamim*; similarly, Shmuel Asher is known to descend from the *Smichat Chachamim*.

• By 1834, Shmuel Leibovich Horenstein was living in Berestechko. Both Shmuel Asher's great grandfather and one of his great grandfather's sons had served as *Av Beit Din* of Berestechko, suggesting that he may have moved there because family members were still living in the town.

• There is considerable evidence that Shmuel, both when he was listed as Shmuel Leibovich, and when he was listed as Shmuel Horenstein, had a brother named David.

1. In 1795, within Ostroh's Old Town, the Census lists "Shmuel Leibovich" (Shmuel, son of Leib) as residing in house #106. Assuming that house numbers were consecutive, "Duvid Leibovich" was residing only four houses away in house #102. The closeness of their homes suggests that Shmuel and Duvid may have been sons of the same Leib and thus brothers. (Both are listed as having been born in 1770; however, birth years were often inaccurate.)

2. In the entire 1850 Berestechko Census, only two families are listed with the Horenstein surname: one is the family of "Shmuel Leibovich Horenstein," while the other is the family of "Duvid Horenstein," suggesting that both men had moved from Ostroh to Berestechko and had acquired the same surname.

3. Based on Jewish naming customs, the names of Duvid's two sons and grandson are entirely consistent with those of members of Shmuel's family:

• Duvid's first son was named Pinchas (b. 1797), the same name as that of Shmuel's grandfather who had died in Ostroh 11 years earlier.

• Duvid's second son was named Saul, the same name as that of Shmuel's great grandfather who had been *Av Beit Din* of Berestechko.

• Duvid's son Saul eventually had his own son who Saul named Gur-arye, an extremely rare given name outside of the same Horenstein family.

Conflicting Evidence

Based on their ages listed on different censuses, Shmuel Asher's son Shimon was born about 1792,[792] as were Shmuel Horenstein's sons Avel[793] and Gur-arye.[794]

However, this data is taken from three different censuses, with each conducted at a different date in the year. Although we do not know that exact dates two of these censuses were conducted, the dates of birth could thus have been up to a year apart. Moreover, it was common for the birth years listed in such records to be inexact and thus they could differ in different census records.

Thus, this conflicting evidence must be viewed with skepticism.

Final Conclusion

Judging on the quality of the evidence, it is highly likely that Shmuel Asher Leibovich became Shmuel Leibovich Horenstein.

Appendix Two

from Part I, Chapter Five

"HORENSTEIN FAMILY RABBIS: FATHERS OF THE FAMILY"

Rachel [Horenstein] Landau (b. 1882), daughter of Joel HaKohen and Royza [Horowitz] Horenstein, and wife of Avraham Mendel Landau, composed the following list of Hasidic rabbis (in Hebrew) and later passed it on to her daughter, Branzunia [Landau] Nahir, without further explanation.

Analysis of this list suggests the following conclusions:

1. "Fathers of the family" appears to be a *yichus* list designed to show the Hasidic rabbinical ancestry of the progeny of Naftali HaKohen Horenstein.

2. These rabbis are generally second or third generation disciples of the *Ba'al Shem Tov*. They are roughly contemporaries of one another, as all died within 15 years of 1800.

3. Rachel was apparently unaware that the *Ba'al Shem Tov* himself belonged on the list:

Yisrael ben Eliezer (the *Ba'al Shem Tov*) → Adel → R' Baruch of Mezhibozh → daughter of R' Baruch → Yisrael Averbuch of Mezhibozh → Avraham Dov Averbuch of Tul'chyn → Moshe Averbuch m. Bina Horenstein (daughter of Naftali HaKohen Horenstein)

Her list follows below:

*(Only the words in **bold type** were in the original list (which is in Hebrew); the rest has been added as explanation.)*

Rabbi [Yechiel] **Michel** [Michal] Rabinowitz, **Magid of Zakotshov** [Zloczow/Zlochuv/Zolochev/Zolotchov/Zlotchov] (1721/31-1786)

Famous disciple of the *Ba'al Shem Tov* and the *Magid* of Mezirech.

Rabbi Levi Itzhak of Berdichev (1740-1810)

Famous disciple of the *Magid* of Mezirech.

Levy Itzhak → Meyer → Esther Rachel → Gitele m. Yisrael Bakovher Sega → Miriam Shipra married Naftali HaKohen Horenstein (1825-1900)

Note 1: This descendant line is the only one provided in the document.

Note 2: There are other lines of descent from Rabbi Levi Yitzchok of Berdichev to the Horensteins:

1. Taube Horowitz, the wife of Gur-arye HaKohen Horenstein (grandson of the first Gur-arye) descends from him.

2. Rachel Trachtenberg, the wife of Avraham Yosef HaKohen Hornstein, as well as her brother, Pinchus Trachtenberg, husband of Fanya Horenstein, may descend from him via his son Yisrael.

3. The husband of Hinde Horenstein Landau, Chaim David HaLevi Landau, is said to descend from the Rabbi. He is Miriam Shipra Horenstein's son from a previous marriage, born with the surname Segal and adopted by the Landau family.

Rabbi [Yehuda Aryeh] **Leib** [*HaSaba*; the Shpoler Zeide] **of Shpali** [Shpola], 1725-1811]

Nicknamed "grandfather" by the *Ba'al Shem Tov* at his circumcision; famed as a miracle worker and devoted to helping the poor; in his early years, he was a disciple of Rabbi Pinchas of Koretz, a leading figure of the second generation.

Rabbi Yevi [Rav Yaivee/Yabi; R. Yakov Yosef] **of Ostrov** [Ostroh]

Disciple of the *Magid* of Mezirech; established the dynasty of Ostroh *Tzadiks*; died 1789-90. Uncle by marriage of Pinchas of Ludmir, father of Arye Judah Leib.

Rabbi Yakov Yosef [ben Tzvi Samson/Shimshon HaKohen Katz] **of Polnea/ Polnav** [Polonnoye/ Polnoye] (1704 - 1781-4)

Leading disciple of the *Ba'al Shem Tov*. The first theoretician and literary propagandist of Hasidism; his *Toledot Yakov Yosef* was the first Hasidic book to be published.

Estherel, a descendant of R. Yakov Yosef of Polonnoye (as well as a grandchild of the 'Ostraha Rebbe" [R. Yakov Yosef II of Ostroh], married Zalman Horenstein..

Rabbi Yankel Yosef of Ostrov [Ostroh]

Identification uncertain: Appears to be a repeat listing for R. Yakov Yosef [R. Yevi] of Ostroh.

Rabbi Zeev [Wolf] **of Jatomir** [Zhitomir] [*died 1800*]

Famous disciple of R. Dov Ber, the *Magid* of Mezirech.

The Rabbi of Chmelnik [Chmilnyk]

Identification uncertain: Probably R. Avraham Dov Auerbach, *Av beit din*, a disciple of both the Magid of Mezeritch and Rabbi Yakov Yosef of Polonnoye.

Rabbi Zusi [Meshulam Zusya/Zushe/Zusha/Zushya ben Eliezer Lipman Lifshutz] **of Annopol** [Hanipoli] [1719-1800]

An outstanding disciple of Rabbi Dov Ber, the *Magid* of Mezirech, and one of the best-known heroes of Hasidic folk tales.

The Magid of Baar [Bar]

R. Menahem Mendel, a second-generation disciple of the *Ba'al Shem Tov* (died 12 Nisan 1765).

The Magid of Stefan [Stepan]

Identification uncertain: Probably R. David Halevi ben R. Shmuel (died 1810-11), a disciple of both the *Ba'al Shem Tov* and the *Magid* of Mezeritch. Son-in-law of R. Yehiel Mikhal of Zlotchov (see his listing above).

[Other possibility: R. Joseph Joel ben Jakob Aron of Stepan (died 1770)]

The Rabbi of Nadvorno [Nadworna, Galicia]

Identification uncertain: Probably R. Zevi Hirsch of Nadworna, Av beit din, died 1802 or 1809. He was a disciple of the *Magid* of Mezeritch and Yechiel Michel, the *Magid* of Zlotchov, and wrote several books.

[Other possibilities: R. Aaron ben Avigdor of Ottynia who extended his patronage over the Jews of Nadworna in 1765; R. Joel Katz of Ottynia (died 1770)]

The Rabbi of Annopol [Anipoli/Hanipoli]

Identification uncertain: Appears to be a repeat listing for Rabbi Zusya of Annopol. If not, he is probably *R. Yehudah Leib HaKohen* – author, *Or Haganuz*, (published in Lemberg in 1866). He was a contemporary of Rabbi Meshulam Zusya and, like Rabbi Zusya, was a disciple of Rabbi Dov Ber of Mezerich and provided an approbation to the Tanya in 1796. (*Son of R. Yosef Gershon HaKohen of Annopol.*) Other possibilities: R. Yakov, R. Meir, R. Samson, or R. David.

Appendix Three:
from Part II, Chapter One

DESCENT OF THE HORENSTEIN BROTHERS
FROM SOME PROMINENT FAMILY LINES

Provided below is a line of descent from an early ancestor of each family down to the Horenstein brothers.[a] While considerable effort has been made to ensure accuracy, early family lines are usually derived from a variety of sources, with some sources more reliable than others; thus expect some errors in this data.

BABAD DESCENT LINE

Rabbi Yosef Yonah (b. 1530)
↓
Rabbi Efraim Naftali Tzvi Hirsh (b. ca. 1560)
↓
Rabbi Jacob of Lublin (b. Kraków, ca. 1575)
↓
Rabbi Abraham Joshua Heshel (b. Brest-Litovsk, ca. 1596)
↓
Rabbi Issachar Berish Heshel (b. Kraków, ca. 1615)
↓
Chief Rabbi Isaac Kraków (b. Brody, 1650)
↓
Rabbi Yakov Yokel Heshel Babad of Tarnograd (b. ca. 1675)
↓
Rabbi Shmuel Babad (b. ca. 1700)
↓
Rabbi Dov Ber Yekels Babad of Ostroh (b. ca. 1720)
↓
Hinde (b. 1750) m. Rabbi Arye Judah Leib (b. Ludmir, 1744)
↓
Rabbi Shmuel Asher (b. 1770)
↓
Rabbi Gur-arye HaKohen (b. ca. 1792)
↓

---

[a] While only a single descent line is shown for each family, often two or more descent lines are known due to marriages between close relatives.

Rabbis Yakov Yosef & Naftali HaKohen Horenstein

EBERLES DESCENT LINE

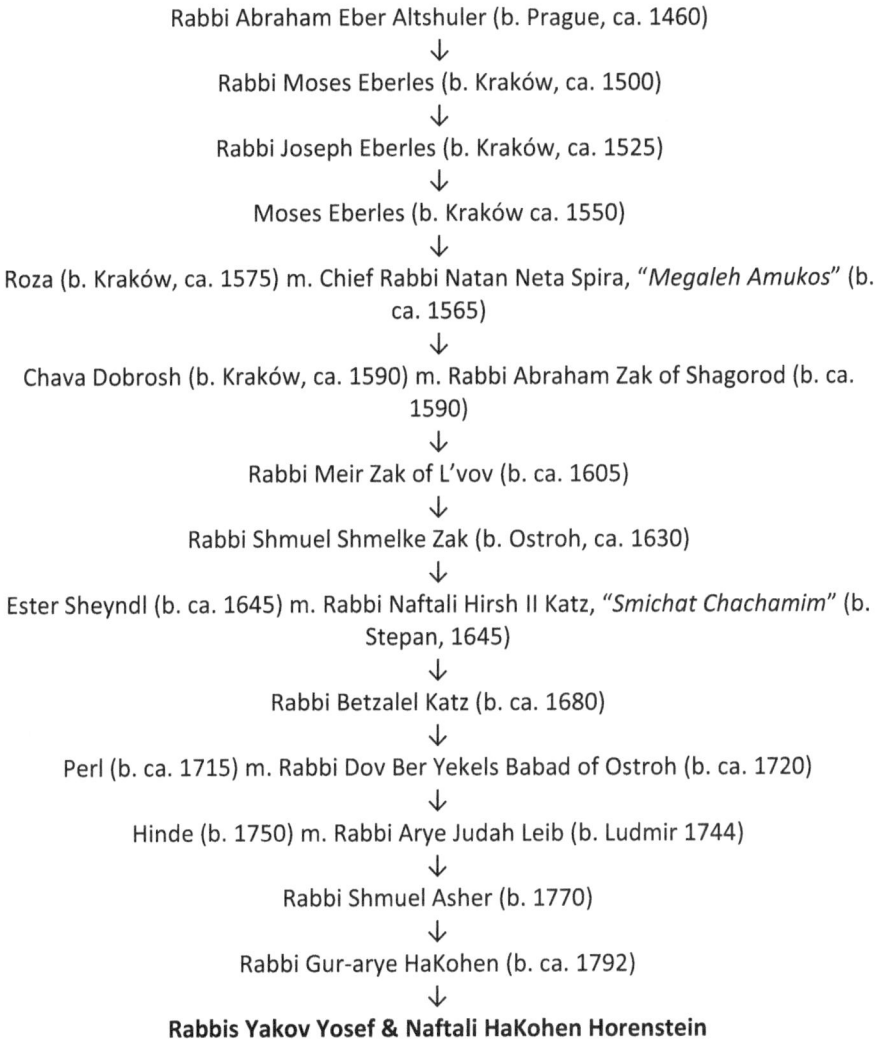

Rabbi Abraham Eber Altshuler (b. Prague, ca. 1460)

↓

Rabbi Moses Eberles (b. Kraków, ca. 1500)

↓

Rabbi Joseph Eberles (b. Kraków, ca. 1525)

↓

Moses Eberles (b. Kraków ca. 1550)

↓

Roza (b. Kraków, ca. 1575) m. Chief Rabbi Natan Neta Spira, *"Megaleh Amukos"* (b. ca. 1565)

↓

Chava Dobrosh (b. Kraków, ca. 1590) m. Rabbi Abraham Zak of Shagorod (b. ca. 1590)

↓

Rabbi Meir Zak of L'vov (b. ca. 1605)

↓

Rabbi Shmuel Shmelke Zak (b. Ostroh, ca. 1630)

↓

Ester Sheyndl (b. ca. 1645) m. Rabbi Naftali Hirsh II Katz, *"Smichat Chachamim"* (b. Stepan, 1645)

↓

Rabbi Betzalel Katz (b. ca. 1680)

↓

Perl (b. ca. 1715) m. Rabbi Dov Ber Yekels Babad of Ostroh (b. ca. 1720)

↓

Hinde (b. 1750) m. Rabbi Arye Judah Leib (b. Ludmir 1744)

↓

Rabbi Shmuel Asher (b. 1770)

↓

Rabbi Gur-arye HaKohen (b. ca. 1792)

↓

Rabbis Yakov Yosef & Naftali HaKohen Horenstein

HEILPRIN DESCENT LINE

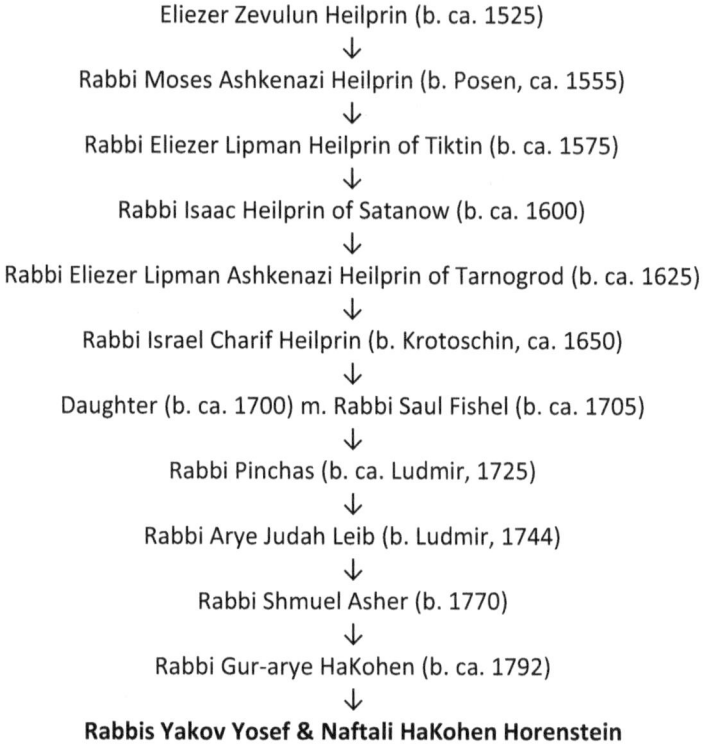

Eliezer Zevulun Heilprin (b. ca. 1525)
↓
Rabbi Moses Ashkenazi Heilprin (b. Posen, ca. 1555)
↓
Rabbi Eliezer Lipman Heilprin of Tiktin (b. ca. 1575)
↓
Rabbi Isaac Heilprin of Satanow (b. ca. 1600)
↓
Rabbi Eliezer Lipman Ashkenazi Heilprin of Tarnogrod (b. ca. 1625)
↓
Rabbi Israel Charif Heilprin (b. Krotoschin, ca. 1650)
↓
Daughter (b. ca. 1700) m. Rabbi Saul Fishel (b. ca. 1705)
↓
Rabbi Pinchas (b. ca. Ludmir, 1725)
↓
Rabbi Arye Judah Leib (b. Ludmir, 1744)
↓
Rabbi Shmuel Asher (b. 1770)
↓
Rabbi Gur-arye HaKohen (b. ca. 1792)
↓
Rabbis Yakov Yosef & Naftali HaKohen Horenstein

KALONYMOS OF LUCCA DESCENT LINE

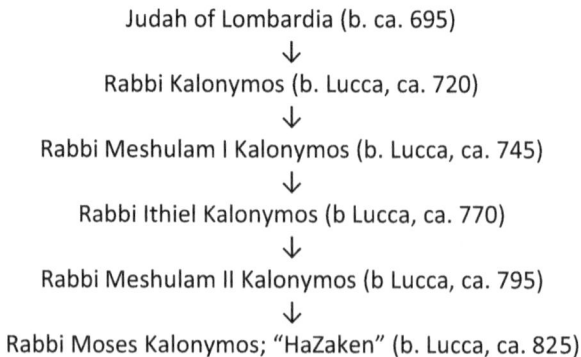

Judah of Lombardia (b. ca. 695)
↓
Rabbi Kalonymos (b. Lucca, ca. 720)
↓
Rabbi Meshulam I Kalonymos (b. Lucca, ca. 745)
↓
Rabbi Ithiel Kalonymos (b Lucca, ca. 770)
↓
Rabbi Meshulam II Kalonymos (b Lucca, ca. 795)
↓
Rabbi Moses Kalonymos; "HaZaken" (b. Lucca, ca. 825)

↓

Rabbi Yekutiel I Kalonymos (b. Lucca, ca. 845)

↓

Rabbi Ibrahim Kalonymos (b. Mainz, ca. 870)

↓

Rabbi Moses (b. Mainz, ca. 885)

↓

Rabbi Kalonymos II (b. Lucca, ca. 905)

↓

Rabbi Meshulam III Kalonymos; "HaGadol" (b. Lucca, ca. 930)

↓

Rabbi Abun Kalonymos; "HaGadol" (b. Le Mans, ca. 945)

↓

Rabbi Joshua Kalonymos; "HaHasid" (b. ca. 970)

↓

Rabbi Isaac Nathan Kalonymos; "HaGadol" (b. ca. 1025)

↓

Rabbi Eliezer ben Nathan; "RaBaN" (b. Germany, ca. 1065)

↓

Rabbi Isaac Kalonymos (b. Mainz, ca. 1085)

↓

Rabbi Kalonymos HaZaken (b. Mainz, ca. 1100)

↓

Rabbi Samuel "HaHasid" (b. Speyer, ca. 1125)

↓

Rabbi Judah HaLevi; "HaHasid" (b. Speyer, ca. 1140)

↓

Rabbi Moses Zaltzman HaLevi (b. ca. 1160)

↓

Rabbi David-Ber HaLevi (b. ca. 1180)

↓

Rabbi Shimon HaLevi of Regensburg (b. ca. 1200)

↓

Rabbi Abraham Ashkenazi; "HaZadik" (b. 1220)

↓

Rabbi Shimshon HaLevi of Rothenberg (b. ca. 1240)

↓

Rabbi David HaLevi (b. ca. 1260)

↓

Rabbi Yakov Yosef Kalonymos HaLevi (b. ca. 1280)

↓

Rabbi Menachem Mendel HaLevi (b. ca. 1295)

↓

Rabbi Zalman Dov HaLevi (b. ca. 1305)

↓

Rabbi David HaLevi (b. ca. 1325)

↓

Yeruchem Kalonymos HaLevi of Germany (b. ca. 1360)

↓

Rabbi Gershon Kalonymos HaLevi (b. ca. 1395)

↓

Rabbi Yosef Kalonymos HaLevi of Germany (b. ca. 1415)

↓

Rabbi Shalom HaLevi of Germany (b. ca. 1440)

↓

Rabbi Judah Leib Kalonymos HaLevi (b. ca. 1460)

↓

Rabbi Yosef HaLevi of Poland (b. ca. 1480)

↓

Moses HaLevi of Poland (b. ca. 1505)

↓

Rabbi Abraham Kalonymos HaLevi of Poland (b. ca. 1530)

↓

Daughter (b. ca. 1545) m. Rabbi Solomon Zalman HaLevi (b. ca. 1545)

↓

Rabbi Shmuel Halevi (b. Ludmir, ca. 1560)

↓

Rabbi David HaLevi Segal; "TaZ" (b. Ludmir, ca. 1586)

↓

Mordechai HaLevi Segal (b. Poznan, 1618)

↓

Beila (b. ca. 1615) m. Rabbi Isaac Heilprin of Satanow (b. ca. 1600)

↓

[Insert the Heilprin descent line here (see above)]

↓

Rabbis Yakov Yosef & Naftali HaKohen Horenstein

───◆───

KATZ DESCENT LINE

Rabbi Akiva the Elder Kohen-Zedek of Salonika (b. ca. 1360)

↓

Rabbi Isaac Katz of Buda & Galata (b. Salonika, ca. 1400)

↓

Gaon Akiva Kohen-Tzedek of Budin (b. ca. 1425)

↓

Rabbi Gershom Katz (b. Prague, ca. 1495)

↓

Rabbi Shimshon Katz of Vienna (b. ca. 1524)

↓

Rabbi Yitzchok I Katz of Nikolsburg (b. ca. 1550)

↓

Rabbi Natali Hirsh I Katz of Prustitz & Lublin (b. Prague or Frankfurt, ca. 1590)

↓

Rabbi Yitzchok II Katz (b. Prague, 1608)

↓

Rabbi Naftali Hirsh II Katz, *"Smichat Chachamim"* (b. Stepan, 1645)

↓

Rabbi Betzalel Katz (b. ca. 1680)

↓

Perl (b. Ostroh, ca. 1715) m. Rabbi Dov Ber Yekels Babad of Ostroh (b. ca. 1720)

↓

Hinde (b. 1750) m. Rabbi Arye Judah Leib (b. Ludmir, 1744)

↓

Rabbi Shmuel Asher (b. 1770)

↓

Rabbi Gur-arye HaKohen (b. ca. 1792)

↓

Rabbis Yakov Yosef & Naftali HaKohen Horenstein

KATZENELLENBOGEN DESCENT LINE

Chief Rabbi Isaac Katzenellenbogen (b. Katzenellenbogen, ca. 1450)

↓

Rabbi Meir Katzenellenbogen; "MaHaRam of Padua" (b. Katzenellenbogen, 1482)

↓

Rabbi Samuel Judah Katenellenbogen; "MaHaRSHIK" (b. Padua, ca. 1521)

↓

Rabbi Saul Wahl Katzenellenbogen; "One Day King" (b. Padua, ca. 1543)

↓

Rabbi Meir Wahl Katzenellenbogen; "MaHaRasH" (b. Brest-Litovsk, ca. 1565)

↓

Rabbi Moses Wahl Katzenellenbogen (b. Chelm, ca. 1590)

↓

Rabbi Saul Brody Katzenellenbogen (b. Chelm, 1617)

↓

Hinde (b. ca. 1665) m. Rabbi Jacob Fishel Kloizner of Ludmir (b. ca. 1690)

↓

Rabbi Saul Fishel (b. ca. 1705)

↓

Rabbi Pinchas (b. Ludmir, ca. 1725)

↓

Rabbi Arye Judah Leib (b. Ludmir, 1744)

↓

Rabbi Shmuel Asher (b. 1770)

↓

Rabbi Gur-arye HaKohen (b. ca. 1792)

↓

Rabbis Yakov Yosef & Naftali HaKohen Horenstein

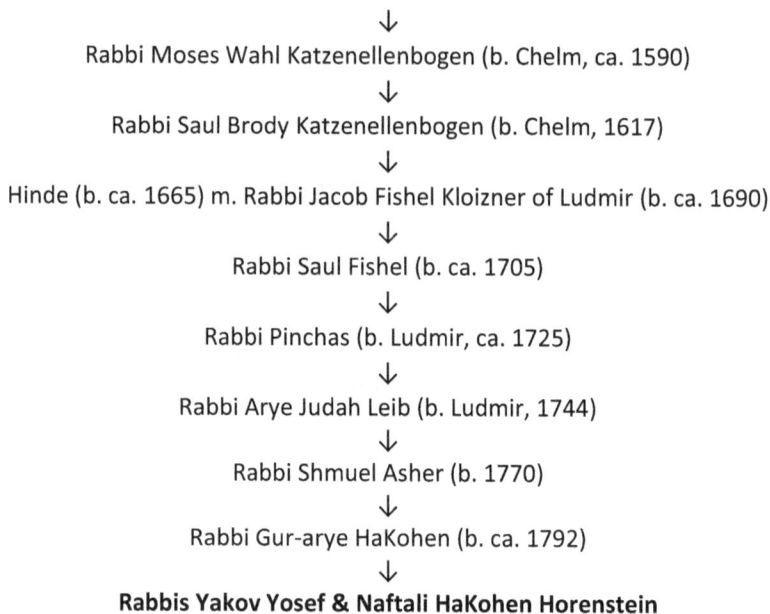

LOEW DESCENT LINE

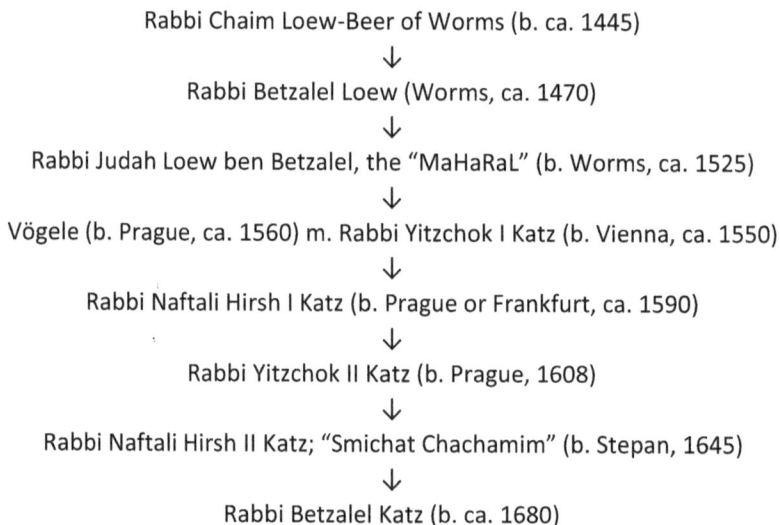

Rabbi Chaim Loew-Beer of Worms (b. ca. 1445)

↓

Rabbi Betzalel Loew (Worms, ca. 1470)

↓

Rabbi Judah Loew ben Betzalel, the "MaHaRaL" (b. Worms, ca. 1525)

↓

Vögele (b. Prague, ca. 1560) m. Rabbi Yitzchok I Katz (b. Vienna, ca. 1550)

↓

Rabbi Naftali Hirsh I Katz (b. Prague or Frankfurt, ca. 1590)

↓

Rabbi Yitzchok II Katz (b. Prague, 1608)

↓

Rabbi Naftali Hirsh II Katz; "Smichat Chachamim" (b. Stepan, 1645)

↓

Rabbi Betzalel Katz (b. ca. 1680)

↓

Perl (b. ca. 1715) m. Rabbi Dov Ber Yekels Babad of Ostroh (b. ca. 1720)

↓

Hinde (b. 1750) m. Rabbi Arye Judah Leib (b. Ludmir, 1744)

↓

Rabbi Shmuel Asher (b. 1770)

↓

Rabbi Gur-arye HaKohen (b. ca. 1792)

↓

Rabbis Yakov Yosef & Naftali HaKohen Horenstein

LURIA DESCENT LINE

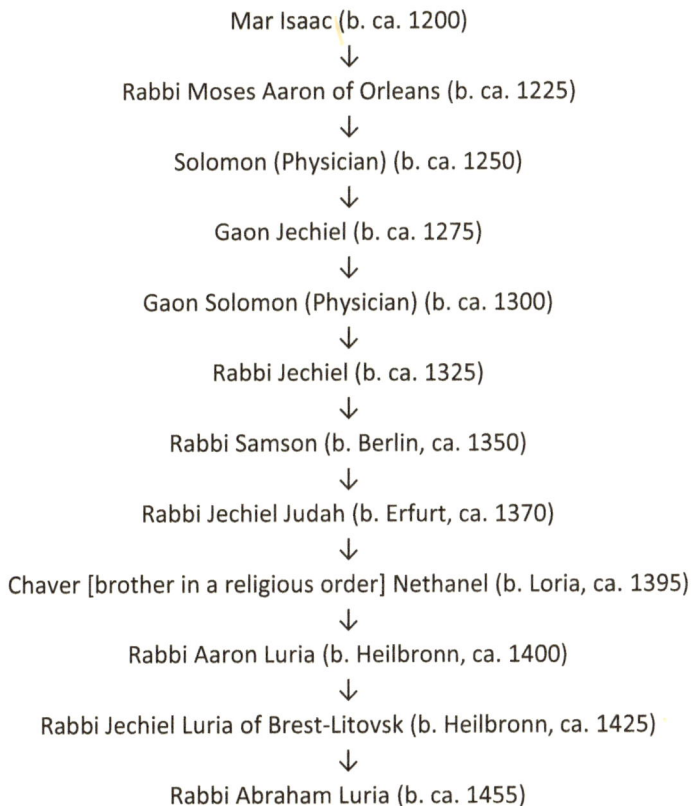

Mar Isaac (b. ca. 1200)

↓

Rabbi Moses Aaron of Orleans (b. ca. 1225)

↓

Solomon (Physician) (b. ca. 1250)

↓

Gaon Jechiel (b. ca. 1275)

↓

Gaon Solomon (Physician) (b. ca. 1300)

↓

Rabbi Jechiel (b. ca. 1325)

↓

Rabbi Samson (b. Berlin, ca. 1350)

↓

Rabbi Jechiel Judah (b. Erfurt, ca. 1370)

↓

Chaver [brother in a religious order] Nethanel (b. Loria, ca. 1395)

↓

Rabbi Aaron Luria (b. Heilbronn, ca. 1400)

↓

Rabbi Jechiel Luria of Brest-Litovsk (b. Heilbronn, ca. 1425)

↓

Rabbi Abraham Luria (b. ca. 1455)

↓

Rabbi Jechiel Luria of Slutzk (b. 1485)

↓

Rabbi Solomon Luria; "MaHaRShal" (b. Germany or Poland, ca. 1510)

↓

Miriam Bella (b. Kraków, ca. 1540) m. Rabbi Eliezer Isserles (b. Kraków, 1530)

↓

Rabbi Moses Lazers Isserles of Brest (b. ca. 1565)

↓

Hesia Miriam (b. Brest, ca. 1600) m. Rabbi Abraham Joshua Heshel (b. Brest, ca. 1596)

↓

Rabbi Dov Berish Heshel Babad (b. Kraków, ca. 1615)

↓

Rabbi Isaac Heshel Babad (b. Brody, ca. 1655)

↓

Rabbi Yakov Yokel Heshel Babad (b. ca. 1675)

↓

Rabbi Shmuel Babad (b. ca. 1700)

↓

Rabbi Dov Ber Yekels Babad of Ostroh (b. ca. 1720)

↓

Hinde (b. 1750) m. Rabbi Arye Judah Leib (b. Ludmir, 1744)

↓

Rabbi Shmuel Asher (b. 1770)

↓

Rabbi Gur-arye HaKohen (b. ca. 1792)

↓

Rabbis Yakov Yosef & Naftali HaKohen Horenstein

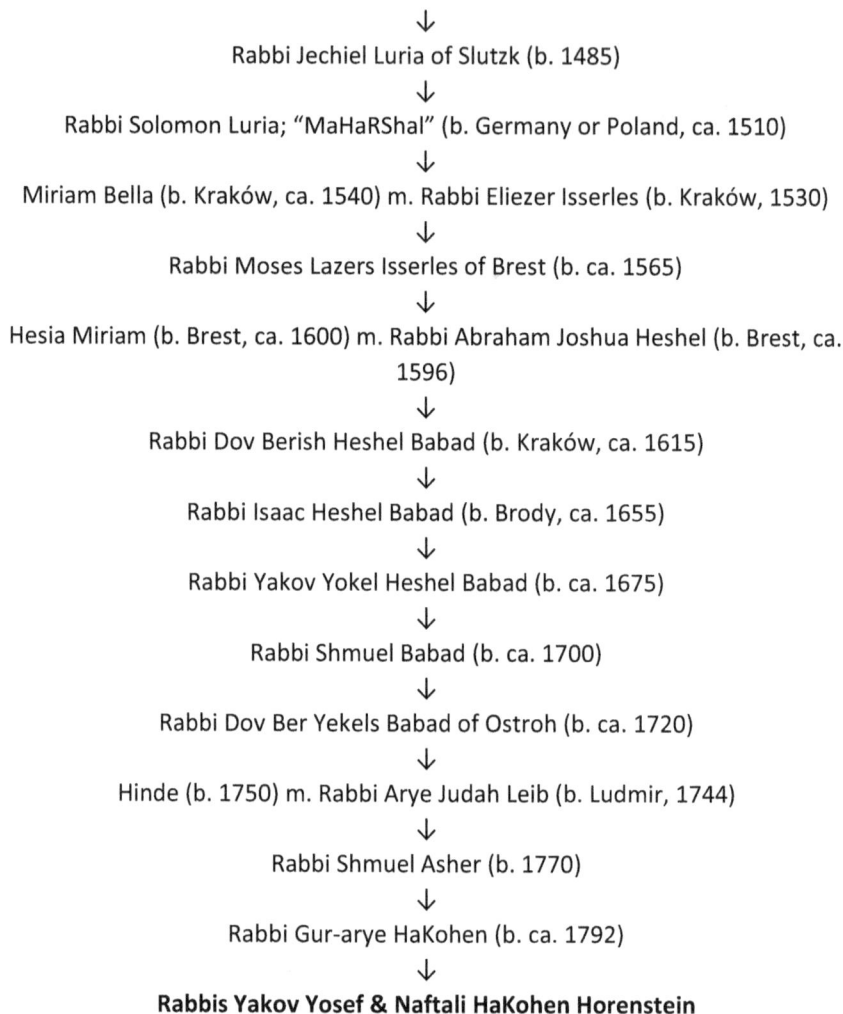

MARGOLIOT (MARGOLIES) DESCENT LINE

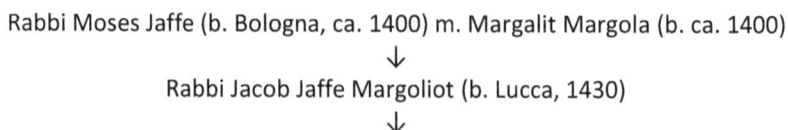

Rabbi Moses Jaffe (b. Bologna, ca. 1400) m. Margalit Margola (b. ca. 1400)

↓

Rabbi Jacob Jaffe Margoliot (b. Lucca, 1430)

↓

Rabbi Yitzchok Eizik Margoliot (b. Worms, ca. 1456)
↓
Rabbi Jacob Margoliot-Eisenstadt (b. Prague, 1490)
↓
Jutta (b. 1515) m. Rabbi Samuel Margoliot (b. Posen, ca. 1512)
↓
Rabbi Moses Mordechai Margoliot (b. Posen, ca. 1540)
↓
Sheindel (b. 1575) m. Rabbi Menachem Mendel Margoliot-Stengen (b. Germany, ca. 1568)
↓
Rabbi Eliezer Margoliot (b. 1600)
↓
Rabbi Shmuel Shmelke Margoliot (b. ca. 1630)
↓
Rabbi Eliezer Rokach (AKA Margoliot) (b. Kraków, 1649,)
↓
Rabbi Moses Rokach (b. Zloczew, 1690)
↓
Daughter of Moses Rokach (b. ca. 1700) m. Rabbi Shmuel Heilprin Babad (b. ca. 1700)
↓
Dov Ber Yekels Babad (b. ca. 1720) m. Perl, daughter of Betzalel Katz (b. ca. 1715)
↓
Hinde (b. 1750) m. Rabbi Arye Judah Leib (b. Ludmir, 1744)
↓
Rabbi Shmuel Asher (b. 1770)
↓
Rabbi Gur-arye HaKohen (b. ca. 1792)
↓
Rabbis Yakov Yosef & Naftali Horenstein

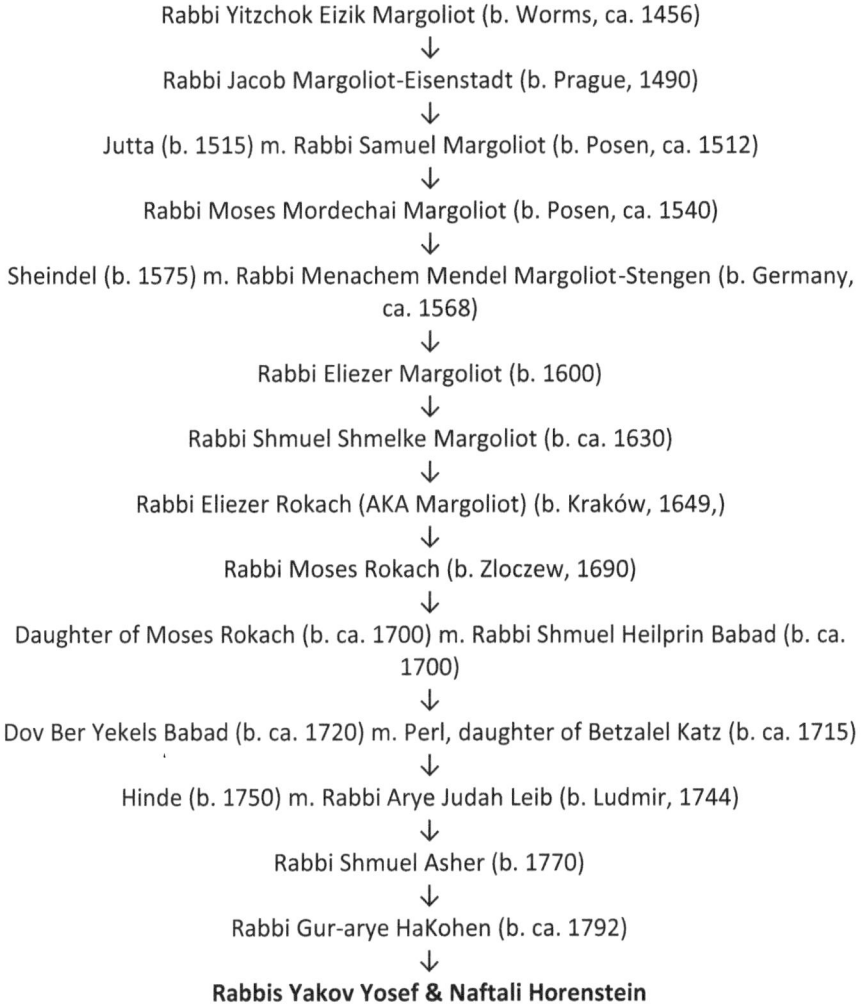

SPIRA (SHAPIRA) DESCENT LINE

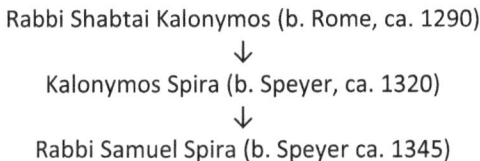

Rabbi Shabtai Kalonymos (b. Rome, ca. 1290)
↓
Kalonymos Spira (b. Speyer, ca. 1320)
↓
Rabbi Samuel Spira (b. Speyer ca. 1345)

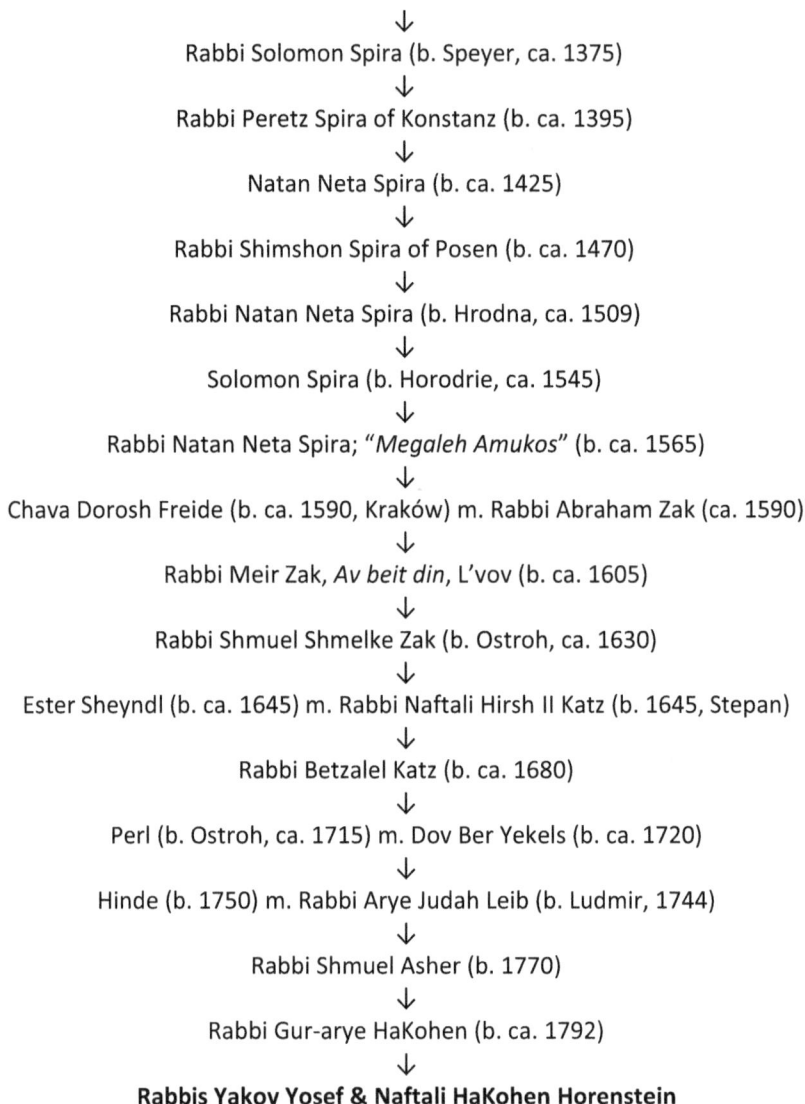

↓
Rabbi Solomon Spira (b. Speyer, ca. 1375)
↓
Rabbi Peretz Spira of Konstanz (b. ca. 1395)
↓
Natan Neta Spira (b. ca. 1425)
↓
Rabbi Shimshon Spira of Posen (b. ca. 1470)
↓
Rabbi Natan Neta Spira (b. Hrodna, ca. 1509)
↓
Solomon Spira (b. Horodrie, ca. 1545)
↓
Rabbi Natan Neta Spira; "*Megaleh Amukos*" (b. ca. 1565)
↓
Chava Dorosh Freide (b. ca. 1590, Kraków) m. Rabbi Abraham Zak (ca. 1590)
↓
Rabbi Meir Zak, *Av beit din*, L'vov (b. ca. 1605)
↓
Rabbi Shmuel Shmelke Zak (b. Ostroh, ca. 1630)
↓
Ester Sheyndl (b. ca. 1645) m. Rabbi Naftali Hirsh II Katz (b. 1645, Stepan)
↓
Rabbi Betzalel Katz (b. ca. 1680)
↓
Perl (b. Ostroh, ca. 1715) m. Dov Ber Yekels (b. ca. 1720)
↓
Hinde (b. 1750) m. Rabbi Arye Judah Leib (b. Ludmir, 1744)
↓
Rabbi Shmuel Asher (b. 1770)
↓
Rabbi Gur-arye HaKohen (b. ca. 1792)
↓
Rabbis Yakov Yosef & Naftali HaKohen Horenstein

TRÈVES DESCENT LINE

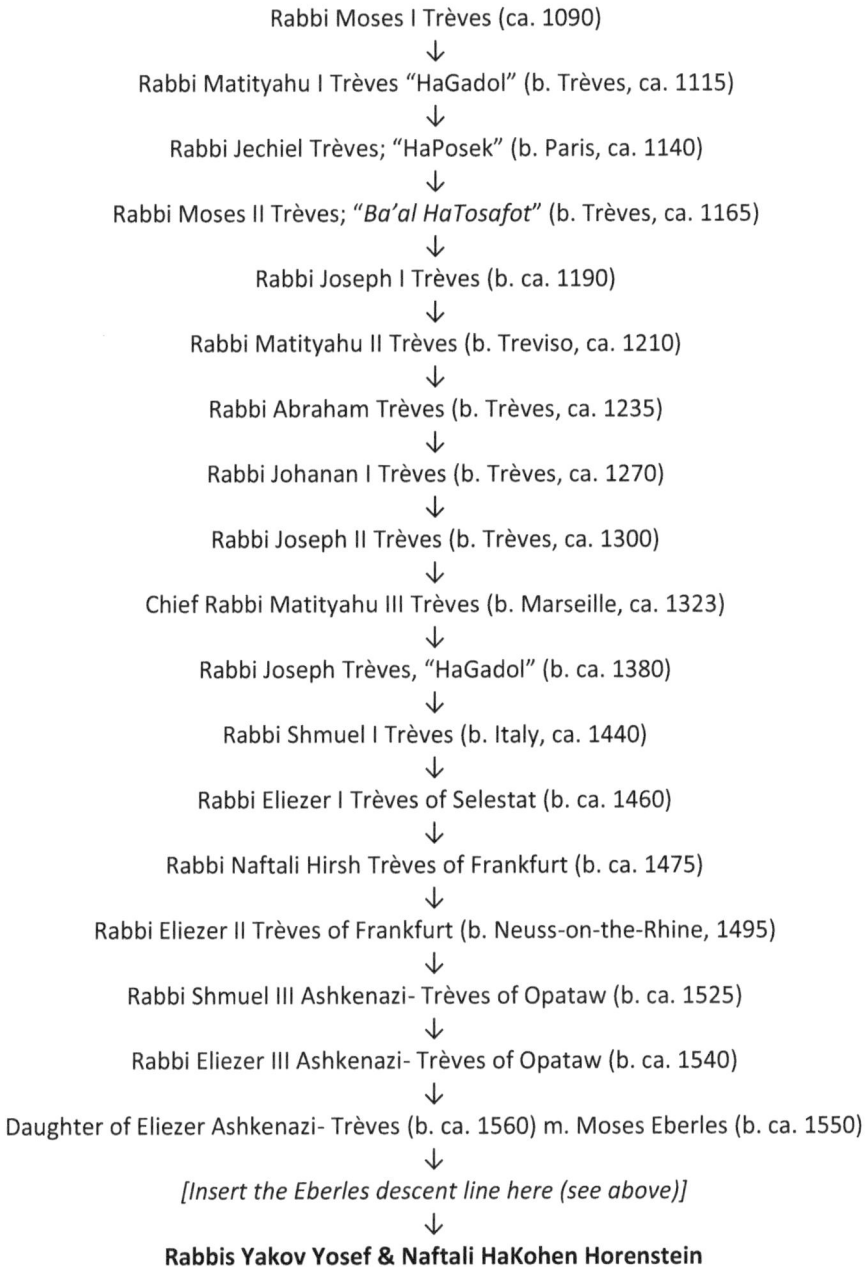

Rabbi Moses I Trèves (ca. 1090)
↓
Rabbi Matityahu I Trèves "HaGadol" (b. Trèves, ca. 1115)
↓
Rabbi Jechiel Trèves; "HaPosek" (b. Paris, ca. 1140)
↓
Rabbi Moses II Trèves; *"Ba'al HaTosafot"* (b. Trèves, ca. 1165)
↓
Rabbi Joseph I Trèves (b. ca. 1190)
↓
Rabbi Matityahu II Trèves (b. Treviso, ca. 1210)
↓
Rabbi Abraham Trèves (b. Trèves, ca. 1235)
↓
Rabbi Johanan I Trèves (b. Trèves, ca. 1270)
↓
Rabbi Joseph II Trèves (b. Trèves, ca. 1300)
↓
Chief Rabbi Matityahu III Trèves (b. Marseille, ca. 1323)
↓
Rabbi Joseph Trèves, "HaGadol" (b. ca. 1380)
↓
Rabbi Shmuel I Trèves (b. Italy, ca. 1440)
↓
Rabbi Eliezer I Trèves of Selestat (b. ca. 1460)
↓
Rabbi Naftali Hirsh Trèves of Frankfurt (b. ca. 1475)
↓
Rabbi Eliezer II Trèves of Frankfurt (b. Neuss-on-the-Rhine, 1495)
↓
Rabbi Shmuel III Ashkenazi- Trèves of Opataw (b. ca. 1525)
↓
Rabbi Eliezer III Ashkenazi- Trèves of Opataw (b. ca. 1540)
↓
Daughter of Eliezer Ashkenazi- Trèves (b. ca. 1560) m. Moses Eberles (b. ca. 1550)
↓
[Insert the Eberles descent line here (see above)]
↓
Rabbis Yakov Yosef & Naftali HaKohen Horenstein

ZAK DESCENT LINE

Rabbi Chaim Zak (b. ca. 1490)
↓
Rabbi Shmuel Shmelke Zak (b. Prague, ca. 1515)
↓
Rabbi Yehoshua Zak (b. Premisle, ca. 1540)
↓
Rabbi Meir Zak (b. ca. 1565)
↓
Rabbi Abraham Zak of Shagorod (b. ca. 1590)
↓
Rabbi Meir Zak of Lvov (b. ca. 1605)
↓
Rabbi Samuel Shmelke Zak (b. Ostroh, ca. 1630)
↓
Ester Sheyndl (b. ca. 1645 m. Rabbi Naftali Hirsh I Katz (b. 1645, Stepan)
↓
[Insert the Katz descent line here (see above)]
↓
Rabbis Yakov Yosef & Naftali HaKohen Horenstein

Appendix Four:
from Part II, Chapter Two

THE HOROWITZ FAMILY: A Re-evaluation of Its Origins

It is commonly believed that the Horowitz family of Bohemia descends from the HaLevi HaYitzhari family of Spain. However, a review of the given names of male family members suggests that it is unlikely that this lineage is that of a single family. It appears rather that the lineages of two different families were improperly merged to fabricate a single descent line from the Halevi HaYitzhari family to the Benveniste family; then another improper merger created a second fabricated descent line from the Benveniste family to the Horowitz family.

In the sequence below, these three descent lines have been separated, and the repeatedly used given names emphasized, in order to highlight the differences between the names chosen by the three families.

[Given names repeated in subsequent generations – in accordance with Jewish custom - are in ***bold, italic type***.]

Members of Family #1: HALEVI HAYITZHARI
of Spain and Provence

Isaac Solomon HaLevi HaYitzhari
b. ca. 1005, Tortosa, Spain
↓
Shem Tov HaLevi HaYitzhari
b. 1220-1235, Gerona or Barcelona, Spain
d. ca. 1110 Provence, France
↓
Zerachya Reuben HaLevi HaYitzhari
b. ca. 1065, Gerona, Spain
d. ca. 1140, Spain
↓
Isaac HaLevi HaYitzhari
"Ba'al HaYitzhari"
b. ca. 1090, Gerona, Spain
d. 1170-1186, Lunel, France
↓
Zerachya HaLevi HaYitzhari
"Ba'al HaMaor"; "RaZaH"

b. ca. 1110, Gerona, Spain
d. after 1186 Lunel, Franc

Members of Family #2: BENVENISTE
of Spain and Provence

Benveniste HaLevi
b. ca. 1125
↓
Joseph Benveniste HaLevi
b. ca. 1145, Provence, France
d. ca. 1205, Barcelona, Spain
↓
Benveniste HaLevi
b. ca. 1165, Sauvagnon, France
d. ca. 1230, Marseille, France
↓
Joseph Benveniste HaLevi
b. ca. 1190
d. 1250-1260, Barcelona, Spain
↓
Benveniste HaLevi
b. ca. 1220
d. ca. 1290
↓
Isaac ***Benveniste*** HaLevi
"HaGadol of Narvona"
b. ca. 1245, Narbonne, France
d. 1293, Narbonne, France
↓
Moses ***Benveniste*** HaLevi
b. ca. 1270, Narbonne, France
d. ca. 1315, Barcelona, Spain
↓
Joseph Benveniste HaLevi
b. ca. 1310, Barcelona, Spain
d. ca. 1380, Barcelona, Spain
↓
Benveniste HaLevi
b. 1340, Barcelona, Spain
d. ca. 1380, Barcelona, Spain

Notice how closely the above Benveniste naming pattern matches that of another Ben-veniste family which lived nearby during the same time period:

BENVENISTE FAMILY *of Saragosa*

Benveniste "HaSaroqosti" (i.e. from Saragosa, Spain)
b. ca. 1040
↓
Joseph Ibn *Benveniste* of Saragosa
b. ca. 1065
d. after 1108
↙ ↘
Moses *Benveniste*   *Isaac* Ibn *Benveniste*
b. ca. 1080   b. ca. 1090
residences: Saragosa; Barcelona; Malaga
d. after 1128, Malaga
↙ ↘
Joseph [?] (AKA *Benveniste*) Ibn *Benveniste*   Sheshet *Benveniste*
b. ca. 1115   b. ca. 1125, Saragosa
d. after 1210   d. ca. 1209, Saragosa
↙ ↘
Isaac Ibn *Benveniste*   *Joseph Benveniste*
b. ca. 1170   b. ca. 1170
d. ca. 1224   residence: Montpellier, France

First Documented members of Family #3: HOROWITZ

Notice how different names listed below are from the Benveniste family names.

Isaiah HaLevi [Ish Horowitz]
b. ca. 1450, Provence
d. ca. 1518, Prague

siblings:
Aaron Meshulam Zalman,
Shabtai Sheftiel,
Asher Zeligman,
Meir,
Pinchas,
Jacob (& possibly 2 more siblings)

GLOSSARY

Aliyah: Immigration to Israel

Av Beit Din: Head of the rabbinical court

Ba'al Shem Tov: "Master of the Good Name;" a man who knows the secret names of God and can manipulate them to serve his desires.

Beit Midrash: A study hall devoted to the study and interpretation of Torah.

Besht: Acronym based on the initials of Israel *Ba'al Shem Tov*

Bikur Holim: Visiting the sick to provide comfort.

Cantor: The synagogue official who chants liturgical music and leads the choir in prayer.

Chevra Kadisha: Burial society

Chuppa: A canopy beneath which Jewish wedding ceremonies are performed.

Cossacks: Christian horsemen who lived on the steppes of Ukraine and were hired by the Czar as soldiers whenever there was a war or military campaign that necessitated ruthless warriors.

Dayan: Judge in a Jewish religious court

Gabbai: Sexton; the person who organizes the running of a Jewish religious service and determines who will receive honors during the portion of the service when the Torah is brought out of the ark.

Gartel: Belt; A special type of belt used by Jewish men, usually *Hasidim*, during prayer.

Gvir: A very wealthy person

Hagaddah: The text recited on the first two nights of the Jewish holiday of Passover.

Halakhah: The collective body of Jewish religious laws derived from the Written and Oral Torah.

Hanukah: Dedication; An eight-day Jewish celebration which commemorates the rededication during the second century B.C. of the Second Temple in Jerusalem, where according to legend, Jews had risen up against their Greek-Syrian oppressors in the Maccabean Revolt.

Hasidim: Adherents to Hasidism

Hasidism: A movement of observant Jews, called *Hasidim* ("pious ones" in Hebrew), founded by Israel *Baal Shem Tov* in Eastern Europe in the 18ᵗʰ century.

Hekdesh: Funds for the poor and sick

Homilies: Sermons

Kabbalah: The ancient Jewish tradition of mystical interpretation of the Bible.

Kahal: Assembly; community. The local governing body of a European Jewish community in charge of administering religious, legal, and communal affairs.

Kapote: A man's long coat of medieval origin worn primarily by Eastern European Jews

Kasket: A head covering with a brim

Kinnui: A "nickname," consisting of a man's Hebrew name followed by the same name in the local language.

Kloyz: House of Jewish religious study

Kollel: Full-time institute for advanced adult students of Talmud and rabbinic literature

Kvitel: "Little note;" a request in the form of a petitionary prayer which is handed to a Hasidic *rebbe* in order to receive the latter's blessing. It is usually given together with some money which is used by the *rebbe* for the upkeep of his court or for distribution to charity.

Lag B'Omer: A festive minor Jewish holiday, occurs in late April to early May, on the 33rd day of the counting of the Omer, a 49-day period between Passover and Shavuot. It serves as a break from the semi-mourning during that interval.

Maftir aliyah: The honor of being the last person to be called up to the Torah on Sabbath mornings. This person also chants the day's *haftorah* (a reading following the Torah reading which is thematically linked to the Torah portion that precedes it).

Midrash: Discussion of the ancient commentary on Hebrew scriptures attached to the biblical text.

Mikveh: A bath dedicated to ritual immersion.

Minyon: The quorum of ten Jewish adults required for public prayer and certain other religious obligations.

Mizrachi: A Religious Zionist organization

Parnas: The president or head of a Jewish congregation

Pilpul: Study of the Talmud through intense textual analysis.

Pinkas: Minutes; records

Piyyut: A liturgical poem recited in the synagogue.

Pogrom: An organized massacre directed at a specific group.

Responsa: Authoritative replies in letter form, made by noted rabbis or Jewish scholars, to questions sent to them concerning Jewish law.

Ruzhiner: Follower of the Hasidic dynasty of Rabbi Yisrael Friedman of Ruzhin.

Sejm: Parliament of the Kingdom of Poland

Shavuot: A Jewish festival that begins on the sixth day of the Hebrew month of Sivan. Originally a harvest festival, it now also commemorates God's giving of the Torah to the Jews.

Siddur: Prayer book

Silichot: The Jewish penitential poems and prayers recited in the period before the High Holidays.

Smichat Chachamim: Applying intelligence; the name of the most famous book written by Rabbi Naftali HaKohen Katz. Its name became his nickname.

Sofer: Scribe

Shtadlan: A specially-qualified official lobbyist for the Jewish community.

Shtiblekh: Small Jewish houses of prayer which also serve as places for community gatherings.

Siddur: Jewish prayer book

Starost: A Polish nobleman who possesses a *starosty* (castle and domain conferred for life).

Sukkah: A temporary booth or hut constructed for use duing Sukkot.

Sukkot: Booths or huts. A weeklong Jewish harvest festival which commemorates God's protection of the children of Israel when they left Egypt.

Tallit: Jewish prayer shawls

Talmud Torah: A school for teaching the fundamentals of Judaism.

Tzadik: "Righteous one;" holy man

Yamulke: Skullcap; a small brimless cap worn by Jews, especially during religious services.

Yichus: Pedigree as modified by personal achievement.

Yishuv: The Jewish community in Palestine prior to the declaration of the state of Israel in 1948.

INDEX

311

BIBLIOGRAPHY

[1] 1850 Kremenets District Revision List

[2] 1858 Shumsk Jewish census - Zitomir Archive

[3] 1858 Shumsk Jewish census - Zitomir Archive

[4] The Whole South-West Territory Business Directory, Borough of Shumsk, District of Kremenets, province of Volhynia, 1913

[5] Lieberman, Yosef. *Shalshelet haYuchasin*. Jerusalem, 1977-8

[6] Orally transmitted family legend as related by Gur-Aryeh Skulsky, son of Nachma Hornstein, Winnipeg, Canada, 1980

[7] Biber, Menachem Mendel. *Markezet LeGedolei Ostraha* (1907), entry 149

[8] Biber, Menachem Mendel. *Markezet LeGedolei Ostraha* (1907), entry 149

[9] Lieberman, Yosef. *Shalshelet HaYuchasin*. Jerusalem, 1977-8, p. 39

[10] Rosenstein, Neil. The Unbroken Chain, second edition. New York, CIS Publishers, Inc., 1990

[11] Rosenstein, Neil. The Unbroken Chain, second edition. New York, CIS Publishers, Inc., 1990

[12] Hundert, Gershon David. Jews in Poland-Lithuania in the Eighteenth Century: A Genealogy of Modernity. Berkeley, Los Angeles, University of California Press, 2004, p. 21

[13] Hundert, Gershon David. Jews in Poland-Lithuania in the Eighteenth Century: A Genealogy of Modernity. Berkeley, Los Angeles, University of California Press, 2004, p. 14

[14] Hundert, Gershon David. Jews in Poland-Lithuania in the Eighteenth Century: A Genealogy of Modernity. Berkeley, Los Angeles, University of California Press, 2004, p. 20

[15] Hundert, Gershon David. Jews in Poland-Lithuania in the Eighteenth Century: A Genealogy of Modernity. Berkeley, Los Angeles, University of California Press, 2004, p. 20

[16] Hundert, Gershon David. Jews in Poland-Lithuania in the Eighteenth Century: A Genealogy of Modernity. Berkeley, Los Angeles, University of California Press, 2004, pp. 32-33

[17] Hundert, Gershon David. Jews in Poland-Lithuania in the Eighteenth Century: A Genealogy of Modernity. Berkeley, Los Angeles, University of California Press, 2004, pp. 32-33

[18] Hundert, Gershon David. 18th-Century Polish Jewry: Demographic and Genealogical Problems. Avotaynu Volume XV, Number 4. Winter 1999

[19] Hundert, Gershon David. 18th-Century Polish Jewry: Demographic and Genealogical Problems. Avotaynu Volume XV, Number 4. Winter 1999

[20] Marcus, Jacob Rader. The Jew in the Medieval World: A Source Book: 315-1791. Cincinnati, Hebrew Union College Press, 1999, p. 233

[21] Gelles, Edward. An Ancient Lineage. London & Portland, Oregon, Vallentine Mitchell, 2006

[22] Councils. The YIVO Encyclopedia of Jews in Eastern Europe. http://www.yivoencyclopedia.org/article.aspx/Councils#id0ewsai

[23] Marcus, Jacob Rader. The Jew in the Medieval World: A Source Book: 315-1791. Cincinnati, Hebrew Union College Press, 1999, p. 233

[24] Kaminski, Andrzej. The Szlachta of the Polish-Lithuanian Commonwealth and Their Government, in Banac, Iwo & Bushkovitch, Paul. The Nobility in Russia and East Central Europe. New Haven, Yale University Press, 1983, pp. 17-45

[25] Weinryb, BD. The Jews of Poland. Philadelphia, Jewish Publication Society, 1973, p. 120

[26] Partitions of Poland. Encyclopedia Britannica Online, 2008

[27] *Liberum* veto. Wikipedia.org

[28] Dubnow, S. M. History of the Jews in Russia and Poland: From the Earliest Times until the Present Day. Philadelphia, The Jewish Publication Society of America, 1916, Volume 1, pp. 262-264

[29] Dubnow, S. M. History of the Jews in Russia and Poland: From the Earliest Times until the Present Day. Philadelphia, The Jewish Publication Society of America, 1916, Volume 1, p. 261

[30] Dubnow, S. M. History of the Jews in Russia and Poland: From the Earliest Times until the Present Day. Philadelphia, The Jewish Publication Society of America, 1916, Volume 1, p. 292

[31] Dubnow, S. M. History of the Jews in Russia and Poland: From the Earliest Times until the Present Day. Philadelphia, The Jewish Publication Society of America, 1916, Volume 1, p. 297

[32] Dubnow, S. M. History of the Jews in Russia and Poland: From the Earliest Times until the Present Day. Philadelphia, The Jewish Publication Society of America, 1916, Volume 1, p. 318

[33] Councils. Yivo Encyclopedia of Jews in Eastern Europe. http://www.yivoencyclopedia.org/article.aspx/Councils

[34] Marcus, Jacob Rader. The Jew in the Medieval World: A Source Book: 315-1791. Cincinnati, Hebrew Union College Press, 1999, p. 233

[35] Councils. Yivo Encyclopedia of Jews in Eastern Europe. http://www.yivoencyclopedia.org/article.aspx/Councils

[36] Rosenthal, Herman. Kahal. JewishEncyclopedia.com (1906)

[37] Hundert, Gershon David. Jews in Poland-Lithuania in the Eighteenth Century: A Genealogy of Modernity. Berkeley, Los Angeles, University of California Press, 2004, pp. 80-81

[38] Hundert, Gershon David. Jews in Poland-Lithuania in the Eighteenth Century: A Genealogy of Modernity. Berkeley, Los Angeles, University of California Press, 2004, p. 86

[39] Hundert, Gershon David. Jews in Poland-Lithuania in the Eighteenth Century: A Genealogy of Modernity. Berkeley, Los Angeles, University of California Press, 2004, p. 81

[40] Hundert, Gershon David. Jews in Poland-Lithuania in the Eighteenth Century: A Genealogy of Modernity. Berkeley, Los Angeles, University of California Press, 2004, p. 83

[41] Hundert, Gershon David. Jews in Poland-Lithuania in the Eighteenth Century: A Genealogy of Modernity. Berkeley, Los Angeles, University of California Press, 2004, pp. 84-86

[42] Hundert, Gershon David. Jews in Poland-Lithuania in the Eighteenth Century: A Genealogy of Modernity. Berkeley, Los Angeles, University of California Press, 2004, p. 84

[43] Rosenthal, Herman. Kahal. Jewish Encyclopedia, 1906
http://www.JewishEncyclopedia.com

[44] Rosenthal, Herman. Kahal. Jewish Encyclopedia, 1906
http://www.JewishEncyclopedia.com

[45] *Pinkas Va'ad Arba' Aratsot,* sigs. 407, 515. Revised and edited by Israel Bartal. Jerusalem, The Bialik Institute, 1945 *(in Hebrew)*

[46] Johnson, Paul. A History of the Jews. New York, Harper & Row, 1987, pp. 295-296

[47] Johnson, Paul. A History of the Jews. New York, Harper & Row, 1987, p. 296

[48] Johnson, Paul. A History of the Jews. New York, Harper & Row, 1987, p. 296-297

[49] Hundert, Gershon David. Jews in Poland-Lithuania in the Eighteenth Century: A Genealogy of Modernity. Berkeley, Los Angeles, University of California Press, 2004, p. 161

[50] Johnson, Paul. A History of the Jews. New York, Harper & Row, 1987, p. 297

[51] Dubnow, S. M. History of the Jews in Russia and Poland. Philadelphia, The Jewish Publication Society of America, 1916, Volume 1, p. 235

[52] Dubnow, S. M. History of the Jews in Russia and Poland. Philadelphia, The Jewish Publication Society of America, 1916, Volume 1, p. 235

[53] Dynner, Glenn. Men of Silk: The Hasidic Conquest of Polish Jewish Society. Oxford & New York, Oxford University Press, 2006, p. 90

[54] Dynner, Glenn. Men of Silk: The Hasidic Conquest of Polish Jewish Society. Oxford & New York, Oxford University Press, 2006, p. 14

[55] Dynner, Glenn. Men of Silk: The Hasidic Conquest of Polish Jewish Society. Oxford & New York, Oxford University Press, 2006, pp. 14-15

[56] Dynner, Glenn. Men of Silk: The Hasidic Conquest of Polish Jewish Society. Oxford & New York, Oxford University Press, 2006, p. 89

[57] Hundert, Gershon David. Jews in Poland-Lithuania in the Eighteenth Century: A Genealogy of Modernity. Berkeley, Los Angeles, University of California Press, 2004, p. 175

[58] Dynner, Glenn. Men of Silk: The Hasidic Conquest of Polish Jewish Society. Oxford & New York, Oxford University Press, 2006, p. 115

[59] Johnson, Paul. A History of the Jews. New York, Harper & Row, 1987, p. 298

[60] Lukin, Benyamin. Volodymry Volyns'kyi. The Yivo Encyclopedia of Jews in Eastern Europe. http://www.yivoencyclopedia.org/article.aspx/Volodymyr_Volynskyi

[61] Chenowicz, Moshe. Rabbis & Notables of Wlodimierz, in Wladimir Wolynsk: in memory of the Jewish community. 1962

[62] Bogdan Khmelnitsky. World ORT. Electronic Jewish Encyclopedia. 2003. https://eleven.co.il/diaspora/judeophobia-anti-semitism/14533/ *(in Ukrainian)*

[63] Rosenthal, Herman. Cossacks' Uprising. Jewish Encyclopedia, 1906 http://www.JewishEncyclopedia.com

[64] Lukin, Benyamin. Volodymry Volyns'kyi. The Yivo Encyclopedia of Jews in Eastern Europe. http://www.yivoencyclopedia.org/article.aspx/Volodymyr_Volynskyi

[65] Dworzhetsky, M. The History of Jewish Wladimir, in *Pinkas Ludmir; sefer zikaron le-kehilat Ludmir (in Hebrew)*

[66] Chenowicz, Moshe, Rabbis and Notables of Wlodimierz, in in *Pinkas Ludmir; sefer zikaron le-kehilat Ludmir (in Hebrew)*

67 Chenowicz, Moshe. Personalities and Figures: Rabbis and Notables of Wlodimierz, in *Pinkas Ludmir; sefer zikaron le-kehilat Ludmir*. Tel Aviv, 1962 *(in Hebrew)*

68 *Pinkas Kremenets (in Hebrew)*

69 Chenowicz, Moshe. Personalities and Figures: Rabbis and Notables of Wlodimierz, in *Pinkas Ludmir; sefer zikaron le-kehilat Ludmir*. Tel Aviv, 1962 *(in Hebrew)*

70 Dworzhetsky, M. The History of Jewish Wladimir, in *Pinkas Ludmir; sefer zikaron le-kehilat Ludmir*. Tel Aviv, 1962 *(in Hebrew)*

71 Chenowicz, Mosh. Personalities and Figures: Rabbis and Notables of Wlodimierz, in *Pinkas Ludmir; sefer zikaron le-kehilat Ludmir*. Tel Aviv, 1962 *(in Hebrew)*

72 Documents and Inscriptions, vol. III, no. 2058; summarized in: Jewish Encyclopedia, 1906; http://www.JewishEncyclopedia.com

73 The Municipal Records of Kremenets. 1758

74 Biber, Menachem Mendel. *Markezet LeGedolei Ostraha* [The Great Men of Ostroh]. Berdichev, 1907, pp. 187-8 *(in Hebrew)*

75 *Pinkas Ludmir; Sefer Zikaron LeKehilat Ludmir*. Former Residents of Ludmir in Israel, Tel Aviv, 1962, p. 291 *(in Hebrew)*

76 Biber, Menachem Mendel. *Markezet LeGedolei Ostraha* [The Great Men of Ostroh]. Berdichev, 1907, pp. 173-174 *(in Hebrew)*

77 Biber, Menachem Mendel. *Markezet LeGedolei Ostraha* [The Great Men of Ostroh]. Berdichev, 1907, pp. 187-8 *(in Hebrew)*

78 *Pinkas Ludmir; Sefer Zikaron LeKehilat Ludmir*, p. 292 *(in Hebrew)*

79 Lukin, Benyamin. Ostroh. The YIVO Encyclopedia of Jews in Eastern Europe. http://www.yivoencyclopedia.org/article.aspx/Ostroh

80 Shochat, Azriel & Spector, Shmue. Ostroh. Encyclopedia Judaica, Second Edition. Detroit, Thomson Gale, 2007

[81] Ostroh. *Pinkas Hakehillot Polin*. Jerusalem, Yad Vashem, 1990 *(in Hebrew)*

[82] Ostroh. World ORT. Electronic Jewish Encyclopedia. 2003.
http://www.eleven.co.il/?mode=article&id=13106 *(in Ukrainian)*

[83] Rosenthal, Herman & Lipman, J. G. Ostroh. Jewish Encyclopedia, 1906
http://www.JewishEncyclopedia.com

[84] Ostroh. *Pinkas Hakehillot Polin*. Jerusalem, Yad Vashem, 1990 *(in Hebrew)*

[85] Shochat, Azriel & Spector, Shmuel. Ostroh. Encyclopedia Judaica, Second Edition.
Detroit, Thomson Gale, 2007

[86] Rosenthal, Herman & Lipman, J. G. Ostroh. Jewish Encyclopedia, 1906
http://www.JewishEncyclopedia.com

[87] Hundert, Gershon David. Jews in Poland-Lithuania in the 18th Century: A
Genealogy of Modernity. Berkeley & Los Angeles, University of California Press,
2004, p. 164

[88] Rosenthal, Herman & Lipman, J. G. Ostroh. Jewish Encyclopedia, 1906
http://www.JewishEncyclopedia.com

[89] Dynner, Glenn. Men of Silk: The Hasidic Conquest of Polish Jewish Society. Oxford
& New York, Oxford University Press, 2006, Chapter 4: Yichus: The Social
Composition of Hasidic Leadership.

[90] Biber, Menachem Mendel. *Markezet LeGedolei Ostraha* [The Great Men of
Ostroh]. Berdichev, 1907, pp. 187-8 *(in Hebrew)*

[91] Biber, Menachem Mendel. *Markezet LeGedolei Ostraha* [The Great Men of
Ostroh]. Berdichev, 1907, pp. 187-8 *(in Hebrew)*

[92] Biber, Menachem Mendel. *Markezet LeGedolei Ostraha* [The Great Men of
Ostroh]. Berdichev, 1907, pp. 187-8 *(in Hebrew)*

[93] Biber, Menachem Mendel. *Mazkeret LeGedolei Ostraha* (1907), pp. 187-88

[94] *Pinkas Ludmir; Sefer Zikaron LeKehilat Ludmir.* Former Residents of Ludmir in
Israel, Tel Aviv, 1962, p. 292 *(in Hebrew)*

95 Biber, Menachem Mendel. *Markezet LeGedolei Ostraha* [The Great Men of Ostroh]. Berdichev, 1907 *(in Hebrew)*

96 Shochat, Azriel & Spector, Shmuel. Ostroh. Encyclopedia Judaica, Second Edition. Detroit, Thomson Gale, 2007

97 Ostroh. *Pinkas Hakehillot Polin*. Jerusalem, Yad Vashem. https://www.jewishgen.org/Yizkor/pinkas_poland/pol5_00034.html *(in Hebrew)*

98 Finkel, Chaim. Ostroh – A Metropolis of the People of Israel, in Ostroh Book: A Memorial to the Ostroh Holy Community. Tel-Aviv, The Ostroh Society in Israel, 1987

99 Ginzberg, Louis. Arye. Jewish Encyclopedia, 1906

http://www.JewishEncyclopedia.com

100 Shochat, Azriel & Spector, Shmuel. Ostroh. Encyclopedia Judaica, Second Edition. Detroit, Thomson Gale, 2007

101 Rosenthal, Herman & Lipman, J. G. Ostroh. Jewish Encyclopedia, 1906 http://www.JewishEncyclopedia.com

102 Rosenthal, Herman & Lipman, J. G. Ostroh. Jewish Encyclopedia, 1906 http://www.JewishEncyclopedia.com

103 Hundert, Gershon David. Jews in Poland-Lithuania in the 18th Century: A Genealogy of Modernity. Berkeley & Los Angeles, University of California Press, 2004, p. 164

104 Warszawski, N. "Historical Jewish Millionaires in Russia (Events, Facts and Episodes)." IX. Ya'akov Yosef Horenstein. *Haint*, 1 Tevet, 5686 (December 18, 1925). *(in Yiddish)*

105 YIVO. Hasidism: Teachings and Literature. www.yivoencyclopedia.org/article.aspx/Hasidism/Teachings_and_Literature

106 What Hasidic Jews Believe. My Jewish Learning. www.myjewishlearning.com/article/hasidic-ideas/

107 Berestechko. Spector, Shmuel, Editor-in-Chief. The Encyclopedia of Jewish Life Before and During the Holocaust. New York, New York University Press, 2001

108 Weiss, Aharon & Spector, Shmuel. Berestechko. Encyclopedia Judaica, Second Edition. Detroit, Thomson Gale, 2007

109 Virtual Shtetl https://sztetl.org.pl/en/towns/b/1108-beresteczko/99-history/137053-history-of-community

110 Spector, Shmuel, Ed. *Pinkas HaKehilot Polin*. Yad Vashem, Jerusalem 1990, Vol. 5, p. 43 *(in Hebrew)*

111 Rąkowsk, Grzegorz. Volhynia. p. 340i *(in Polish)*

112 Rąkowsk, Grzegorz. Volhynia. p. 340i *(in Polish)*

113 Avitachi, Arie. History: Rovno and Population, in Avitachi, Arie, Ed. Rowne; Sefer Zikaron. Tel Aviv, 1956 *(in Hebrew)*

114 1816 Aleksandriya, Rovno Uezd, *Revizskaya Skazka (in Russian)*

115 1834 Aleksandriya, Rovno Uezd, *Revizskaya Skazka (in Russian)*

116 1850 Berestechko *Revizskaya Skazka (in Russian)*

117 1850 Kremenets District Census

118 1811 Kremenets District Census

119 1850 Kremenets District Census

120 Kiev archives

121 1913 Radomyshl Business directory

122 Ironi, Noa, in Nathan Livneh, Ed. *Pinkas Hackehilah Alexandrija/Sefer Iskor*. Alexssandrija Committee in Israel, Israel, 1972 *(in Hebrew)*

123 Ironi, Noa, in Nathan Livneh, Ed. *Pinkas Hackehilah Alexandrija/Sefer Iskor*. Alexssandrija Committee in Israel, Israel, 1972 *(in Hebrew)*

[124] Ironi, Noa, in Nathan Livneh, Ed. *Pinkas Hackehilah Alexandrija/Sefer Iskor*. Alexssandrija Committee in Israel, Israel, 1972 *(in Hebrew)*

[125] Ironi, Noa, in Nathan Livneh, Ed. *Pinkas Hackehilah Alexandrija/Sefer Iskor*. Alexssandrija Committee in Israel, Israel, 1972 *(in Hebrew)*

[126] Ironi, Noa, in Nathan Livneh, Ed. *Pinkas Hackehilah Alexandrija/Sefer Iskor*. Alexssandrija Committee in Israel, Israel, 1972 *(in Hebrew)*

[127] Avitachi, Arie. Rovno and Population, in *Rowne; Sefer Zikaron* (Rovno, a Memorial to the Jewish Community of Rovno, Yolyn). Tel Aviv, 1956, p. 21 *(in Hebrew)*

[128] 1850 Berestechko *Revizskaya Skazka (in Russian)*

[129] Ett, S. Volhynia. Encyclopedia Judaica. New York, Macmillan Company, 1971-1972, pp. 206-212

[130] Ruzhin (Hasidic dynasty). Wikipedia.org

[131] Assaf, David (2010). "Ruzhin Hasidic Dynasty." YIVO Encyclopedia of Jews in Eastern Europe; http://www.yivoencyclopedia.org/article.aspx/Ruzhin_Hasidic_Dynasty

[132] Friedman, Yisroel. The Golden Dynasty. Chapter One: The Rebbe Reb Yisroel of Ruzhin, 1997; http://www.nishmas.org./gdynasty/

[133] Yisrael Friedman of Ruzhyn. Wikipedia.org

[134] Eulogy to Rabbi Naftali Horenstein. Jerusalem, the *"Mishkebnot HaRo'im"* Institute of Boyan, 2000 *(in Hebrew)*

[135] 1850 Aleksandriya, Rovno Uezd, *Revizskaya Skazka* taken January 20, 1851 *(in Russian)*

[136] 1850 Ludvipol, Rovno uezd, Census

[137] Lieberman, Yosef. *Shalshelet HaYuchasin*. Jerusalem, 1977-8. *(in Hebrew)*

[138] Lieberman, Yosef. *Shalshelet HaYuchasin*. Jerusalem, 1977-8. *(in Hebrew)*

[139] History of the Lubomirski Family http://janlubomirski.pl/ang/history-of-the-lubomirski-family-2

[140] https://pl.wikipedia.org/wiki/Równe

[141] Weiss, Aharon. Rovno. Encyclopedia Judaica, Second Edition. Detroit, Thomson Gale, 2007

[142] https://pl.wikipedia.org/wiki/Równe

[143] http://jewua.org/mezhyrichi/

[144] https://en.wikipedia.org/wiki/Lubomirski

[145] Weiss, Aharon. Rovno. Encyclopedia Judaica, Second Edition. Detroit, Thomson Gale, 2007

[146] Spector, Shmuel, Ed. *Pinkas HaKehilot Polin*. Yad Vashem, Jerusalem 1990, Vol. 5, p. 43

[147] https://pl.wikipedia.org/wiki/Fryderyk_Lubomirski

[148] https://pl.wikipedia.org/wiki/Fryderyk_Lubomirski

[149] *Inedita. Studia Norwidiana* 34:2016. (English version.) *Blade Kłosy na odłogu…* - An Unknown Poem by Norwid.
http://czasopisma.tnkul.pl/index.php/sn/article/view/6484/6582 [download PDF]

[150] *Inedita. Studia Norwidiana* 34:2016. (English version.) *Blade Kłosy na odłogu…* - An Unknown Poem by Norwid.
http://czasopisma.tnkul.pl/index.php/sn/article/view/6484/6582 [download PDF]

[151] https://pl.wikipedia.org/wiki/Fryderyk_Lubomirski

[152] Kazimierz Lubomirski (composer). Wikipedia.org *(in Polish)*
https://pl.wikipedia.org/wiki/Kazimierz_Lubomirski_(kompozytor)

[153] *Inedita. Studia Norwidiana* 34:2016. (English version.) *Blade Kłosy na odłogu…* - An Unknown Poem by Norwid.

http://czasopisma.tnkul.pl/index.php/sn/article/view/6484/6582 [download PDF]

[154] Rąkowsk, Grzegorz. Volhynia. p. 340i *(in Polish)*

[155] Sulimierski, Filip et al. Geographical dictionary of the Kingdom of Poland and other Slavic countries, vol. IX. Warsaw: 1880-1902, pp. 818-22

[156] Rovno. Volhynia, Poland.
http://www.wolhynia.pl/index.php?option=com_content&view=article&id=319&catid=24&Itemid=101

[157] 1834 Aleksandriya, Rovno uezd, Census

[158] 1850 Ludvipol, Rovno uezd, Census

[159] Avitachi, Arie. History: Rovno and Population, in Avitachi, A., Ed. *Rowne; Sefer Zikaron*. Tel Aviv, 1956 *(in Hebrew)*

[160] Ayalon, N. Ed. *Sefer Zikaron le-kehilat Ludvipol (Slisht Gadol)*. Tel Aviv, 1965

[161] Ayalon, N. Ed. *Sefer Zikaron le-kehilat Ludvipol (Slisht Gadol)*. Tel Aviv, 1965

[162] Ayalon, N. Ed. *Sefer Zikaron le-kehilat Ludvipol (Slisht Gadol)*. Tel Aviv, 1965

[163] Ayalon, N. Ed. *Sefer Zikaron le-kehilat Ludvipol (Slisht Gadol)*. Tel Aviv, 1965

[164] 1850 Ludvipol, Rovno Uezd, Census

[165] Fond 1286 - Executive Police Dept., inventory 11 for the year 1848, file 268, Catalog of the Russian State Historic Files

[166] 1858 Ludvipol, Rovno Uezd, Census

[167] The British and Foreign Review, July-Oct. 1838, pp. 423-4 (bottom)

[168] 1858 Ludvipol, Rovno Uezd Census

[169] 1858 Ludvipol, Rovno Uezd Census

[170] 1858 Ludvipol, Rovno Uezd Census

[171] Ironi, Noa, in Nathan Livneh, Ed. *Pinkas HaKehilah Alekandrija/Sefer Iskor*. Israel, Aleksandrija Committee in Israel, 1972. *(in Hebrew)*

[172] Ironi, Noa, in Nathan Livneh, Ed. *Pinkas HaKehilah Aleksandrija/Sefer Iskor*. Israel, Aleksandriia Committee in Israel, 1972. *(in Hebrew)*

[173] Lieberman, Yosef. *Shalshelet HaYuchasin*. Jerusalem, 1977-8. *(in Hebrew)*

[174] Ironi, Noa, in Nathan Livneh, Ed. *Pinkas HaKehilah Aleksandrija/Sefer Iskor*. Israel, Aleksandrija Committee in Israel, 1972. *(in Hebrew)*

[175] Horodyshche. Geographical Dictionary of the Polish Kingdom and other Slavic Countries 1880-1914 *(in Polish)*

[176] Horodyshche. Geographical Dictionary of the Polish Kingdom and other Slavic Countries 1880-1914 *(in Polish)*

[177] Ironi, Noa, in Nathan Livneh, Ed. *Pinkas HaKehilah Aleksandrija/Sefer Iskor*. Israel, Aleksandriia Committee in Israel, 1972. *(in Hebrew)*

[178] Warszawski, N. Historical Jewish Millionaires in Russia (Events, Facts and Episodes).
IX. Ya'akov Yosef Horenstein. *Haint*, 1 Tevet, 5686 (December 18, 1925). *(in Yiddish)*

[179] Asher Ben-Oni, Editor. *Mizoch – Sefer Iskor*. Y. Nediv, Tel Aviv, 1961

[180] Asher Ben-Oni, Editor. *Mizoch – Sefer Iskor*. Y. Nediv, Tel Aviv, 1961

[181] Warszawski, N. Historical Jewish Millionaires in Russia (Events, Facts and Episodes).
IX. Ya'akov Yosef Horenstein. *Haint,* 1 Tevet, 5686 (December 18, 1925). *(in Yiddish)*

[182] Warszawski, N. Historical Jewish Millionaires in Russia (Events, Facts and Episodes).
IX. Ya'akov Yosef Horenstein. *Haint*, 1 Tevet, 5686 (December 18, 1925). *(in Yiddish)*

[183] Warszawski, N. Historical Jewish Millionaires in Russia (Events, Facts and Episodes).

IX. Ya'akov Yosef Horenstein. *Haint*, 1 Tevet, 5686 (December 18, 1925). *(in Yiddish)*

[184] *Kiryat Melech* (The King's City), Sayings of the Tzadikim, Sheet 12, 2004. *(in Hebrew)*

[185] *Kiryat Melech* (The King's City), Sayings of the Tzadikim, Sheet 12, 2004. *(in Hebrew)*

[186] Warszawski, N. Historical Jewish Millionaires in Russia (Events, Facts and Episodes).
IX. Ya'akov Yosef Horenstein. *Haint*, 1 Tevet, 5686 (December 18, 1925). *(in Yiddish)*

[187] Warszawski N. Historical Jewish Millionaires in Russia (Events, Facts and Episodes). X. Naftali Horenstein. *Haint* 8 Tevet, 5686 (December 25, 1925), p. 5. *(in Yiddish)*

[188] Virtual Shtetl: Korzec. https://sztetl.org.pl/en/towns/k/1047-korzec/99-history/137508-history-of-community

[189] Warszawski, N. Historical Jewish Millionaires in Russia (Events, Facts and Episodes).
IX - Ya'akov Yosef Horenstein. *Haint*, 1 Tevet, 5686 (December 18, 1925). *(in Yiddish)*

[190]
http://www.wolhynia.pl/index.php?option=com_content&view=article&id=35:korzec-1928&catid=14&Itemid=113

[191] http://www.sztetl.org.pl/en/city/korzec/

[192] http://www.sztetl.org.pl/en/city/korzec/

[193] http://www.sztetl.org.pl/en/city/korzec/

[194] Leoni, E. Ed. *Korets (Wolyn); sefer zikaron le-kehilatenu she-ala aleha ha-koret*. Tel Aviv, 1959

[195] *HaCarmel* May 31, 1866. *(in Hebrew)*

[196] Warszawski, N. Historical Jewish Millionaires in Russia (Events, Facts and Episodes).
IX. Ya'akov Yosef Horenstein. *Haint*, 1 Tevet, 5686 (December 18, 1925). *(in Yiddish)*

[197] http://www.sztetl.org.pl/en/city/korzec/

[198] Kiev state oblast archive, fond 2, opys 207, sprava #572. 1891

[199] Kiev state oblast archive, fond 2, opys 207, sprava #572. 1891

[200] The British and Foreign Review, July-Oct. 1838, pp. 423-4 (bottom)

[201] Rubinow, Isaac M. Economic Conditions of Jews in Russia. Published 1907, Vol. 15, US Dept. of Commerce and Labor, Bulletin of Labor, pp. 487-582

[202] Nathans, Benjamin. Beyond the Pale: The Jewish Encounter with Late Imperial Russia. U. of California Press, Berkeley & Los Angeles, CA, 2002

[203] Ryndziunskii, P. G. *Gorodskoe grazhdanstw doreformennoi Rossii*. Moscow, 1958. The Great Soviet Encyclopedia, 3rd Edition (1970-1979). *(in Russian)*

[204] Warszawski, N. Historical Jewish Millionaires in Russia (Events, Facts and Episodes).
IX. Ya'akov Yosef Horenstein. *Haint*, 1 Tevet, 5686 (December 18, 1925). *(in Yiddish)*

[205] Warszawski, N. Historical Jewish Millionaires in Russia (Events, Facts and Episodes).
IX. Ya'akov Yosef Horenstein. *Haint*, 1 Tevet, 5686 (December 18, 1925). *(in Yiddish)*

[206] Warszawski, N. Historical Jewish Millionaires in Russia (Events, Facts and Episodes
IX - Ya'akov Yosef Horenstein. *Haint*, 1 Tevet, 5686 (December 18, 1925). *(in Yiddish)*

[207] *HaIvri*. 13 Nissan 5636 (April 7, 1876)

[208] Hershenhorn, Nechemiah. Obituary for Ya'akov Yosef Horenstein *HaTzefirah* April 19, 1876. *(in Hebrew)*

[209] Hershenhorn, Nechemiah. Obituary for Ya'akov Yosef Horenstein. *HaTzefirah* April 19, 1876. *(in Hebrew)*

[210] *HaIvri*. 13 Nissan 5636 (April 7, 1876)

[211] *HaIvri*. 13 Nissan 5636 (April 7, 1876)

[212] Ankori, Zvi. Chestnuts of Yesteryear: A Jewish Odyssey. Jerusalem, Gefen Publishing House, 2003; Klingerman, Hinda. The great fire in Korets, in E. Leoni, Editor. The Korets Book; in Memory of our Community that is No More. 1959, Tel Aviv, p. 97

[213] Basiuk E. p. 101

[214] Kligerman Y. p. 165

[215] Frankel. Korets yisgor book

[216] *HaMelitz* 18; March 16, 1883, p. 280

[217] *HaMelitz* 18; March 16, 1883, p. 280

[218] *HaMelitz* 18; March 16, 1883, p. 280

[219] Warzawski N. Historical Jewish Millionaires in Russia (Events, Facts and Episodes). X. Naftali Horenstein. *Haint* 8 Tevet, 5686 (December 25, 1925), p. 5. *(in Yiddish)*

[220] Warzawski N. Historical Jewish Millionaires in Russia (Events, Facts and Episodes). X. Naftali Horenstein. *Haint* 8 Tevet, 5686 (December 25, 1925), p. 5. *(in Yiddish)*

[221] Warzawski N. Historical Jewish Millionaires in Russia (Events, Facts and Episodes). X. Naftali Horenstein. *Haint* 8 Tevet, 5686 (December 25, 1925), p. 5. *(in Yiddish)*

[222] http://www.ivelt.com/forum/viewtopic.php?f=31&t=20320&start=25

[223] *Erekh Avot*:
http://www.hebrewbooks.org/pdfpager.aspx?req=2121&st=&pgnum=28

[224] http://zchusavos.blogspot.com/2010/07/av-yartzeits.html

[225] Jascha Der Horensteiner. *Aufbau*, 1943. *(in Yiddish)*

[226] Mayzel, Nakhman. The Horensteins of Radomysl—A Famous Jewish Family of the Ukraine. *Morgn Frayhayt*, 1943. *(in Yiddish)*

[227] Warzawski N. Historical Jewish Millionaires in Russia (Events, Facts and Episodes). X. Naftali Horenstein. *Haint* 8 Tevet, 5686 (December 25, 1925), p. 5. *(in Yiddish)*

[228] Jascha Der Horensteiner. *Aufbau*, 1943. *(in Yiddish)*

[229] Mayzel, Nakhman. The Horensteins of Radomysl—A Famous Jewish Family of the Ukraine. *Morgn Frayhayt*, 1943. *(in Yiddish)*

[230] Warzawski N. Historical Jewish Millionaires in Russia (Events, Facts and Episodes). X. Naftali Horenstein *Haint* 8 Tevet, 5686 (December 25, 1925), p. 5. *(in Yiddish)*

[231] 1858 Aleksandriya, Rovno uezd, Census

[232] Warzawski N. Historical Jewish Millionaires in Russia (Events, Facts and Episodes). X. Naftali Horenstein. *Haint* 8 Tevet, 5686 (December 25, 1925), p. 5. *(in Yiddish)*

[233] Mayzel, Nakhman. The Horensteins of Radomysl—A Famous Jewish Family of the Ukraine. *Morgn Frayhayt*, 1943. *(in Yiddish)*

[234] Mayzel, Nakhman. The Horensteins of Radomysl—A Famous Jewish Family of the Ukraine. *Morgn Frayhayt*, 1943. *(in Yiddish)*

[235] Mayzel, Nakhman. The Horensteins of Radomysl—A Famous Jewish Family of the Ukraine. *Morgn Frayhayt*, 1943. *(in Yiddish)*

[236] Warzawski N. Historical Jewish Millionaires in Russia (Events, Facts and Episodes). X. Naftali Horenstein. *Haint* 8 Tevet, 5686 (December 25, 1925), p. 5. *(in Yiddish)*

[237] Warzawski N. Historical Jewish Millionaires in Russia (Events, Facts and Episodes). X. Naftali Horenstein. *Haint* 8 Tevet, 5686 (December 25, 1925), p. 5. *(in Yiddish)*

238 *Kiryat Melech: Omrei Tzadikim*. May 6, 2004; The United Societies of the Youth of Sadigura. *(in Hebrew)*

239 *Kiryat Melech: Omrei Tzadikim*. May 6, 2004; The United Societies of the Youth of Sadigura. *(in Hebrew)*

240 Warzawski N. Historical Jewish Millionaires in Russia (Events, Facts and Episodes). X. Naftali Horenstein. *Haint* 8 Tevet, 5686 (December 25, 1925), p. 5. *(in Yiddish)*

241 Pokhilevich, Lavrentiy. Kiev and Radomysl Uyezds: Statistical and Historical Notes. Kiev, Press of A. Davidenko, 1887. *(in Russian)*

242 Pokhilevich, Lavrentiy. Inventory of Land Ownership in Radomysl district of Kiev Gubernia. 1882. *(in Russian)*

243 Pokhilevich, Lavrentiy. Kiev and Radomysl Uyezds: Statistical and Historical Notes. Kiev, Press of A. Davidenko, 1887. *(in Russian)*

244 1909 Tax Records of the Radomysl area

245 Business catalog of the Leather Industry in Radomysl District. The 300-year History of the Maloratsky Family, Chapter I. http://maloratsky-vinitsky.weebly.com/generations-1-7.html

246 The 300-year History of the Maloratsky Family, Chapter I. http://maloratsky-vinitsky.weebly.com/generations-1-7.html

247 1909 Tax Records of the Radomysl area

248 Pokhilevich, Lavrentiy. Kiev and Radomysl Uyezds: Statistical and Historical Notes. Kiev, Press of A. Davidenko, 1887. *(in Russian)*

249 Kiev state oblast archive, fond 2, opys 207, sprava #208. 1891

250 Kiev state oblast archive, fond 2, opys 207, sprava #570. 1891

251 Pokhilevich, Lavrentiy. Kiev and Radomysl Uyezds: Statistical and Historical Notes. Kiev, Press of A. Davidenko, 1887. *(in Russian)*

252 Kiev state oblast archive, fond 1, opys 295, sprava #79944. 1881. 20 ark/17 docs

[253] Mayzel, Nakhman. The Horensteins of Radomysl—A Famous Jewish Family of the Ukraine. *Morgn Frayhayt*, 1943. *(in Yiddish)*

[254] Mayzel, Nakhman. The Horensteins of Radomysl—A Famous Jewish Family of the Ukraine. *Morgn Frayhayt*, 1943. *(in Yiddish)*

[255] Pokhilevich, Lavrentiy. Kiev and Radomysl Uyezds: Statistical and Historical Notes. Kiev, Press of A. Davidenko, 1887. *(in Russian)*

[256] Pokhilevich, Lavrentiy. Kiev and Radomysl Uyezds: Statistical and Historical Notes. Kiev, Press of A. Davidenko, 1887. *(in Russian)*

[257] Mayzel, Nakhman. The Horensteins of Radomysl—A Famous Jewish Family of the Ukraine. *Morgn Frayhayt*, 1943. *(in Yiddish)*

[258] Kiev state oblast archive, fond 1, opys 295, #71367, 1878

[259] Kiev state oblast archive, fond 1, opys 295, sprava #79944. 1881

[260] Kiev state oblast archive, fond 1, opys 295, sprava #79944. 1881

[261] 1913 All South-Western Territory Industrial trade directory. *(in Russian)*

[262] 1899-1913 All Russia Industrial Trade Directory. *(in Russian)*

[263] 1909-1914 Enterprises of the Russian Empire. *(in Russian)*

[264] 1913 All South-Western Territory Industrial trade directory. *(in Russian)*

[265] 1899-1913 All Russia Industrial Trade Directory. *(in Russian)*

[266] 1909-1914 Enterprises of the Russian Empire. *(in Russian)*

[267] Heifitz, Elias. The Slaughter of the Jews in the Ukraine in 1919. New York, Thomas Seltzer, 1921

[268] Pokhilevich, Lavrentiy. Kiev and Radomysl Uyezds: Statistical and Historical Notes. Kiev, Press of A. Davidenko, 1887. *(in Russian)*

[269] Jascha Der Horensteiner. *Aufbau*, 1943. *(in Yiddish)*

[270] Mayzel, Nakhman. The Horensteins of Radomysl—A Famous Jewish Family of the Ukraine. *Morgn Frayhayt*, 1943. *(in Yiddish)*

[271] Warzawski N. Historical Jewish Millionaires in Russia (Events, Facts and Episodes). X. Naftali Horenstein. *Haint* 8 Tevet, 5686 (December 25, 1925), p. 5. *(in Yiddish)*

[272] http://piskivska-gromada.gov.ua/smt-piskivka-23-18-34-23-06-2016/

[273] Warzawski N. Historical Jewish Millionaires in Russia (Events, Facts and Episodes). XI. The Horenstein Children. Warzawski N. Historical Jewish Millionaires in Russia (Events, Facts and Episodes). XI. The Horenstein Children. *Haint* 15 Tevet, 5686 (January 1, 1926), p. 5. *(in Yiddish)*

[274] Warzawski N. Historical Jewish Millionaires in Russia (Events, Facts and Episodes). XI. The Horenstein Children. Warzawski N. Historical Jewish Millionaires in Russia (Events, Facts and Episodes). XI. The Horenstein Children. *Haint* 15 Tevet, 5686 (January 1, 1926), p. 5. *(in Yiddish)*

[275] Warzawski N. Historical Jewish Millionaires in Russia (Events, Facts and Episodes). XI. The Horenstein Children. *Haint* 15 Tevet, 5686 (January 1, 1926), p. 5. *(in Yiddish)*

[276] Warzawski N. Historical Jewish Millionaires in Russia (Events, Facts and Episodes). XI. The Horenstein Children. *Haint* 15 Tevet, 5686 (January 1, 1926), p. 5. *(in Yiddish)*

[277] Mayzel, Nakhman. The Horensteins of Radomysl—A Famous Jewish Family of the Ukraine. *Morgn Frayhayt*, 1943. *(in Yiddish)*

[278] Warzawski N. Historical Jewish Millionaires in Russia (Events, Facts and Episodes). X. Naftali Horenstein. *Haint* 8 Tevet, 5686 (December 25, 1925), p. 5. *(in Yiddish)*

[279] Warzawski N. Historical Jewish Millionaires in Russia (Events, Facts and Episodes). X. Naftali Horenstein. *Haint* 8 Tevet, 5686 (December 25, 1925), p. 5. *(in Yiddish)*

[280] Warzawski N. Historical Jewish Millionaires in Russia (Events, Facts and Episodes). XI. The Horenstein Children. *Haint* 15 Tevet, 5686 (January 1, 1926), p. 5. *(in Yiddish)*

[281] Warzawski N. Historical Jewish Millionaires in Russia (Events, Facts and Episodes). X. Naftali Horenstein. *Haint* 8 Tevet, 5686 (December 25, 1925), p. 5. *(in Yiddish)*

[282] Warzawski N. Historical Jewish Millionaires in Russia (Events, Facts and Episodes). X. Naftali Horenstein. *Haint* 8 Tevet, 5686 (December 25, 1925), p. 5. *(in Yiddish)*

[283] Warzawski N. Historical Jewish Millionaires in Russia (Events, Facts and Episodes). X. Naftali Horenstein. *Haint* 8 Tevet, 5686 (December 25, 1925), p. 5. *(in Yiddish)*

[284] Warzawski N. Historical Jewish Millionaires in Russia (Events, Facts and Episodes). X. Naftali Horenstein. *Haint* 8 Tevet, 5686 (December 25, 1925), p. 5. *(in Yiddish)*

[285] Mayzel, Nakhman. The Horensteins of Radomysl—A Famous Jewish Family of the Ukraine. *Morgn Frayhayt*, 1943. *(in Yiddish)*

[286] Jascha Der Horensteiner. *Aufbau*, 1943. *(in Yiddish)*

[287] Jascha Der Horensteiner. *Aufbau*, 1943. *(in Yiddish)*

[288] Lieberman, Yosef. *Shalshelet HaYuchasin*. Jerusalem, 1977-8. *(in Hebrew)*

[289] Mayzel, Nakhman. The Horensteins of Radomysl—A Famous Jewish Family of the Ukraine. *Morgn Frayhayt*, 1943. *(in Yiddish)*

[290] Jascha Der Horensteiner. *Aufbau*, 1943. *(in Yiddish)*

[291] Mayzel, Nakhman. The Horensteins of Radomysl—A Famous Jewish Family of the Ukraine. *Morgn Frayhayt*, 1943. *(in Yiddish)*

[292] Jascha Der Horensteiner. *Aufbau*, 1943. *(in Yiddish)*

[293] Kiev state oblast archive, fond 1, opys 295, sprava #79944, 1881. *(in Russian)*

[294] Bedrik-Bilan Kh., et al. 100 Most Famous Ukrainians. Orpheus, 2005, pp. 251-253. *(in Ukrainian)*

[295] Personal communication: Lipa Horenstein, Naftali Horenstein's greatgrandson, and his son Misha

[296] Druh, Olga & Malakov, Dmitry. Mansions of Kiev. K., Ky, 2004 *(translated)*

[297] Dynner, Glenn. Men of Silk: The Hasidic Conquest of Polish Jewish Society. Oxford & New York, Oxford University Press, 2006, Chapter 4: Yichus: The Social Composition of Hasidic Leadership.

[298] Dynner, Glenn. Men of Silk: The Hasidic Conquest of Polish Jewish Society. Oxford & New York, Oxford University Press, 2006, Chapter 4: Yichus: The Social Composition of Hasidic Leadership.

[299] Dynner, Glenn. Men of Silk: The Hasidic Conquest of Polish Jewish Society. Oxford & New York, Oxford University Press, 2006, Chapter 4: Yichus: The Social Composition of Hasidic Leadership.

[300] Mayzel, Nakhman. The Horensteins of Radomysl—A Famous Jewish Family of the Ukraine. *Morgn Frayhayt*, 1943. *(in Yiddish)*

[301] Mayzel, Nakhman. The Horensteins of Radomysl—A Famous Jewish Family of the Ukraine. *Morgn Frayhayt*, 1943. *(in Yiddish)*

[302] Mayzel, Nakhman. The Horensteins of Radomysl—A Famous Jewish Family of the Ukraine. *Morgn Frayhayt*, 1943. *(in Yiddish)*

[303] Mayzel, Nakhman. The Horensteins of Radomysl—A Famous Jewish Family of the Ukraine. *Morgn Frayhayt*, 1943. *(in Yiddish)*

[304] Mordechai Horenstein, in Tidhar D. Encyclopedia of the Founders and Builders of Israel. Vol. 2, pp. 1004-5, 1947. Retrieved from http://www.tidhar.tourolib.org/tidhar/view/2/1004 *(in Hebrew)*.

[305] Rachman, R. Ben-Tzyon. Approbation to *Tiferet Menachem*, 1972 ed. *(in Hebrew)*

[306] Rachman, R. Ben-Tzyon. Approbation to *Tiferet Menachem*, 1972 ed. *(in Hebrew)*

[307] Mishkenot HaRoim Institute of Boyan, 24 Nov, 2000. *(in Hebrew)*

[308] Warzawski N. Historical Jewish Millionaires in Russia (Events, Facts and Episodes). X. Naftali Horenstein. *Haint* 8 Tevet, 5686 (December 25, 1925), p. 5. *(in Yiddish)*

309 Warzawski N. Historical Jewish Millionaires in Russia (Events, Facts and Episodes). X. Naftali Horenstein. *Haint* 8 Tevet, 5686 (December 25, 1925), p. 5. *(in Yiddish)*

310 Hershenhorn, Nechemiah. Obituary for Ya'akov Yosef Horenstein. *HaTzefirah* April 19, 1876. *(in Hebrew)*

311 Leo Horenstein - personal communication

312 Aleichem, Shalom. Latkes for Hanukah, 1904. *(in Yiddish)*

313 Mayzel, Nakhman. The Horensteins of Radomysl—A Famous Jewish Family of the Ukraine. *Morgn Frayhayt*, 1943. *(in Yiddish)*

314 Mordechai Horenstein, in Tidhar D. Encyclopedia of the Founders and Builders of Israel. Vol. 2, pp. 1004-5, 1947. http://www.tidhar.tourolib.org/tidhar/view/2/1004 *(in Hebrew)*

315 1909 Tax Records of the Radomysl area. *(in Russian)*

316 Warzawski N. Historical Jewish Millionaires in Russia (Events, Facts and Episodes). X. Naftali Horenstein. *Haint* 8 Tevet, 5686 (December 25, 1925), p. 5. *(in Yiddish)*

317 Mayzel, Nakhman. The Horensteins of Radomysl—A Famous Jewish Family of the Ukraine. *Morgn Frayhayt*, 1943. *(in Yiddish)*

318 Mayzel, Nakhman. The Horensteins of Radomysl—A Famous Jewish Family of the Ukraine. *Morgn Frayhayt*, 1943. *(in Yiddish)*

319 Warzawski N. Historical Jewish Millionaires in Russia (Events, Facts and Episodes). XI. The Horenstein Children. *Haint* 15 Tevet, 5686 (January 1, 1926), p. 5. *(in Yiddish)*

320 Warzawski N. Historical Jewish Millionaires in Russia (Events, Facts and Episodes). XI. The Horenstein Children. *Haint* 15 Tevet, 5686 (January 1, 1926), p. 5. *(in Yiddish)*

321 Mayzel, Nakhman. The Horensteins of Radomysl—A Famous Jewish Family of the Ukraine. *Morgn Frayhayt*, 1943. *(in Yiddish)*

[322] Warzawski N. Historical Jewish Millionaires in Russia (Events, Facts and Episodes). XI. The Horenstein Children. *Haint* 15 Tevet, 5686 (January 1, 1926), p. 5. *(in Yiddish)*

[323] Orz Tzadik (Horenstein descendant) – personal communication

[324] Mayzel, Nakhman. The Horensteins of Radomysl—A Famous Jewish Family of the Ukraine. *Morgn Frayhayt*, 1943. *(in Yiddish)*

[325] 1895 Kiev Gubernia. All *Vsia Rossiia*. *(in Russian)*

[326] 1913 All South-Western Territory Industrial trade directory

[327] 1913 All South-Western Territory Industrial trade directory

[328] 1903 Minsk Gubernia. All *Vsia Rossiia*. *(in Russian)*

[329] Warzawski N. Historical Jewish Millionaires in Russia (Events, Facts and Episodes). XI. The Horenstein Children. *Haint* 15 Tevet, 5686 (January 1, 1926), p. 5. *(in Yiddish)*

[330] Warzawski N. Historical Jewish Millionaires in Russia (Events, Facts and Episodes). XI. The Horenstein Children. *Haint* 15 Tevet, 5686 (January 1, 1926), p. 5. *(in Yiddish)*

[331] *Sefer Ner Yisrael*: Teachings from *Rebbe* Yisrael of Ruzhin and his descendants: volume 6, pp. 96 & 100

[332] Warzawski N. Historical Jewish Millionaires in Russia (Events, Facts and Episodes). XI. The Horenstein Children. *Haint* 15 Tevet, 5686 (January 1, 1926), p. 5. *(in Yiddish)*

[333] Warzawski N. Historical Jewish Millionaires in Russia (Events, Facts and Episodes). XI. The Horenstein Children. *Haint* 15 Tevet, 5686 (January 1, 1926), p. 5. *(in Yiddish)*

[334] Warzawski N. Historical Jewish Millionaires in Russia (Events, Facts and Episodes). XI. The Horenstein Children. Haint 15 Tevet, 5686 (January 1, 1926), p. 5. *(in Yiddish)*

[335] Zwik, Gennady. The History of Radomyshl. Zhytomir, Polissya, 2002. *(in Ukrainian)*

[336] Warzawski N. Historical Jewish Millionaires in Russia (Events, Facts and Episodes). XI. The Horenstein Children. *Haint* 15 Tevet, 5686 (January 1, 1926), p. 5. *(in Yiddish)*

[337] Ora Tzadik (Horenstein descendant) - personal communication

[338] Warzawski N. Historical Jewish Millionaires in Russia (Events, Facts and Episodes). XI. The Horenstein Children. *Haint* 15 Tevet, 5686 (January 1, 1926), p. 5. *(in Yiddish)*

[339] Liebersohn, Aharon. Yanushpol, in *Yalqut Vohlyn*, Volume 2 (1945), Collection 9, pp. 26-27

[340] Liebersohn, Aharon. Yanushpol, in *Yalqut Vohlyn*, Volume 2 (1945), Collection 9, pp. 26-27

[341] Warzawski N. Historical Jewish Millionaires in Russia (Events, Facts and Episodes). XI. The Horenstein Children. *Haint* 15 Tevet, 5686 (January 1, 1926), p. 5. *(in Yiddish)*

[342] Liebersohn, Aharon. Yanushpol, in *Yalqut Vohlyn*, Volume 2 (1945), Collection 9, pp. 26-27

[343] Warzawski N. Historical Jewish Millionaires in Russia (Events, Facts and Episodes). XI. The Horenstein Children. *Haint* 15 Tevet, 5686 (January 1, 1926), p. 5. *(in Yiddish)*

[344] Warzawski N. Historical Jewish Millionaires in Russia (Events, Facts and Episodes). XI. The Horenstein Children. *Haint* 15 Tevet, 5686 (January 1, 1926), p. 5. *(in Yiddish)*

[345] Warzawski N. Historical Jewish Millionaires in Russia (Events, Facts and Episodes). XI. The Horenstein Children. *Haint* 15 Tevet, 5686 (January 1, 1926), p. 5. *(in Yiddish)*

[346] Warzawski N. Historical Jewish Millionaires in Russia (Events, Facts and Episodes). XI. The Horenstein Children. *Haint* 15 Tevet, 5686 (January 1, 1926), p. 5. *(in Yiddish)*

[347] Warzawski N. Historical Jewish Millionaires in Russia (Events, Facts and Episodes). XI. The Horenstein Children. *Haint* 15 Tevet, 5686 (January 1, 1926), p. 5. *(in Yiddish)*

[348] Liebersohn, Aharon. Yanushpol, in *Yalqut Vohlyn*, Volume 2 (1945), Collection 9, pp. 26-27

[349] Heifitz, Elias. The Slaughter of the Jews in the Ukraine in 1919. New York, Thomas Seltzer, 1921

[350] 1913 All South-Western Territory Industrial trade directory. *(in Russian)*

[351] 1899-1913 All Russia Industrial Trade Directory. *(in Russian)*

[352] 1909-1914 Enterprises of the Russian Empire. *(in Russian)*

[353] Yanushpol. Spector, Shmuel, Editor in Chief. The Encyclopedia of Jewish Life Before and During the Holocaust. New York, New York University Press, 2001, Volume 3, p. 1474

[354] Warzawski N. Historical Jewish Millionaires in Russia (Events, Facts and Episodes). XI. The Horenstein Children. *Haint* 15 Tevet, 5686 (January 1, 1926), p. 5. *(in Yiddish)*

[355] Warzawski N. Historical Jewish Millionaires in Russia (Events, Facts and Episodes). XI. The Horenstein Children. *Haint* 15 Tevet, 5686 (January 1, 1926), p. 5. *(in Yiddish)*

[356] Warzawski N. Historical Jewish Millionaires in Russia (Events, Facts and Episodes). XI. The Horenstein Children. *Haint* 15 Tevet, 5686 (January 1, 1926), p. 5. *(in Yiddish)*

[357] Liebersohn, Aharon. Yanushpol, in *Yalqut Vohlyn*, Volume 2 (1945), Collection 9, pp. 26-27

[358] Chapter 3, A Biography of Mendel Horenstein, in *Teshurah*. 5 Nisan, 5772 (March 28, 2012). http://www.teshura.com/teshurapdf/Shweke-Noki%20-%20Nissan%205,%205772.pdf *(in Hebrew)*

[359] Rabbi Yanki Towber. Leaven "paranoia." Chabad-Lubavitch in Cyberspace. http://www.chabad.org/gopher/weekly/exodus/003/w4.htm

[360] It once happened, in *L'Chaim*: The Weekly Publication for Every Jewish Person, Issue #745, Lubavitch Youth Organization, Brooklyn, NY, USA, November 22, 2002; http://www.lchaimweekly.org/lchaim/5763/745

[361] Chapter 3, A Biography of Mendel Horenstein, in *Teshurah*. 5 Nisan, 5772 (March 28, 2012). http://www.teshura.com/teshurapdf/Shweke-Noki%20-%20Nissan%205,%205772.pdf *(in Hebrew)*

[362] Chapter 3, A Biography of Mendel Horenstein, in *Teshurah*. 5 Nisan, 5772 (March 28, 2012). http://www.teshura.com/teshurapdf/Shweke-Noki%20-%20Nissan%205,%205772.pdf *(in Hebrew)*

[363] Warzawski N. Historical Jewish Millionaires in Russia (Events, Facts and Episodes). XI. The Horenstein Children. *Haint* 15 Tevet, 5686 (January 1, 1926), p. 5. *(in Yiddish)*

[364] Mayzel, Nakhman. The Horensteins of Radomysl—A Famous Jewish Family of the Ukraine. *Morgn Frayhayt*, 1943. *(in Yiddish)*

[365] Warzawski N. Historical Jewish Millionaires in Russia (Events, Facts and Episodes). XI. The Horenstein Children. *Haint* 15 Tevet, 5686 (January 1, 1926), p. 5. *(in Yiddish)*

[366] 1910 Book of State Schools of Kiev Gubernia

[367] State Archives in the City of Kiev, fond 163, opys 7, sprava #534, 1876-87

[368] Horenstein, Rose Landwehr. Unpublished manuscript in the possession of Misha Horenstein.

[369] State Archives in the City of Kiev, fond 163, opys 7, sprava #1070, 1887

[370] 1886 and 1887 documents in the Kiev Archive.

[371] 1895 Kiev Gubernia. *All Vsia Rossiia. (in Russian)*

[372] Kiev. *Kraj*, nr.9, 1900, str. 17. (*in Polish*)

[373] Mayzel, Nakhman. The Horensteins of Radomysl—A Famous Jewish Family of the Ukraine. *Morgn Frayhayt*, 1943. (*in Yiddish*)

[374] Jascha Der Horensteiner. *Aufbau*, 1943. *(in Yiddish)*

375 Mayzel, Nakhman. The Horensteins of Radomysl—A Famous Jewish Family of the Ukraine. *Morgn Frayhayt*, 1943. *(in Yiddish)*

376 Warzawski N. Historical Jewish Millionaires in Russia (Events, Facts and Episodes). XI. The Horenstein Children. *Haint* 15 Tevet, 5686 (January 1, 1926), p. 5. *(in Yiddish)*

377 *Jascha Der Horensteiner. Aufbau*, 1943. *(in Yiddish)*

378 Lieberman, Yosef, *Shalshelet HaYuchasin*. Jerusalem, 1977-8. *(in Hebrew)*

379 Mayzel, Nakhman. The Horensteins of Radomysl—A Famous Jewish Family of the Ukraine. *Morgn Frayhayt*, 1943. *(in Yiddish)*

380 Warzawski N. Historical Jewish Millionaires in Russia (Events, Facts and Episodes). XI. The Horenstein Children. *Haint* 15 Tevet, 5686 (January 1, 1926), p. 5. *(in Yiddish)*

381 Mayzel, Nakhman. The Horensteins of Radomysl—A Famous Jewish Family of the Ukraine. *Morgn Frayhayt*, 1943. *(in Yiddish)*

382 Advertisement in The Times (London), March 28, 1899, p. 4

383 Gordon, Beate Sirota. The Only Woman in the Room. Tokyo, Kodansha International, 1997

384 Sirota, Augustina Horenstein - Interview

385 Warzawski N. Historical Jewish Millionaires in Russia (Events, Facts and Episodes). XI. The Horenstein Children. *Haint* 15 Tevet, 5686 (January 1, 1926), p. 5. *(in Yiddish)*

386 Asher Ben-Oni, Editor. *Mizoch – Sefer Iskor.* Y. Nediv, Tel Aviv, 1961; Kiev. Kraj, nr.9, 1900, str. 17. *(in Polish)*

387 Personal communication: Misha Horenstein

388 Sirota, Augustina Horenstein - Interview

389 Sirota, Augustina Horenstein - Interview

[390] Sirota, Augustina Horenstein - Interview

[391] Sirota, Augustina Horenstein - Interview

[392] Gordon, Beate Sirota. The Only Woman in the Room. Tokyo, Kodansha International, 1997

[393] Gordon, Beate Sirota. The Only Woman in the Room. Tokyo, Kodansha International, 1997

[394] Gordon, Beate Sirota. The Only Woman in the Room. Tokyo, Kodansha International, 1997

[395] Gordon, Beate Sirota. The Only Woman in the Room. Tokyo, Kodansha International, 1997

[396] Warzawski N. Historical Jewish Millionaires in Russia (Events, Facts and Episodes). XI. The Horenstein Children. *Haint* 15 Tevet, 5686 (January 1, 1926), p. 5. *(in Yiddish)*

[397] Gladysh, Liudmyla. Keys to the Town of Radomyshl: Town History Essays. Zhtomyr, Polissya, 2007. *(in Ukrainian)*

[398] Zwik, Gennady. The History of Radomyshl. Zhytomir, Polissya, 2002. (*in Ukrainian)*

[399] Gladysh, Liudmyla. Keys to the Town of Radomyshl: Town History Essays. Zhtomyr, Polissya, 2007. *(in Ukrainian)*

[400] Zwik, Gennady. The History of Radomyshl. Zhytomir, Polissya, 2002. *(in Ukrainian)*

[401] Molodiko, Vladimir. Radomyshl City from the Depths of Centuries: Tiles from the Horenstein House. http://radomyshl.blogspot.com/2014/07/blog-post_9.html *(in Ukrainian)*

[402] Gladysh, Liudmyla. Keys to the Town of Radomyshl: Town History Essays. Zhtomyr, Polissya, 2007. *(in Ukrainian)*

[403] Zwik, Gennady. The History of Radomyshl. Zhytomir, Polissya, 2002. *(in Ukrainian)*

[404] The 300-Year History of the Maloratsky Family, Chapter I. http://maloratsky-vinitsky.weebly.com/generations-1-7.html

[405] The 300-Year History of the Maloratsky Family, Chapter I. http://maloratsky-vinitsky.weebly.com/generations-1-7.html

[406] Maya Kaganskaya. Centropa.org. http://www.centropa.org/biography/maya-kaganskaya

[407] The 300-Year History of the Maloratsky Family, Chapter I. http://maloratsky-vinitsky.weebly.com/generations-1-7.html

[408] Maya Kaganskaya. Centropa.org. http://www.centropa.org/biography/maya-kaganskaya

[409] The 300-Year History of the Maloratsky Family, Chapter I. http://maloratsky-vinitsky.weebly.com/generations-1-7.html

[410] Pirogov, Alexander. History of the House on Prisutstvena Street. *(in Ukrainian)* http://radomyshl-nash-dim.blogspot.com/2012/11/blog-post28.html

[411] Zwik, Gennady. The History of Radomyshl. Zhytomir, Polissya, 2002. *(in Ukrainian)*

[412] 1909 Tax Records of the Radomysl area. *(in Russian)*

[413] 1913 All South-Western Territory Industrial trade directory. *(in Russian)*

[414] Mordechai Horenstein, in Tidhar D. Encyclopedia of the Founders and Builders of Israel. Vol. 2, pp. 1004-5, 1947. http://www.tidhar.tourolib.org/tidhar/view/2/1004 *(in Hebrew)*

[415] Rabinovitz, Dov. *Mishkenot HaRo'im*. Jerusalem, 1984, pp. 160-162, footnote no. 45 *(in Hebrew)*

[416] Tidhar D. Encyclopedia of the Founders and Builders of Israel. Vol. 2, p. 1004, 1947. http://www.tidhar.tourolib.org/tidhar/view/2/1004 *(in Hebrew)*

[417] Advertisement in the Radomysylian, #99. August 25, 1913

[418] Maya Kaganskaya. Centropa.org. http://www.centropa.org/biography/maya-kaganskaya

[419] Gladysh, Liudmyla. Keys to the Town of Radomyshl: Town History Essays. Zhtomyr, Polissya, 2007. *(in Ukrainian)*

[420] Moshe (Trachtenberg) Dagan (Horenstein descendant) - personal communication

[421] 1913 All South-Western Territory Industrial trade directory. *(in Russian)*

[422] Warzawski N. Historical Jewish Millionaires in Russia (Events, Facts and Episodes). XI. The Horenstein Children. Haint 15 Tevet, 5686 (January 1, 1926). *(in Yiddish)*

[423] Pirogov, Alexander. History of the House on Prisutstvena Street. *(in Ukrainian)* http://radomyshl-nash-dim.blogspot.com/2012/11/blog-post28.html)

[424] Pirogov, Alexander. History of the House on Prisutstvena Street. *(in Ukrainian)* http://radomyshl-nash-dim.blogspot.com/2012/11/blog-post28.html)

[425] Molodiko, Vladimir. Radomyshl City from the Depths of Centuries: Tiles from the Horenstein House. http://radomyshl.blogspot.com/2014/07/blog-post_9.html *(in Ukrainian)*

[426] Molodiko, Vladimir. Radomyshl City from the Depths of Centuries: Tiles from the Horenstein House. http://radomyshl.blogspot.com/2014/07/blog-post_9.html *(in Ukrainian)*

[427] Pirogov, Alexander. History of the House on Prisutstvena Street. *(in Ukrainian)* http://radomyshl-nash-dim.blogspot.com/2012/11/blog-post28.html

[428] Gladysh, Liudmyla. Keys to the Town of Radomyshl: Town Historical Essays. Zytomyr, Polissya, 2007. *(in Ukrainian)*

[429] Pirogov, Alexander. History of the House on Prisutstvena Street. *(in Ukrainian)* http://radomyshl-nash-dim.blogspot.com/2012/11/blog-post28.html)

[430] Pirogov, Alexander. History of the House on Prisutstvena Street. *(in Ukrainian)* http://radomyshl-nash-dim.blogspot.com/2012/11/blog-post28.html)

[431]Pirogov, Alexander. History of the House on Prisutstvena Street. *(in Ukrainian)* http://radomyshl-nash-dim.blogspot.com/2012/11/blog-post28.html)

[432] Pirogov, Alexander. History of the House of Prisutstvena Street. *(in Ukrainian)* http://radomyshl-nash-dim.blogspot.com/2012/11/blog-post28.html)

[433] Molodiko, Vladimir. Radomyshl City from the Depths of Centuries: Tiles from the Horenstein House. *(in Ukrainian)* http://radomyshl.blogspot.com/2014/07/blog-post_9.html

[434] Gladysh, Liudmyla. Keys to the Town of Radomyshl: Town Historical Essays. Zytomyr, Polissya, 2007. *(in Ukrainian)*

[435] Pirogov, Alexander. From the City of Radomysl on Postcards. Unpublished monograph. *(in Ukrainian)*

[436] The 300-Year History of the Maloratsky Family, Chapter I. http://maloratsky-vinitsky.weebly.com/generations-1-7.html

[437] The 300-Year History of the Maloratsky Family, Chapter I. http://maloratsky-vinitsky.weebly.com/generations-1-7.html

[438] Pirogov, Alexander. History of the House on Prisutstvena Street. *(in Ukrainian)* http://radomyshl-nash-dim.blogspot.com/2012/11/blog-post28.html

[439] 1850 Kremenets District Census

[440] All Russia. 1912. *(in Russian)*

[441] Plants and Factories of All Russia. 1913. *(in Russian)*

[442] All South-Western Region. Gazetteer and Address Book of Kiev, Podolia and Volhyn Gubernias, 1913 *(in Russian)*

[443] Gladysh, Liudmyla. Keys to the Town of Radomyshl: Town History Essays. Zhtomyr, Polissya, 2007. *(In Ukrainian.)*

[444] Zwik, Gennady. The History of Radomyshl. Zhytomir, Polissya, 2002. *(in Ukrainian)*

[445] 1913 All South-Western Territory Industrial trade directory. *(in Russian)*

[446] Harry Sapir, Abraham Yosef Horenstein's grandson – personal communication

[447] *Zentralfriedhof Israelite Tor*, (Central Cemetery), Vienna

[448] Berdichev Uyezd, *Vsia Rossiia*, 1911. *(in Russian)*

[449] Harry Sapir, Abraham Yosef Horenstein's grandson – personal communication

[450] Ittai Hershman, Abraham Yosef Horenstein's great grandson – personal communication

[451] Mordechai Horenstein, in Tidhar D. Encyclopedia of the Founders and Builders of Israel. Vol. 2, pp. 1004-5, 1947.
http://www.tidhar.tourolib.org/tidhar/view/2/1004 *(In Hebrew.)*

[452] Mordechai Horenstein, in Tidhar D. Encyclopedia of the Founders and Builders of Israel. Vol. 2, pp. 1004-5, 1947.
http://www.tidhar.tourolib.org/tidhar/view/2/1004 *(in Hebrew)*

[453] Mordechai Horenstein, in Tidhar D. Encyclopedia of the Founders and Builders of Israel. Vol. 2, pp. 1004-5, 1947.
http://www.tidhar.tourolib.org/tidhar/view/2/1004 *(in Hebrew)*

[454] Mordechai Horenstein, in Tidhar D. Encyclopedia of the Founders and Builders of Israel. Vol. 2, pp. 1004-5, 1947.
http://www.tidhar.tourolib.org/tidhar/view/2/1004 *(in Hebrew)*

[455] Mordechai Horenstein, in Tidhar D. Encyclopedia of the Founders and Builders of Israel. Vol. 2, pp. 1004-5, 1947.
http://www.tidhar.tourolib.org/tidhar/view/2/1004 *(in Hebrew)*

[456] Mordechai Horenstein, in Tidhar D. Encyclopedia of the Founders and Builders of Israel. Vol. 2, pp. 1004-5, 1947.
http://www.tidhar.tourolib.org/tidhar/view/2/1004 *(in Hebrew)*

[457] Mordechai Horenstein, in Tidhar D. Encyclopedia of the Founders and Builders of Israel. Vol. 2, pp. 1004-5, 1947.
http://www.tidhar.tourolib.org/tidhar/view/2/1004 *(In Hebrew.)*

[458] Mordechai Horenstein, in Tidhar D. Encyclopedia of the Founders and Builders of Israel. Vol. 2, pp. 1004-5, 1947.
http://www.tidhar.tourolib.org/tidhar/view/2/1004 *(in Hebrew)*

[459] Pirogov, Alexander. Noble Assembly in the County Town of Radomysl. *(in Ukrainian)*
http://radomyshl-nash-dim.blogspot.com/2016/09/blog-post_22.html

[460] Ettinger, Shmuel Volhynia. Encyclopedia Judaica, Second Edition. Detroit, Thomson Gale, 2007, pp. 206-21

[461] Ettinger, Shmuel. Volhynia. Encyclopedia Judaica, Second Edition. Detroit, Thomson Gale, 2007, pp. 206-21

[462] Ettinger, Shmuel. Volhynia. Encyclopedia Judaica, Second Edition. Detroit, Thomson Gale, 2007, pp. 206-212

[463] Pirogov, Alexander. Noble Assembly in the County Town of Radomysl. *(in Ukrainian)*
http://radomyshl-nash-dim.blogspot.com/2016/09/blog-post_22.html

[464] Mayzel, Nakhman. The Horensteins of Radomysl—A Famous Jewish Family of the Ukraine. *Morgn Frayhayt*, 1943. *(in Yiddish)*

[465] Warzawski N. Historical Jewish Millionaires in Russia (Events, Facts and Episodes). X. Naftali Horenstein. *Haint* 8 Tevet, 5686 (December 25, 1925), p. 5. *(in Yiddish)*

[466] Warzawski N. Historical Jewish Millionaires in Russia (Events, Facts and Episodes). XI. The Horenstein Children. *Haint* 15 Tevet, 5686 (January 1, 1926), p. 5. *(in Yiddish)*

[467] Warzawski N. Historical Jewish Millionaires in Russia (Events, Facts and Episodes). XI. The Horenstein Children. *Haint* 15 Tevet, 5686 (January 1, 1926), p. 5. *(in Yiddish)*

[468] Rabinovitz, Dov. *Mishkenot HaRo'im*. Jerusalem, 1984, p. 56. *(in Hebrew)*

[469] Rabinovitz, Dov. *Mishkenot HaRo'im*. Jerusalem, 1984, p. 56. *(in Hebrew)*

470 R. Menachum Nachum of Tchernovitz. *Tiferet Menachem*. (BS 1225 M3935, volume 1, 1972 edition). *(in Hebrew)*

471 R. Menachum Nachum of Tchernovitz. *Tiferet Menachem*. (BS 1225 M3935, volume 1, 1972 edition). *(in Hebrew)*

472 Ettinger, Shmuel. Volhynia. Encyclopedia Judaica, Second Edition. Detroit, Thomson Gale, 2007, pp. 206-212

473 https://www.chabad.org/search/results.asp?searchWord= menachem+mendel+horenstein

474 Mayzel, Nakhman. The Horensteins of Radomysl—A Famous Jewish Family of the Ukraine. *Morgn Frayhayt*, 1943. *(in Yiddish)*

475 Jascha Horenstein. Wikipedia.org

476 Brewer, Roy. Jascha Horenstein. Artist Biography. http://www.allmusic.com/artist/jascha-horenstein-mn0000118920/biography

477 Jascha Horenstein. Wikipedia.org

478 Brewer, Roy. Jascha Horenstein. Artist Biography. http://www.allmusic.com/artist/jascha-horenstein-mn0000118920/biography

479 Jascha Horenstein. Wikipedia.org

480 Jascha Horenstein. Wikipedia.org

481 Loppert, Max. Horenstein, Jascha. Encyclopedia Judaica, Volume 9, 2007

482 Loppert, Max. Horenstein, Jascha. Encyclopedia Judaica, Volume 9, 2007

483 Brewer, Roy. Jascha Horenstein. Artist Biography. http://www.allmusic.com/artist/jascha-horenstein-mn0000118920/biography

484 Jascha Horenstein biography on Spotify.com: https://open.spotify.com/artist/7fa3rN13UOA9Y1GzdtSJHv/about

485 Ross, Alex. Arts: Recordings View; A Minor Legend in His Time, Now a Major Cult Hero. The New York Times, October 16, 1994

[486] Ettinger, Shmuel. Volhynia. Encyclopedia Judaica, Second Edition. Detroit, Thomson Gale, 2007, pp. 206-212

[487] Ettinger, Shmuel. Volhynia. Encyclopedia Judaica, Second Edition. Detroit, Thomson Gale, 2007, pp. 206-212

[488] Mayzel, Nakhman. The Horensteins of Radomysl—A Famous Jewish Family of the Ukraine. *Morgn Frayhayt*, 1943. *(in Yiddish)*

[489] Jascha Der Horensteiner. *Aufbau*, 1943 *(in German)*

[490] McKenzie, Steven L. King David: A Biography. 2000, Oxford University Press, pp. 186-188

[491] McKenzie, Steven L. King David: A Biography. 2000, Oxford University Press, pp. 186-188

[492] McKenzie, Steven L. King David: A Biography. 2000, Oxford University Press, p. 28

[493] Finkelstein, Israel and Silberman, Neil Asher. David and Solomon. In Search of the Bible's Sacred Kings and the Roots of the Western Tradition. New York Simon & Schuster, 2006

[494] Finkelstein, Israel and Silberman, Neil Asher. David and Solomon. In Search of the Bible's Sacred Kings and the Roots of the Western Tradition. New York Simon & Schuster, 2006, p. 274

[495] Finkelstein, Israel, interviewed in Stern Shefler, Gil. Are You a Descendant of the House of David? The Jerusalem Post, January 10, 2012

[496] http://www.jewishvirtuallibrary.org/myth-and-reality-of-king-david-s-jerusalem

[497] Finkelstein, Israel. The Forgotten Kingdom: The Archeology and History of Northern Israel. Atlanta, Society of Biblical Literature, 2013

[498] Finkelstein, Israel, interviewed in Stern Shefler, Gil. Are You a Descendant of the House of David? The Jerusalem Post, January 10, 2012

[499] Finkelstein, Israel and Silberman, Neil Asher. David and Solomon. In Search of the Bible's Sacred Kings and the Roots of the Western Tradition. New York Simon & Schuster, 2006, p. 265

[500] Finkelstein, Israel. The Quest for the Historical Israel: Debating Archeology and the History of Early Israel. 2007, the Society of Biblical Literature, p. 17

[501] II Samuel 12-13

[502] Jeremiah 33:17

[503] 1 Kings 9:6

[504] 2 Chronicles 7:17-18

[505] Eusubius. *Historia Ecclessiastica*. I, 7, 13

[506] Plummer, Alfred. A Critical and Exegetical Commentary on the Gospel According to S. Luke. Edinburgh, T. & T. Clark, 1896, p. 102

[507] The Life of Flavius Josephus AKA Vita

[508] Isaiah 11:1

[509] Messiah. Encyclopedia Judaica, Second Edition. Detroit, Thomson Gale, 2007

[510] Luria, Solomon. *Responsum* No. 29

[511] Hurwitz, Simon (1938). The Responsa of Solomon Luria. New York, New York. pp. 146–151

[512] Rosenstein, Neil. The Luria Legacy. Bergenfield, New Jersey, Avotaynu, 2004, pp. 36-37

[513] Franklin, Arnold E. This Noble House. Jewish Descendants of King David in the Medieval Islamic East. Philadelphia, University of Pennsylvania Press, 2013, p. 39

[514] Goodblatt, David. The Monarchic Principle.: Studies in Jewish Self-Government in Antiquity. Tübingen, J. C. B. Mohr (Paul Sieback), 1994

[515] Ephraim Zalman Margoliot. *Ma'alot HaYuhasin (in Hebrew)*

[516] Einsiedler, David. Can We Prove Descent from King David? Avotaynu. Vol 8, no. 3, Fall, 1992

[517] Hurwitz, Simon. The Responsa of Solomon Luria. New York, New York, 1938, pp. 146–151

[518] Lévi, Israel. *L'origine davidique de Hillel. Revue des études juives* XXXI,1895 pp. 209ff and XXXIII 1896 pp. 143-144

[519] Margoshes, Joseph. A World Apart: A Memoir of Jewish Life in Nineteenth Century Galicia. Boston, Academic Studies Press, 2008, p. 184

[520] Gelles, Edward. An Ancient Lineage.

[521] Jacobs, Joseph & Wiernik, Peter. Heilprin. Jewish Encyclopedia, 1906 http://www.JewishEncyclopedia.com

[522] Heilprin. Wikipedia.org

[523] Horowitz. Wikipedia.org

[524] Bonet, Andrés J. The Bonet-Kalonymos-Shem Tovs: Direct Descendants of King David and the Princes of Septimania. *Sharsharet Hadorot* Vol. 17, no. 2

[525] The Bonet-Kalonymos-Shem Tovs: Direct Descendants of King David and the Princes of Septimania by Andrés J. Bonet. *Sharsharet Hadorot* Vol. 17, No. 2, June 2003

[526] The Itinerary of Rabbi Benjamin of Tudela. Translated and edited by A. Asher, Vol. 1. New York, "Hakesheth" Publishing Co., undated

[527] Adler, Marcus Nathan, Ed. The Itinerary of Benjamin of Tudela. New York, Philipp Feldheim, 1907

[528] Zuckerman, Arthur J. A Jewish Princedom in Feudal France: 768-900. New York, Columbia University Press, 1972

[529] Settipani, Christian. *Continuité gentilice et continuité familiale dans les familles sénatoriales romaines à l'époque impériale: mythe et réalité*, Unit for Prosopographical Research, Linacre College, University of Oxford, 2000, p. 78. *(in French)*

530 Bierbrier, M.L. Genealogical Flights of Fancy. Old Assumptions, New Sources, in Foundations: Journal of the Foundation for Medieval Genealogy. 2:379-87

531 Zuckerman, Arthur J. A Jewish Princedom in Feudal France: 768-900. New York, Columbia University Press, 1972, pp. 120-121

532 Ginzberg, L. Genizah Studies. II, p. 620

533 Kalonymos family. Wikipedia.org

534 Gottheil, Richard & Broydé, Isaac. Kalonymus. Jewish Encyclopedia, 1906 http://www.JewishEncyclopedia.com

535 Dan, Joseph. Kalonymus. Encyclopedia Judaica, Second Edition. Detroit, Thomson Gale, 2007

536 Cohen, J. Simcha. Intermarriage and Conversion: A Halakhic Solution. Hoboken, New Jersey, Ktav Publishing House, Inc., 1987, p. 173

537 HaKohen, HaGaon Rav Shmuel. *Tiferet Avot*, Introduction, *Ma'adanai Shmuel*, discussed by Rabbi J. Simcha Cohen in Intermarriage and Conversion: A Halakhic Solution. Hoboken, New Jersey, Ktav Publishing House, Inc. 1987, p. 173

538 Böhmer, "Regesten," No. 501; Wiener, "Regesten," pp. 23, 33; Kayserling, Meyer et al. Katzenellenbogen. Jewish Encyclopedia, 1906 http://www.JewishEncyclopedia.com

539 https://www.jewishvirtuallibrary.org/katzenellenbogen

540 https://www.jewishvirtuallibrary.org/Katzenellenbogen

541 Epstein, Abraham. *Mishpachat Luria*. Vienna, 1901

542 Rosenstein, Neil. The Luria Legacy. Bergenfield, New Jersey, Avotaynu, 2004, p. xxi

543 Luria, Solomon. Appendix to *Responsum* No. 29

544 Rosenstein, Neil. The Luria Legacy. Bergenfield, New Jersey, *Avotaynu*, 2004, pp. 36-37

[545] Hurwitz, Simon. The *Responsa* of Solomon Luria. New York, New York, 1938, pp. 146–151

[546] Rosenstein, Neil. A 17th Century Luria Manuscript Based on an Earlier Manuscript. *Avotaynu* vol. 7 no. 2, Summer 1991

[547] Rosenstein, Neil. A 17th Century Luria Manuscript Based on an Earlier Manuscript. *Avotaynu* vol. 7 no. 2, Summer 1991

[548] https://www.geni.com/people/Jacob-Jaffe-Margaliyot/6000000010614845043?through=6000000009987430114

[549] Jacobs, Joseph et al. Margolioth. The Jewish Encyclopedia, 1906 http://www.JewishEncyclopedia.com

[550] http://web.archive.org/web/20110725222014/http://www.davidicdynasty.org/shapiro_art.php

[551] Jacobi, Paul. The Historicity of the Rashi Descent. *Avotaynu*, Spring 1990

[552] Singer, Isidore et al. Trèves. Jewish Encyclopedia, 1906 http://www.JewishEncyclopedia.com

[553] Wigoder, Geoffrey, Editor-in-Chief. The New Standard Jewish Encyclopedia. New York & Oxford, Facts on File, 1992

[554] History of the Jews in Spain. Wikipedia.org

[555] Ashtor, Eliyahu. The Jews of Moslem Spain. Volume 1

[556] Brody, Robert. The Geonim of Babylonia and the Shaping of Medieval Jewish Culture. New Haven, Yale University Press, 1998, p. 132

[557] Ben-Sasson, H. H., ed. A History of the Jewish People. Cambridge, Massachusetts, Harvard University Press, 1976 (English translation), p. 393

[558] Wigoder, Geoffrey, Editor-in-Chief. The New Standard Jewish Encyclopedia. New York & Oxford, Facts on File, 1992

[559] Wigoder, Geoffrey, Editor-in-Chief. The New Standard Jewish Encyclopedia. New York & Oxford, Facts on File, 1992

[560] Malka, Jeffrey S. Sephardic Surnames: Evolution through the Millenia and Role in Genealogy. *Sharsheret Hadorot*, vol. 21, no. 1, VIII-XV

[561] Gartenhaus, Rabbi Eliezer, the Mikolayev Rabbi. Margoshes Family Genealogy. Written by 1936. Published in Margoshes, Joseph. A World Apart: A Memoir of Jewish Life in Nineteenth Century Galicia. Boston, Academic Studies Press, 2008, p. 184

[562] Cohen, J. Simcha. Intermarriage and Conversion: A Halakhic Solution. Hoboken, New Jersey, Ktav Publishing House, Inc., 1987, p. 173

[563] *Tiferet Avot*. Introduction, *Ma'adanai Shmuel*.

[564] Demsqî, Aharon et al. These are the Names: Studies in Jewish Onomastics, Volume 2. Bar-Han University Press, 1999, p. 115

[565] Kirschen, Bryan. Judeo-Spanish and the Making of a Community. Cambridge Scholars Publishing, 2015

[566] Gartenhaus, Eliezer, the Mikolayev Rabbi, written by 1936 and published in Margoshes, Joseph. A World Apart: A Memoir of Jewish Life in Nineteenth Century Galicia. Boston, Academic Studies Press, 2008

[567] Steifel, Barry L. Jews and the Renaissance of Synagogue Architecture, 1450-1730, p. 59

[568] Margoshes, Joseph. A World Apart: A Memoir of Jewish Life in Nineteenth Century Galicia. Boston, Academic Studies Press, 2008, p. 184

[569] https://berdichevsky.tribalpages.com/tribe/browse?userid=berdichevsky&view=0&pid=335&ver=9947

[570] 1 Chronicles 24:20; I Chronicles 26:29

[571] 1 Samuel 8

[572] Izhar. Wikipedia.org

[573] History of the Jews in Spain. Wikipedia.org

[574] Benveniste. Encyclopedia Judaica, Second Edition. Detroit, Thomson Gale, 2007

[575] Honey, Michael. Jewish Historical Clock: Branches from The Start Of The Horowitz Family Name In Prague Up To The Horowitz Dynasty In Dzikow/Tarnobrzeg Poland, Revision 5, 2005

[576] Honey, Michael. Jewish Historical Clock: Branches from The Start Of The Horowitz Family Name In Prague Up To The Horowitz Dynasty In Dzikow/Tarnobrzeg Poland, Revision 5, 2005

[577] Marmorstein, Avrohom. Does the Horowitz Family from Bohemia Really Descend from the Benvenisti Halevy Family from Spain? *Avotaynu* Online, July 19, 2016 [https://www.avotaynuonline.com/2016/03/does-the-horowitz-family-from-bohemia-really-descend-from-the-benvenisti-halevy-family-from-spain/]

[578] Marmorstein, Avrohom. Does the Horowitz Family from Bohemia Really Descend from the Benvenisti Halevy Family from Spain? *Avotaynu* Online, July 19, 2016 [https://www.avotaynuonline.com/2016/03/does-the-horowitz-family-from-bohemia-really-descend-from-the-benvenisti-halevy-family-from-spain/]

[579] Questioning the Experts: Interview with Itzhak Epstein. *Dorot* 36:4 Summer 2015

[580] https://jewsoffrankfurt.com/family-trees/levite-buchsbaum-eppsteingelhauser-goldsmith-horowitz/horowitz/

[581] http://www.earlyjewishwritings.com/1maccabees.html

[582] Johnson, Paul. A History of the Jews. New York, Harper Perennial, 1987, pp. 170-171

[582] Ben-Sasson, H. H., ed. A History of the Jewish People. Cambridge, Massachusetts, Harvard University Press, 1976 (English translation), p. 393

[584] Glick, Leonard B. Abraham's Heirs: Jews and Christians in Medieval Europe. Syracuse, NY, Syracuse University Press, 1999, pp. IX-X

[585] Potok, Chaim. Wanderings. Chaim Potok's History of the Jews. New York, Alfred A. Knopf, 1978, p. 294

[586] Marcus, Jacob Rader. The Jew in the Medieval World: A Source Book: 315 – 1791. Revised Edition. Cincinnati, Hebrew Union College Press, 1999

[587] Potok, Chaim. Wanderings. Chaim Potok's History of the Jews. New York, Alfred A. Knopf, 1978, p. 294

[588] Potok, Chaim. Wanderings. Chaim Potok's History of the Jews. New York, Alfred A. Knopf, 1978, p. 294

[589] Glick, Leonard B. Abraham's Heirs: Jews and Christians in Medieval Europe. Syracuse, NY, Syracuse University Press, 1999, pp. 58-59

[590] Glick, Leonard B. Abraham's Heirs: Jews and Christians in Medieval Europe. Syracuse, NY, Syracuse University Press, 1999, pp. 58-59

[591] Glick, Leonard B. Abraham's Heirs: Jews and Christians in Medieval Europe. Syracuse, NY, Syracuse University Press, 1999, pp. 64-65

[592] Glick, Leonard B. Abraham's Heirs: Jews and Christians in Medieval Europe. Syracuse, NY, Syracuse University Press, 1999, pp. 62-63

[593] Glick, Leonard B. Abraham's Heirs: Jews and Christians in Medieval Europe. Syracuse, NY, Syracuse University Press, 1999, pp. 62-63

[594] Gottheil, Richard & Broydé, Isaac. Kalonymus. Jewish Encyclopedia, 1906 http://www.JewishEncyclopedia.com

[595] Grabois, Arye. The Illustrated Encyclopedia of Medieval Civilization. p. 465

[596] Harper, William Rainey et al, Eds. The Biblical World, Volume 8

[597] Kraemer, David Charles. The Jewish Family: Metaphor and Memory

[598] The Memim Encyclopedia. http://memim.com/kalonymos-familymeshullam-the-great.html

[599] The Memim Encyclopedia. http://memim.com/kalonymos-familymeshullam-the-great.html

[600] The Memim Encyclopedia. http://memim.com/kalonymos-familymeshullam-the-great.html

[601] The Memim Encyclopedia. http://memim.com/kalonymos-familymeshullam-the-great.html

[602] Abun. Encyclopedia Judaica, Second Edition. Detroit, Thomson Gale, 2007

[603] Bonet, Andres J. The Bonet-Kalonymos-Shem Tovs. *Sharsharet Hadorot* v. 17 no. 2

[604] Rabbi Solomon Luria, *Responsa* #29, Lublin, 1575

[605] Tauber, Laurence. The (Maternal) Descent of Rashi. Avotaynu, vol. IX, Number 2, Summer 1993

[606] Glick, Leonard B. Abraham's Heirs: Jews and Christians in Medieval Europe. Syracuse, NY, Syracuse University Press, 1999, pp. 92-93

[607] Glick, Leonard B. Abraham's Heirs: Jews and Christians in Medieval Europe. Syracuse, NY, Syracuse University Press, 1999, p. 93

[608] Glick, Leonard B. Abraham's Heirs: Jews and Christians in Medieval Europe. Syracuse, NY, Syracuse University Press, 1999, p. 94

[609] Glick, Leonard B. Abraham's Heirs: Jews and Christians in Medieval Europe. Syracuse, NY, Syracuse University Press, 1999, pp. 95-99

[610] Glick, Leonard B. Abraham's Heirs: Jews and Christians in Medieval Europe. Syracuse, NY, Syracuse University Press, 1999, pp. 101-102

[611] Glick, Leonard B. Abraham's Heirs: Jews and Christians in Medieval Europe. Syracuse, NY, Syracuse University Press, 1999, pp. 103-104

[612] Kalonymus. Encyclopedia Judaica, Second Edition. Detroit, Thomson Gale, 2007

[613] Roemer, Nils H. German City, Jewish Memory: The Story of Worms. Chapter 1: Sacred Realms

[614] Eliezer ben Judah ben Kalonymus of Worms, quoted in http://www.jewishvirtuallibrary.org/kalonymus

[615] Jacobs, Joseph; Liber Morris; Seligsohn, M. Rashi (Solomon bar Isaac). The Jewish Encyclopedia 1906

http://www.JewishEncyclopedia.com

[616] Renaissance of the 12th century. Wikipedia.org

[617] Glick, Leonard B. Abraham's Heirs: Jews and Christians in Medieval Europe. Syracuse, NY, Syracuse University Press, 1999, p. 111

[618] Glick, Leonard B. Abraham's Heirs: Jews and Christians in Medieval Europe. Syracuse, NY, Syracuse University Press, 1999, p. 111

[619] Glick, Leonard B. Abraham's Heirs: Jews and Christians in Medieval Europe. Syracuse, NY, Syracuse University Press, 1999, p. 178

[620] Glick, Leonard B. Abraham's Heirs: Jews and Christians in Medieval Europe. Syracuse, NY, Syracuse University Press, 1999, pp. 113-114

[621] Glick, Leonard B. Abraham's Heirs: Jews and Christians in Medieval Europe. Syracuse, NY, Syracuse University Press, 1999, pp. 114-115

[622] Glick, Leonard B. Abraham's Heirs: Jews and Christians in Medieval Europe. Syracuse, NY, Syracuse University Press, 1999, pp. 117-118

[623] Glick, Leonard B. Abraham's Heirs: Jews and Christians in Medieval Europe. Syracuse, NY, Syracuse University Press, 1999, pp. 117-118

[624] Luke 6:34-35

[625] Glick, Leonard B. Abraham's Heirs: Jews and Christians in Medieval Europe. Syracuse, NY, Syracuse University Press, 1999, p. 118

[626] Glick, Leonard B. Abraham's Heirs: Jews and Christians in Medieval Europe. Syracuse, NY, Syracuse University Press, 1999, pp. 118-119

[627] Glick, Leonard B. Abraham's Heirs: Jews and Christians in Medieval Europe. Syracuse, NY, Syracuse University Press, 1999, p. 121

[628] Glick, Leonard B. Abraham's Heirs: Jews and Christians in Medieval Europe. Syracuse, NY, Syracuse University Press, 1999, pp. 125-126

[629] Glick, Leonard B. Abraham's Heirs: Jews and Christians in Medieval Europe. Syracuse, NY, Syracuse University Press, 1999, p. 126

[630] Glick, Leonard B. Abraham's Heirs: Jews and Christians in Medieval Europe. Syracuse, NY, Syracuse University Press, 1999, pp. 126-129

[631] Glick, Leonard B. Abraham's Heirs: Jews and Christians in Medieval Europe. Syracuse, NY, Syracuse University Press, 1999, p. 159

[632] Glick, Leonard B. Abraham's Heirs: Jews and Christians in Medieval Europe. Syracuse, NY, Syracuse University Press, 1999, p. 160

[633] The Expulsion of the Jews from France: 1182, in Marcus, Jacob Rader. The Jew in the Medieval World: A Source Book: 315 – 1791. Revised Edition. Cincinnati, Hebrew Union College Press, 1999, pp. 27-37

[634] Glick, Leonard B. Abraham's Heirs: Jews and Christians in Medieval Europe. Syracuse, NY, Syracuse University Press, 1999, pp. 168-169

[635] Glick, Leonard B. Abraham's Heirs: Jews and Christians in Medieval Europe. Syracuse, NY, Syracuse University Press, 1999, pp. 170-177

[636] Innocent and the Jews: 1215, in Marcus, Jacob Rader. The Jew in the Medieval World: A Source Book: 315 – 1791. Revised Edition. Cincinnati, Hebrew Union College Press, 1999, pp. 153-158

[637] Ta-Shma, Israel Moses. Eliezer ben Nathan of Mainz. Encyclopedia Judaica, Second Edition. Detroit, Thomson Gale, 2007

[638] Eliezer ben Nathan. *Kuntres Gezerot "Tatnu"* ("Booklet on the Massacres of 1096") publ. Leipzig, 1854; publ. in English translation by Eidelberg, 1986

[639] Schechter, Solomon and Schloessinger, Max. Jacob ben meïr tam. JewishEncyclopedia.com, 1906

[640] Mindel, Nissan. Rabbi Judah HaChassid. Kehot Publication Society; http://www.chabad.org/library/article_cdo/aid/111829/jewish/Rabbi-Judah-HaChassid.htm

[641] Mindel, Nissan. Rabbi Judah HaChassid. Kehot Publication Society; http://www.chabad.org/library/article_cdo/aid/111829/jewish/Rabbi-Judah-HaChassid.htm

[642] History of the Jews in Regensburg. Wikipedia.org

[643] Mindel, Nissan. Rabbi Judah HaChassid. Kehot Publication Society; http://www.chabad.org/library/article_cdo/aid/111829/jewish/Rabbi-Judah-HaChassid.htm

[644] Kohler, Kaufmann & Schloessinger, Max. Judah ben Samuel He-Hasid of Regensburg

[645] Gelles, Edward. The Jewish Journey: A Passage Through European History. I. B. Tauris, 2015

[646] Havlin, Shlomoh Zalman. Meshullam ben Jacob of Lunel. Encyclopedia Judaica, Second Edition. Detroit, Thomson Gale, 2007

[647] Havlin, Shlomoh Zalman. Meshullam ben Jacob of Lunel. Encyclopedia Judaica, Second Edition. Detroit, Thomson Gale, 2007

[648] Grayzel, Solomon; Stow, Kenneth R. The Church and the Jews in the XIII Century, 1989, pp. 308-309

[649] Glick, Leonard B. Abraham's Heirs: Jews and Christians in Medieval Europe. Syracuse, NY, Syracuse University Press, 1999, p. 168

[650] Glick, Leonard B. Abraham's Heirs: Jews and Christians in Medieval Europe. Syracuse, NY, Syracuse University Press, 1999, pp. 234-235

[651] Glick, Leonard B. Abraham's Heirs: Jews and Christians in Medieval Europe. Syracuse, NY, Syracuse University Press, 1999, pp. 252-253

[652] Glick, Leonard B. Abraham's Heirs: Jews and Christians in Medieval Europe. Syracuse, NY, Syracuse University Press, 1999, pp. 255-256

[653] Glick, Leonard B. Abraham's Heirs: Jews and Christians in Medieval Europe. Syracuse, NY, Syracuse University Press, 1999, p. 257

[654] Glick, Leonard B. Abraham's Heirs: Jews and Christians in Medieval Europe. Syracuse, NY, Syracuse University Press, 1999, pp. 234-235

[655] Glick, Leonard B. Abraham's Heirs: Jews and Christians in Medieval Europe. Syracuse, NY, Syracuse University Press, 1999, pp. 190-192

[656] Freimann, Jacob & Schwartz, Dov. Abba Mari ben Moses ben Joseph Astruc of Lunel. Encyclopedia Judaica, Second Edition. Detroit, Thomson Gale, 2007

[657] Freimann, Jacob & Schwartz, Dov. Abba Mari ben Moses ben Joseph Astruc of Lunel. Encyclopedia Judaica, Second Edition. Detroit, Thomson Gale, 2007

[658] Glick, Leonard B. Abraham's Heirs: Jews and Christians in Medieval Europe. Syracuse, NY, Syracuse University Press, 1999, pp. 246-247

[659] Glick, Leonard B. Abraham's Heirs: Jews and Christians in Medieval Europe. Syracuse, NY, Syracuse University Press, 1999, p. 252

[660] Glick, Leonard B. Abraham's Heirs: Jews and Christians in Medieval Europe. Syracuse, NY, Syracuse University Press, 1999, p. 270

[661] Glick, Leonard B. Abraham's Heirs: Jews and Christians in Medieval Europe. Syracuse, NY, Syracuse University Press, 1999, p.p. 238-239

[662] Glick, Leonard B. Abraham's Heirs: Jews and Christians in Medieval Europe. Syracuse, NY, Syracuse University Press, 1999, p. 271

[663] Glick, Leonard B. Abraham's Heirs: Jews and Christians in Medieval Europe. Syracuse, NY, Syracuse University Press, 1999, p. 259

[664] Glick, Leonard B. Abraham's Heirs: Jews and Christians in Medieval Europe. Syracuse, NY, Syracuse University Press, 1999, pp. 268-269

[665] Hildesheimer, Esriel. The Treves Families. Avotaynu vol. V, Number 1, Spring 1989 S17-S22

[666] Hildesheimer, Esriel. The Treves Families. Avotaynu vol. V, Number 1, Spring 1989 S17-S22

[667] Glick, Leonard B. Abraham's Heirs: Jews and Christians in Medieval Europe. Syracuse, NY, Syracuse University Press, 1999, p. 272

[668] Glick, Leonard B. Abraham's Heirs: Jews and Christians in Medieval Europe. Syracuse, NY, Syracuse University Press, 1999, p. 273

[669] Rabinowicz, Harry. Rabbi Joseph Colon (1420-1480). Hebrew Studies Vol. 26, No. 2, 1985, pp. 301-306

[670] Woolf, Jeffery R. New Light on the Life and Times of Rabbi Joseph Colon Trabotto (Maharik). Italia 13-15, 2001, pp. 151-180

[671] Kahn, S. Singer, Isadore. Trévoux. Jewish Encyclopedia, 1906 http://www.JewishEncyclopedia.com

[672] Colon, Joseph B. Solomon. Jewish Encyclopedia, 1906 http://www.JewishEncyclopedia.com

[673] Rabinowicz, Harry. Rabbi Joseph Colon (1420-1480). Hebrew Studies Vol. 26, No. 2, 1985, pp. 301-306

[674] Colon, Joseph B. Solomon. Jewish Encyclopedia, 1906 http://www.JewishEncyclopedia.com

[675] Colon, Joseph B. Solomon. Jewish Encyclopedia, 1906 http://www.JewishEncyclopedia.com

[676] Colon, Joseph ben Solomon. Encyclopedia Judaica, Second Edition. Detroit, Thomson Gale, 2007

[677] Rabbi Shlomo Luria (ca. 1510-1573) as reported in *L'Chaim* [http://www.lchaimweekly.org/lchaim/5756/405.htm]

[678] Eidelberg, Shlomo. Minz, Judah ben Eliezer Ha-levi. Encyclopedia Judaica, Second Edition. Detroit, Thomson Gale, 2007

[679] http://pedhatzur.com/family-tree-sarah-kahana-shapira-2/24-rabbi-avraham-mintz/

[680] Eidelberg, Shlomo. Minz, Abraham ben Judah Ha-levi. Encyclopedia Judaica, Second Edition. Detroit, Thomson Gale, 2007

[681] Johnson, Paul. A History of the Jews. New York, Harper & Row, 1987, p. 250

[682] Hundert, Gershon David. Jews in Poland-Lithuania in the Eighteenth Century: A Genealogy of Modernity. Berkeley, Los Angeles, University of California Press, 2004, p. 6

[683] Hundert, Gershon David. Jews in Poland-Lithuania in the Eighteenth Century: A Genealogy of Modernity. Berkeley, Los Angeles, University of California Press, 2004, p. 6

[684] Davies, Norman. God's Playground: A History of Poland, Volume I. New York: Columbia University Press, 2005, p. 66

[685] Hundert, Gershon David. Jews in Poland-Lithuania in the Eighteenth Century: A Genealogy of Modernity. Berkeley, Los Angeles, University of California Press, 2004, p. 6

[686] Davies, Norman. Europe: A History, p. 429

[687] Overy, Richard. The Times Complete History of the World, Eighth Edition. London, Times Books, 2010, pp. 116-117

[688] Bokser, Ben Zion. The Maharal: The Mystical Philosophy of Rabbi Judah Loew of Prague. Northvale, New Jersey & London, Jason Aronson, 1994, pp. 22-27

[689] Bokser, Ben Zion. The Maharal: The Mystical Philosophy of Rabbi Judah Loew of Prague. Northvale, New Jersey & London, Jason Aronson, 1994, pp. 22-27

[690] Bokser, Ben Zion. The Maharal: The Mystical Philosophy of Rabbi Judah Loew of Prague. Northvale, New Jersey & London, Jason Aronson, 1994, pp. 22-27

[691] Bokser, Ben Zion. The Maharal: The Mystical Philosophy of Rabbi Judah Loew of Prague. Northvale, New Jersey & London, Jason Aronson, 1994, pp. 22-27

[692] Bokser, Ben Zion. The Maharal: The Mystical Philosophy of Rabbi Judah Loew of Prague. Northvale, New Jersey & London, Jason Aronson, 1994, pp. 22-27

[693] Bokser, Ben Zion. The Maharal: The Mystical Philosophy of Rabbi Judah Loew of Prague. Northvale, New Jersey & London, Jason Aronson, 1994, pp. 22-27

[694] Johnson, Paul. A History of the Jews. New York, Harper & Row, 1987, p. 253

[695] Weiner, Rebecca. Virtual Jewish World: Prague, in JewishVirtualLibrary.org

[696] Weiner, Rebecca. Virtual Jewish World: Prague, in JewishVirtualLibrary.org

697 Margolis, Max L., and Alexander Marx. A History of the Jewish People. Philadelphia: The Jewish Publication Society of America, 1927

698 History of the Jews in Prague. Wikipedia.org

699 Johnson, Paul. A History of the Jews. New York, Harper & Row, 1987, p. 250

700 Johnson, Paul. A History of the Jews. New York, Harper & Row, 1987, p. 250

701 Johnson, Paul. A History of the Jews. New York, Harper & Row, 1987, p. 250

702 Johnson, Paul. A History of the Jews. New York, Harper & Row, 1987, p. 250

703 Johnson, Paul. A History of the Jews. New York, Harper & Row, 1987, p. 250

704 Johnson, Paul. A History of the Jews. New York, Harper & Row, 1987, p. 251

705 Johnson, Paul. A History of the Jews. New York, Harper & Row, 1987, pp. 251-252

706 Johnson, Paul. A History of the Jews. New York, Harper & Row, 1987, p. 252

707 Gratiani, Antonio Maria, bishop of Amelia, Italy. *La Vie du cardinal Jean-Françoise Commendon*, trans. Fléchier. Paris, 1614

708 Ben-Sasson, H. H., Ed. A History of the Jewish People. Part VI: The Modern Period by Shmuel Ettinger. Cambridge, Massachusetts, Harvard University Press, 1999, p. 733

709 Mindel, Nissan. Chabad.org; http://www.chabad.org/library/article_cdo/aid/112518/jewish/Rabbi-Shlomo-Luria.htm

710 Shochat, Azriel & Spector, Shmuel. Ostroh. Encyclopedia Judaica, Second Edition. Detroit, Thomson Gale, 2007

711 Rosenthal, Herman & Lipman, J. G. Ostroh. Jewish Encyclopedia, 1906 http://www.JewishEncyclopedia.com

712 Rosenthal, Herman, et al. Luria. Jewish Encyclopedia, 1906 http://www.JewishEncyclopedia.com

713 Bokser, Ben Zion. The Maharal: The Mystical Philosophy of Rabbi Judah Loew of Prague. North Vale, NJ, Jason Aronson Inc., 1994

714 Bokser, Ben Zion. The Maharal: The Mystical Philosophy of Rabbi Judah Loew of Prague. North Vale, NJ, Jason Aronson Inc., 1994

715 Bokser, Ben Zion. The Maharal: The Mystical Philosophy of Rabbi Judah Loew of Prague. North Vale, NJ, Jason Aronson Inc., 1994

716 Bokser, Ben Zion. The Maharal: The Mystical Philosophy of Rabbi Judah Loew of Prague. North Vale, NJ, Jason Aronson Inc., 1994

717 Bokser, Ben Zion. The Maharal: The Mystical Philosophy of Rabbi Judah Loew of Prague. North Vale, NJ, Jason Aronson Inc., 1994

718 Bokser, Ben Zion. The Maharal: The Mystical Philosophy of Rabbi Judah Loew of Prague. North Vale, NJ, Jason Aronson Inc., 1994

719 Englard, Shlomo. *Tsfunot* #12 - reprinted in a collection of his articles, Bnei Brak 2004. *(in Hebrew)*

720 Freedman, Chaim. The Maharal of Prague's Descent from King David. *Avotaynu* Vol. XXII, No. 1, Spring 2006

721 MaHaRaL's Descent from King David: Additional Comments by Neil Rosenstein. *Avotaynu* XXII:3, Fall, 2006, pp. 29-33

722 Einsiedler, David. Online Journal: Descent from King David – Part II

723 Beilinsohn Moshe Eliezer. *Megalat Yukhsin*. Odessa 1863. *(in Hebrew)*

724 Rashkes, Moshe. *Zikhron LeMoshe*. Odessa, 1873. *(in Hebrew)*

725 Golem. Jewish Encyclopedia, 1906
http://www.JewishEncyclopedia.com

726 Golem. Jewish Encyclopedia, 1906
http://www.JewishEncyclopedia.com

727 Golem. JewishEncyclopedia, 1906

http://www.JewishEncyclopedia.com

[728] *Idel, Moshe (1990). Golem: Jewish Magical and Mystical Traditions on the Artificial Anthropoid. Albany, New York: State University of New York Press,* p. 296

[729] Golem. Wikipedia.org

[730] Bokser, Ben Zion. The Maharal: The Mystical Philosophy of Rabbi Judah Loew of Prague. North Vale, NJ, Jason Aronson Inc., 1994

[731] Karpeles, Gustav. Jewish Literature and Other Essays. Forgotten Books. pp. 273-284. ISBN 978-1-4400-7733-3.

[732] Berschadzky. *Woschod*, 1889, No. 10 *ff. (in Russian)*

[733] Edels, Samuel Eliezer ben Judah Ha-Levi. Encyclopedia Judaica, Second Edition. Detroit, Thomson Gale, 2007

[734] Finkel, Chaim. Ostroh – A Metropolis of the People of Israel, in Ostroh Book: A Memorial to the Ostroh Holy Community. Tel-Aviv, The Ostroh Society in Israel, 1987

[735] Rosenthal, Herman & Lipman, J. G. Ostroh. Jewish Encyclopedia, 1906 http://www.JewishEncyclopedia.com

[736] Edels, Samuel Eliezer ben Judah Ha-Levi. Encyclopedia Judaica, Second Edition. Detroit, Thomson Gale, 2007

[737] Yom-Tov Lipmann Heller. Wikipedia.org

[738] Yom-Tov Lipmann Heller. Wikipedia.org

[739] Yom-Tov Lipmann Heller. Wikipedia.org

[740] Hundert, Gershon David. Jews in Poland-Lithuania in the Eighteenth Century: A Genealogy of Modernity. Berkeley, Los Angeles, University of California Press, 2004, p. 14

741 Hundert, Gershon David. Jews in Poland-Lithuania in the Eighteenth Century: A Genealogy of Modernity. Berkeley, Los Angeles, University of California Press, 2004, p. 14

742 Johnson, Paul. A History of the Jews. New York, Harper & Row, 1987, p. 258-259

743 Johnson, Paul. A History of the Jews. New York, Harper & Row, 1987, p. 259

744 Johnson, Paul. A History of the Jews. New York, Harper & Row, 1987, p. 260-272

745 Dubnow, S. M. History of the Jews in Russia and Poland: From the Earliest Times until the Present Day. Philadelphia, The Jewish Publication Society of America, 1916, Volume 1, pp. 241-242

746 Dubnow, S. M. History of the Jews in Russia and Poland: From the Earliest Times until the Present Day. Philadelphia, The Jewish Publication Society of America, 1916, Volume 1, pp. 244-246

747 Russian historian Solovyov quoting Peter the Great, in Dubnow, S. M. History of the Jews in Russia and Poland: From the Earliest Times until the Present Day. Philadelphia, The Jewish Publication Society of America, 1916, Volume 1, p. 247

748 Shabbetai ben Meir Ha-Kohen. Encyclopedia Judaica, Second Edition. Detroit, Thomson Gale, 2007

749 Shabbethai B. Meïr Ha-Kohen (SHaK). Jewish Encyclopedia, 1906 http://www.JewishEncyclopedia.com

750 Mindel, Nissan. Rabbi – The Shach [http://www.chabad.org/library/article_cdo/aid/112365/jewish/RabbiShabtaiHaKohenTheShach.htm]

751 HaKohen, Shabbatai. Megillah 'Afah ("Flying Scroll"), ca. 1648. (in Hebrew)

752 Mindel, Nissan. Rabbi – The Shach; http://www.chabad.org/library/article_cdo/aid/112365/jewish/RabbiShabtai-HaKohenTheShach.htm

753 Liebes, Yehuda. A Profile of R. Naphtali Katz from Frankfurt and His Attitude towards Sabbateanism, in Grözinger, Karl Erich & Dan, Joseph, Eds. Mysticism,

Magic and Kabbalah in Ashkenazi Judaism. Berlin & New York, Walter de Gruyter, 1995, p. 208

754 Cohen, Naphtali. Jewish Encyclopedia, 1906
http://www.JewishEncyclopedia.com

755 Cohen, Naphtali. Jewish Encyclopedia, 1906
http://www.JewishEncyclopedia.com

756 Cohen, Naphtali. Jewish Encyclopedia, 1906
http://www.JewishEncyclopedia.com

757 Katz, Naphtali ben Isaac. Encyclopedia Judaica, Second Edition. Detroit, Thomson Gale, 2007

758 Carlebach, Elisheva. The Pursuit of Heresy: Rabbi Moses Hagiz and the Sabbatian Controversies. New York, Columbia University Press, 1990, p. 155

759 Cohen, Naphtali. JewishEncyclopedia.com, 1906.
http://www.JewishEncyclopedia.com

760 Carlebach, Elisheva. The Pursuit of Heresy: Rabbi Moses Hagiz and the Sabbatian Controversies. New York, Columbia University Press, 1990, p. 120

761 Carlebach, Elisheva. The Pursuit of Heresy: Rabbi Moses Hagiz and the Sabbatian Controversies. New York, Columbia University Press, 1990, p. 120

762 Katz, Naphtali ben Isaac. Encyclopedia Judaica, Second Edition. Detroit, Thomson Gale, 2007

763 Katz, Naphtali ben Isaac. Encyclopedia Judaica, Second Edition. Detroit, Thomson Gale, 2007

764 Bar-Levav, Avriel. Chapter 10: Ritualizing death and dying: the ethical will of Naphtali Ha-Kohen Katz, in Fine, Lawrence, Ed. Judaism in Practice: From the Middle Ages through the Early Modern Period. Princeton & Oxford, Princeton University Press, 2001

765 Bar-Levav, Avriel. Ethical Will of Naphtali Ha-Kohen Katz. Princeton, 2001, p. 165

766 Bar-Levav, Avriel. Ethical Will of Naphtali Ha-Kohen Katz. Princeton, 2001, p. 165

[767] Felix Mendelssohn-Bartholdy, 1809-1847. Library of Congress https://loc.gov/item/ihas.200156439

[768] Felix Mendelssohn. Wikipedia.org

[769] Felix Mendelssohn-Bartholdy, 1809-1847. Library of Congress https://loc.gov/item/ihas.200156439

[770] Karl Marx. Wikipedia.org

[771] Karl Marx. Wikipedia.org

[772] Johnson, Paul. A History of the Jews. New York, Harper Perennial, 1988, pp. 346-355

[773] http://www.bbc.co.uk/history/historic_figures/freud_sigmund.shtml

[774] Sigmund Freud. Wikipedia.org

[775] Auden, W. H. In Memory of Sigmund Freud, in Another Time. Random House, 1940

[776] Rosenstein, Neil. The Unbroken Chain, second edition. New York, CIS Publishers, Inc., 1990

[777] Biber, Menachem Mendel. *Markezet LeGedolei Ostraha* (Berdichev, Ukraine, 1906-7), p. 115

[778] Biber, Menachem Mendel. *Markezet LeGedolei Ostraha* (Berdichev, Ukraine, 1906-7), p. 115

[779] Rosenstein, Neil. The Unbroken Chain, second edition. New York, CIS Publishers, Inc., 1990

[780] Biber, Menachem Mendel. *Markezet LeGedolei Ostraha* (Berdichev, Ukraine, 1906-7), entry 69

[781] 1795 Ostroh District Jewish Revision List

[782] Biber, Menachem Mendel. *Markezet LeGedolei Ostraha* (Berdichev, Ukraine, 1906-7), pp. 115-116

[783] Biber, Menachem Mendel. *Markezet LeGedolei Ostraha* (Berdichev, Ukraine, 1906-7)

[784] Biber, Menachem Mendel. *Markezet LeGedolei Ostraha* (Berdichev, Ukraine, 1906-7)

[785] 1795 Ostroh District Jewish Revision List

[786] Accounts Book of the Ostroh Chevra Kadisha

[787] Biber, Menachem Mendel. *Markezet LeGedolei Ostraha* (Berdichev, Ukraine, 1906-7)

[788] 1795 Ostroh District Jewish Revision List

[789] 1795 Ostroh District Jewish Revision List

[790] 1850 Berestechko *Revizskaya Skazka. (in Russian)*

[791] Biber, Menachem Mendel. *Markezet LeGedolei Ostraha* (Berdichev, Ukraine, 1906-7)

[792] 1795 Ostroh District Jewish Revision List

[793] 1816 Aleksandriya *Revizskaya Skazka. (in Russian)*

[794] 1851 Aleksandriya *Revizskaya Skazka. (in Russian)*

www.ingramcontent.com/pod-product-compliance
Lightning Source LLC
Chambersburg PA
CBHW030909270326
41929CB00008B/634